ECLIPSE™

Published by Top Cow Productions, Inc.
Los Angeles

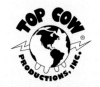

ECLIPSE™

Created by Zack Kaplan

Zack Kaplan
Writer

Giovanni Timpano
Artist

Chris Northrop
Colorist

Giovanni Timpano & Chris Northrop
Covers

Troy Peteri
Letterer

Ashley Victoria Robinson & Ryan Cady
Editors

For Top Cow Productions, Inc.
Marc Silvestri - CEO
Matt Hawkins - President and COO
Bryan Hill - Story Editor
Ashley Victoria Robinson - Editor
Elena Salcedo - Director of Operations
Henry Barajas - Operations Coordinator
Vincent Valentine - Production Artist
Dylan Gray - Marketing Director

To find the comic shop nearest you, call:
1-888-COMICBOOK

Want more info? Check out:
www.topcow.com
for news & exclusive Top Cow merchandise!

Tricia Ramos
Book Design & Layout

Vincent Valentine
Logo Design

IMAGE COMICS, INC.
Robert Kirkman—Chief Operating Officer
Erik Larsen—Chief Financial Officer
Todd McFarlane—President
Marc Silvestri—Chief Executive Officer
Jim Valentino—Vice-President

Eric Stephenson—Publisher
Corey Murphy—Director of Sales
Jeff Boison—Director of Publishing Planning & Book Trade Sales
Chris Ross—Director of Digital Sales
Kat Salazar—Director of PR & Marketing
Branwyn Bigglestone—Controller
Susan Korpela—Accounts Manager
Drew Gill—Art Director
Brett Warnock—Production Manager
Meredith Wallace—Print Manager
Briah Skelly—Publicist
Aly Hoffman— Conventions & Events Coordinator
Sasha Head—Sales & Marketing Production Designer
David Brothers—Branding Manager
Melissa Gifford—Content Manager
Erika Schnatz—Production Artist
Ryan Brewer—Production Artist
Shanna Matuszak—Production Artist
Tricia Ramos—Production Artist
Vincent Kukua—Production Artist
Jeff Stang—Direct Market Sales Representative
Emilio Bautista—Digital Sales Associate
Leanna Caunter—Accounting Assistant
Chloe Ramos-Peterson—Library Market Sales Representative
IMAGECOMICS.COM

ECLIPSE, VOL. 1. First printing. February 2017. Published by Image Comics, Inc. Office of publication: 2701 NW Vaughn St., Suite 780, Portland, OR 97210.

ISBN 978-1-5343-0038-5.

Dear Readers,

ECLIPSE is my first comic book.

Eight years ago, I dreamed of writing a comic book.
I was also working a graveyard shift as a poker dealer.
I toiled at night and slept during the day. I had studied
writing in school, but not yet found success. I was living a
lifestyle different than most. I was disconnected from my
friends and family. Looking back, I can say...
...my life was facing darkness.

But I've always tried to see the bright side of things.

And that's what ECLIPSE is really about to me.
Being hopeful in dark times.

On behalf of the entire ECLIPSE Creative Team, we want to thank
Matt Hawkins and Top Cow for giving us the chance to tell this story.
We want to thank everyone at Top Cow and Image Comics for helping
us every step of the way. We want to thank every comic reviewer and
blogger and podcaster and fan who offered a kind word about ECLIPSE.

And we want to thank you, yes you, the reader, for picking up this comic
book and reading it! I buy a lot of comic books, but many land on the
shelf and wait to be read. It takes a commitment to read a comic book.
I hope you find ECLIPSE thrilling and entertaining, and maybe a little
thought-provoking. We hope you connect to it.

We'd love for you to stay connected. Reach out on social media!

The world and story of ECLIPSE are just getting started...

All the best,

Zack Kaplan

CHAPTER ONE

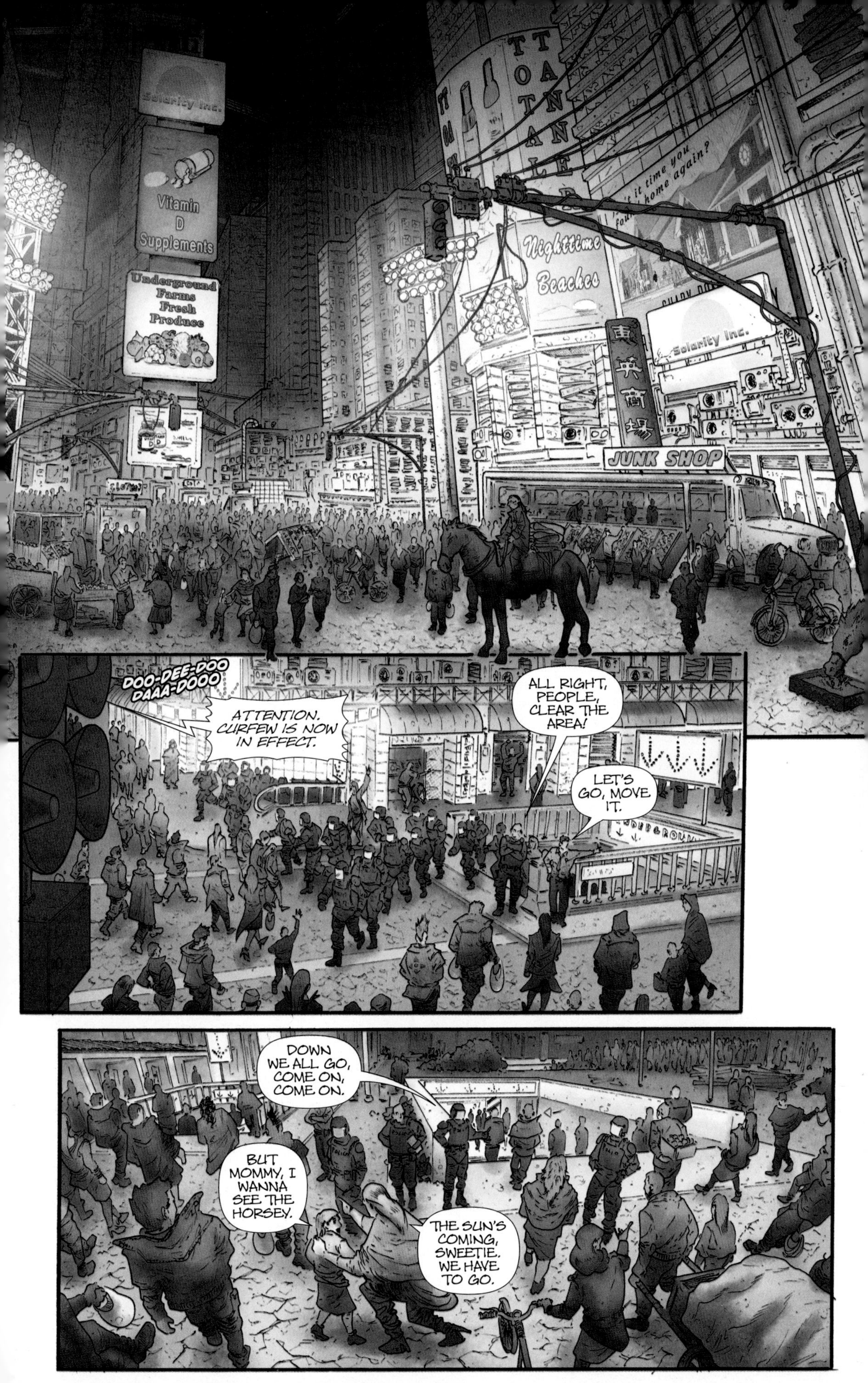

Solarity Inc.
Vitamin D Supplements
Underground Farms Fresh Produce
Nighttime Beaches
Solarity Inc.
JUNK SHOP
DOO-DEE-DOO DAAA-DOOO
ATTENTION. CURFEW IS NOW IN EFFECT.
ALL RIGHT, PEOPLE, CLEAR THE AREA!
LET'S GO, MOVE IT.
DOWN WE ALL GO, COME ON, COME ON.
BUT MOMMY, I WANNA SEE THE HORSEY.
THE SUN'S COMING, SWEETIE. WE HAVE TO GO.

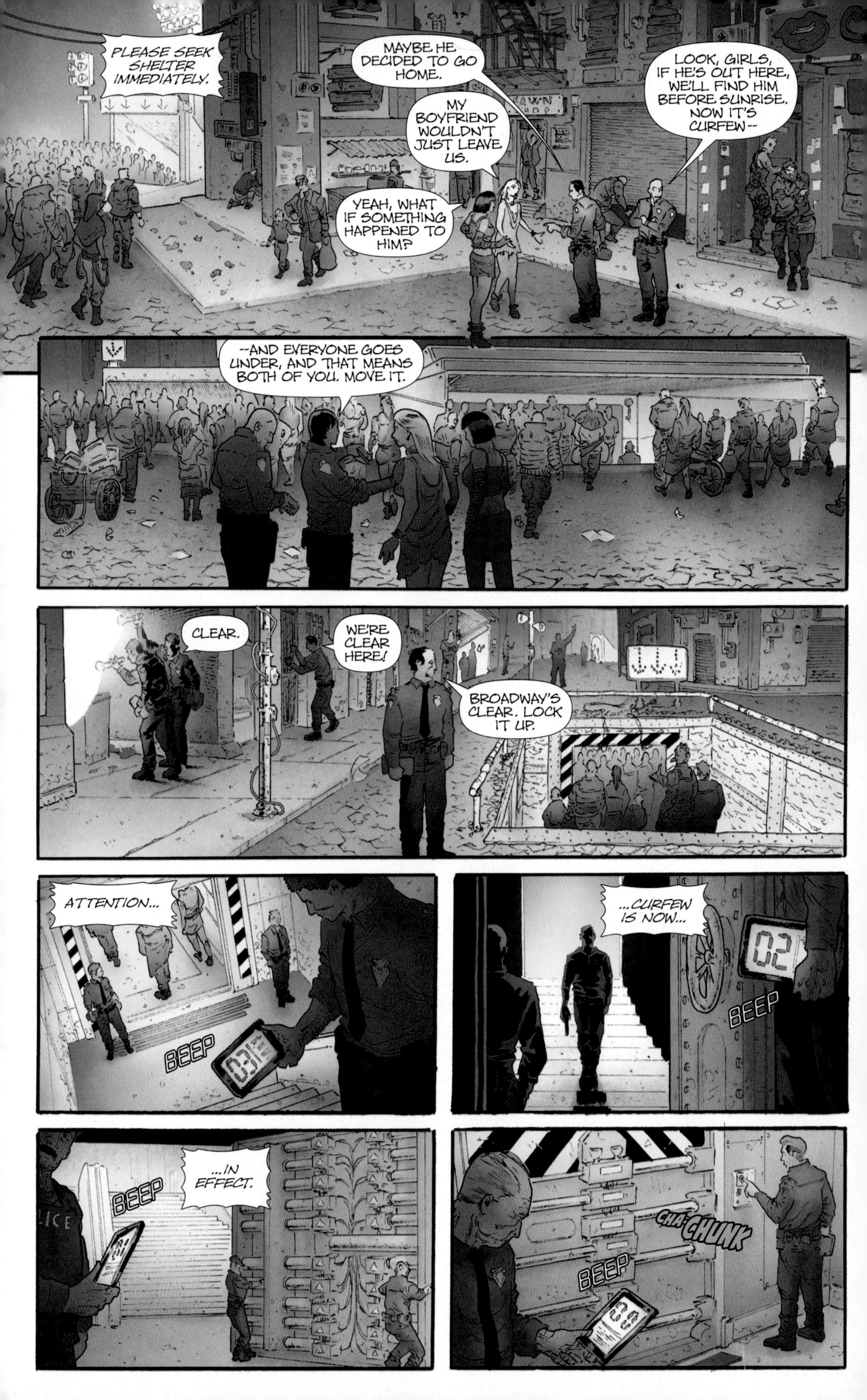
PLEASE SEEK SHELTER IMMEDIATELY.
MAYBE HE DECIDED TO GO HOME.
MY BOYFRIEND WOULDN'T JUST LEAVE US.
YEAH, WHAT IF SOMETHING HAPPENED TO HIM?
LOOK, GIRLS, IF HE'S OUT HERE, WE'LL FIND HIM BEFORE SUNRISE. NOW IT'S CURFEW--
--AND EVERYONE GOES UNDER, AND THAT MEANS BOTH OF YOU. MOVE IT.
CLEAR.
WE'RE CLEAR HERE!
BROADWAY'S CLEAR. LOCK IT UP.
ATTENTION...
BEEP
...CURFEW IS NOW...
02
BEEP
...IN EFFECT.
BEEP
CHA-CHUNK
BEEP

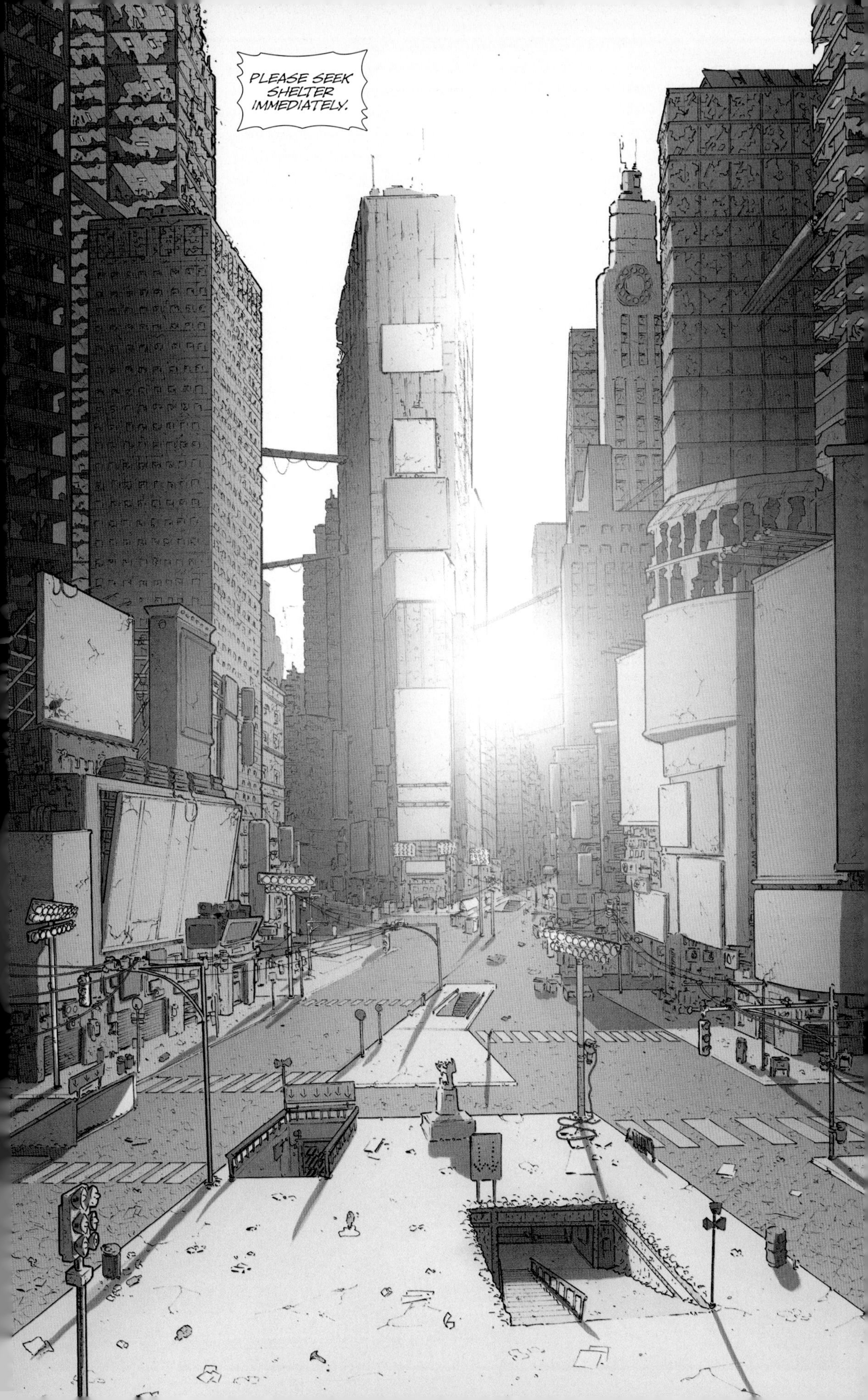
PLEASE SEEK SHELTER IMMEDIATELY.

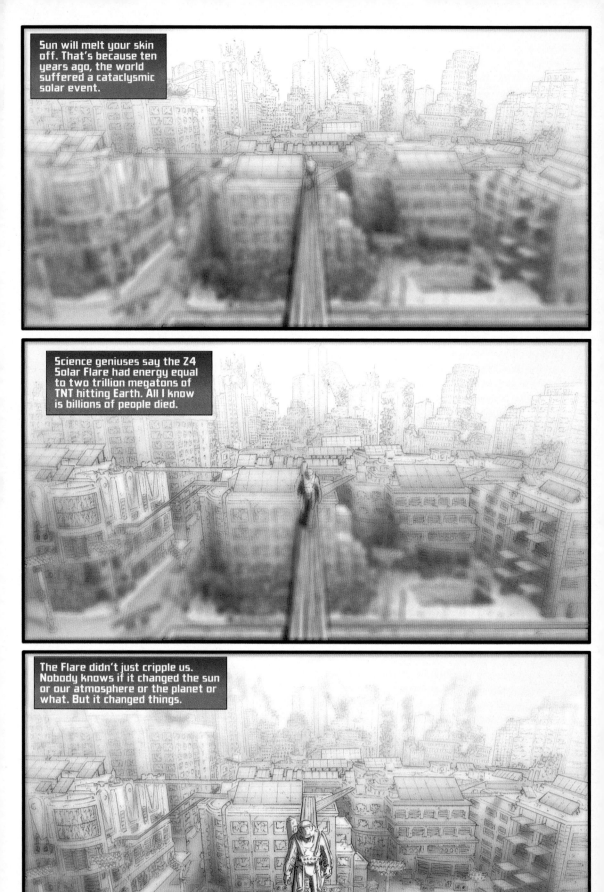

Sun will melt your skin off. That's because ten years ago, the world suffered a cataclysmic solar event.

Science geniuses say the Z4 Solar Flare had energy equal to two trillion megatons of TNT hitting Earth. All I know is billions of people died.

The Flare didn't just cripple us. Nobody knows if it changed the sun or our atmosphere or the planet or what. But it changed things.

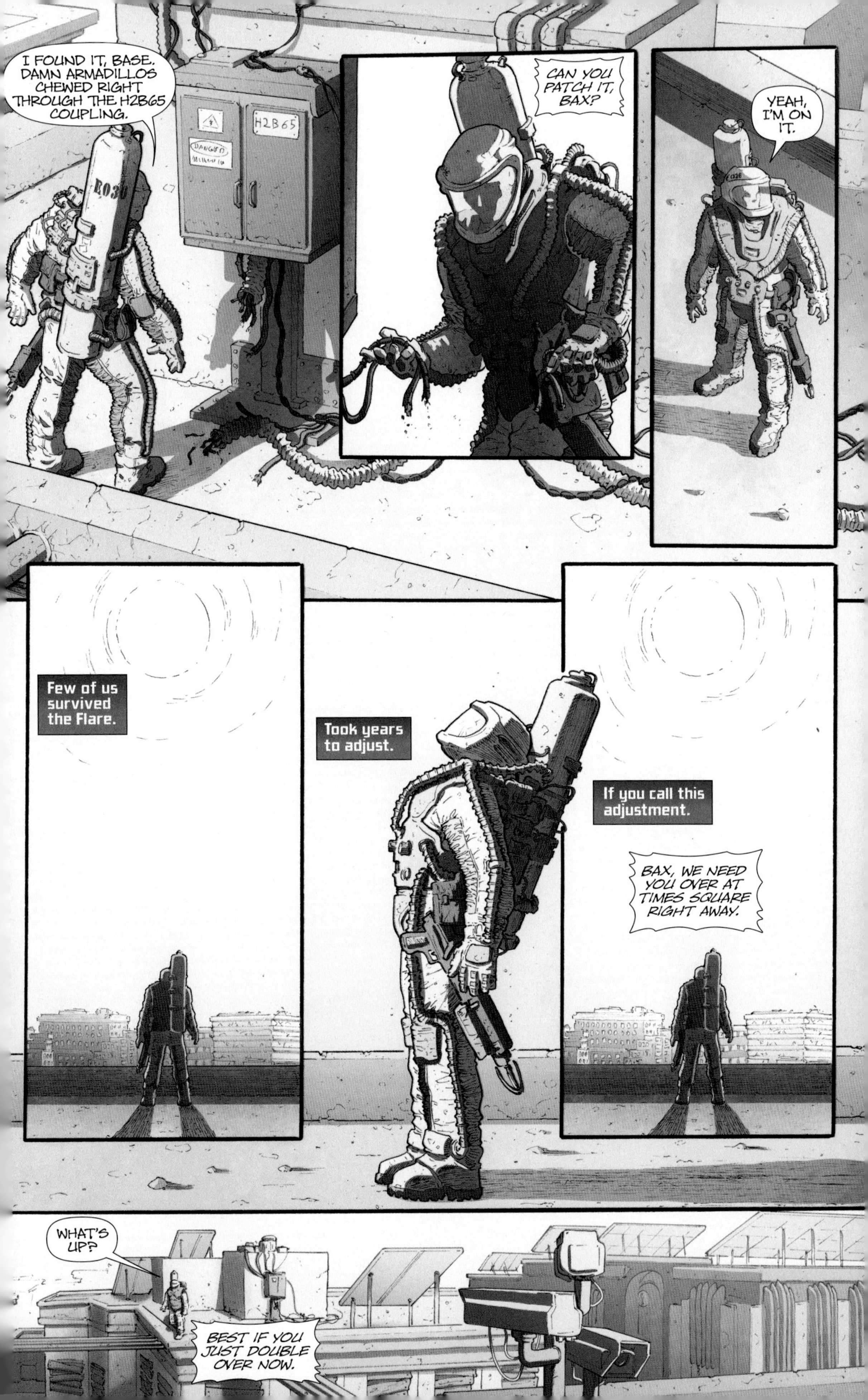
I FOUND IT, BASE. DAMN ARMADILLOS CHEWED RIGHT THROUGH THE H2B65 COUPLING.
H2B65
DANGER
R030
CAN YOU PATCH IT, BAX?
YEAH, I'M ON IT.
Few of us survived the Flare.
Took years to adjust.
If you call this adjustment.
BAX, WE NEED YOU OVER AT TIMES SQUARE RIGHT AWAY.
WHAT'S UP?
BEST IF YOU JUST DOUBLE OVER NOW.

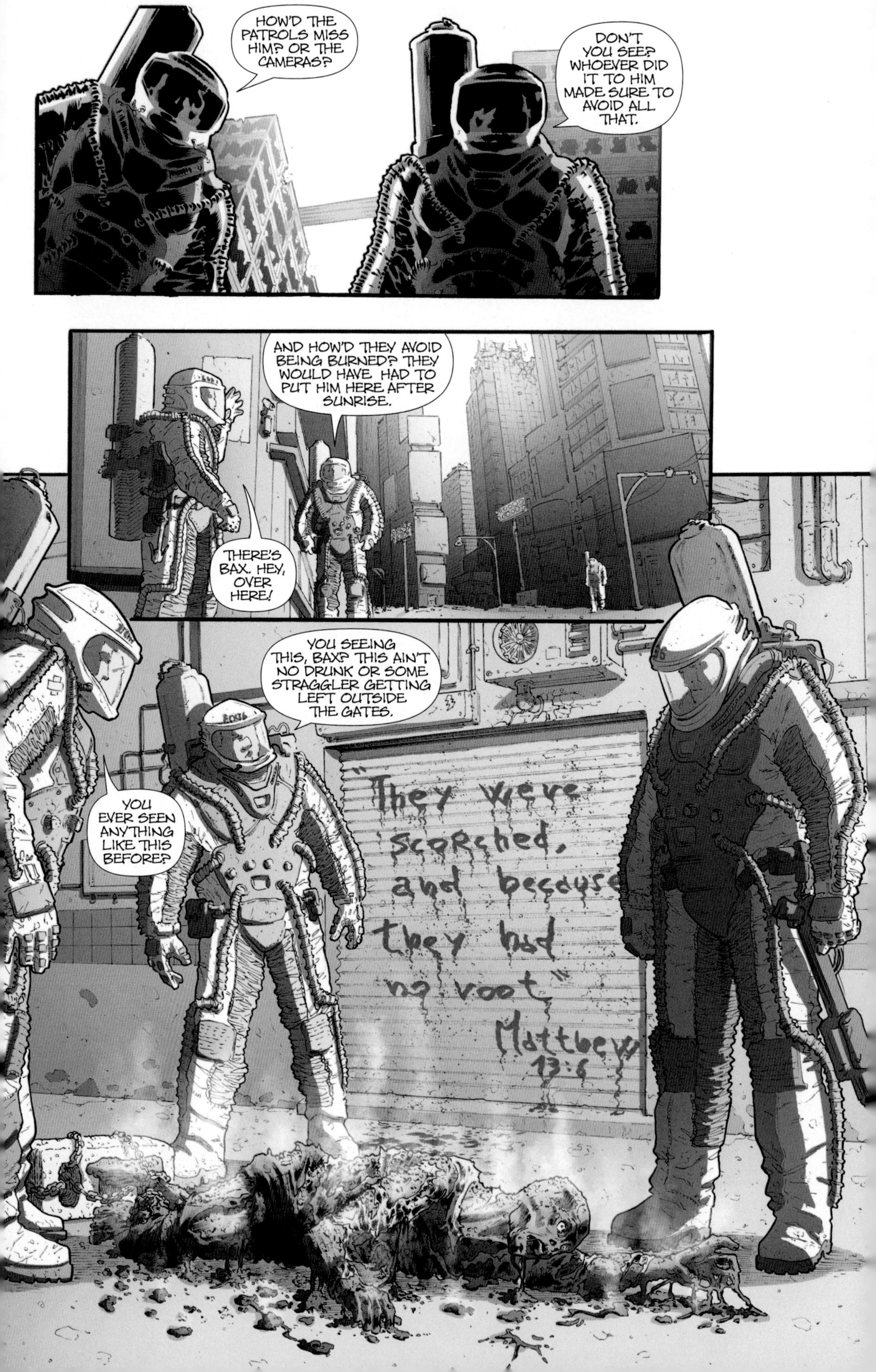

HOW'D THE PATROLS MISS HIM? OR THE CAMERAS?
DON'T YOU SEE? WHOEVER DID IT TO HIM MADE SURE TO AVOID ALL THAT.
AND HOW'D THEY AVOID BEING BURNED? THEY WOULD HAVE HAD TO PUT HIM HERE AFTER SUNRISE.
THERE'S BAX. HEY, OVER HERE!
YOU SEEING THIS, BAX? THIS AIN'T NO DRUNK OR SOME STRAGGLER GETTING LEFT OUTSIDE THE GATES.
YOU EVER SEEN ANYTHING LIKE THIS BEFORE?
"They were scorched, and because they had no root." Matthew 13:6

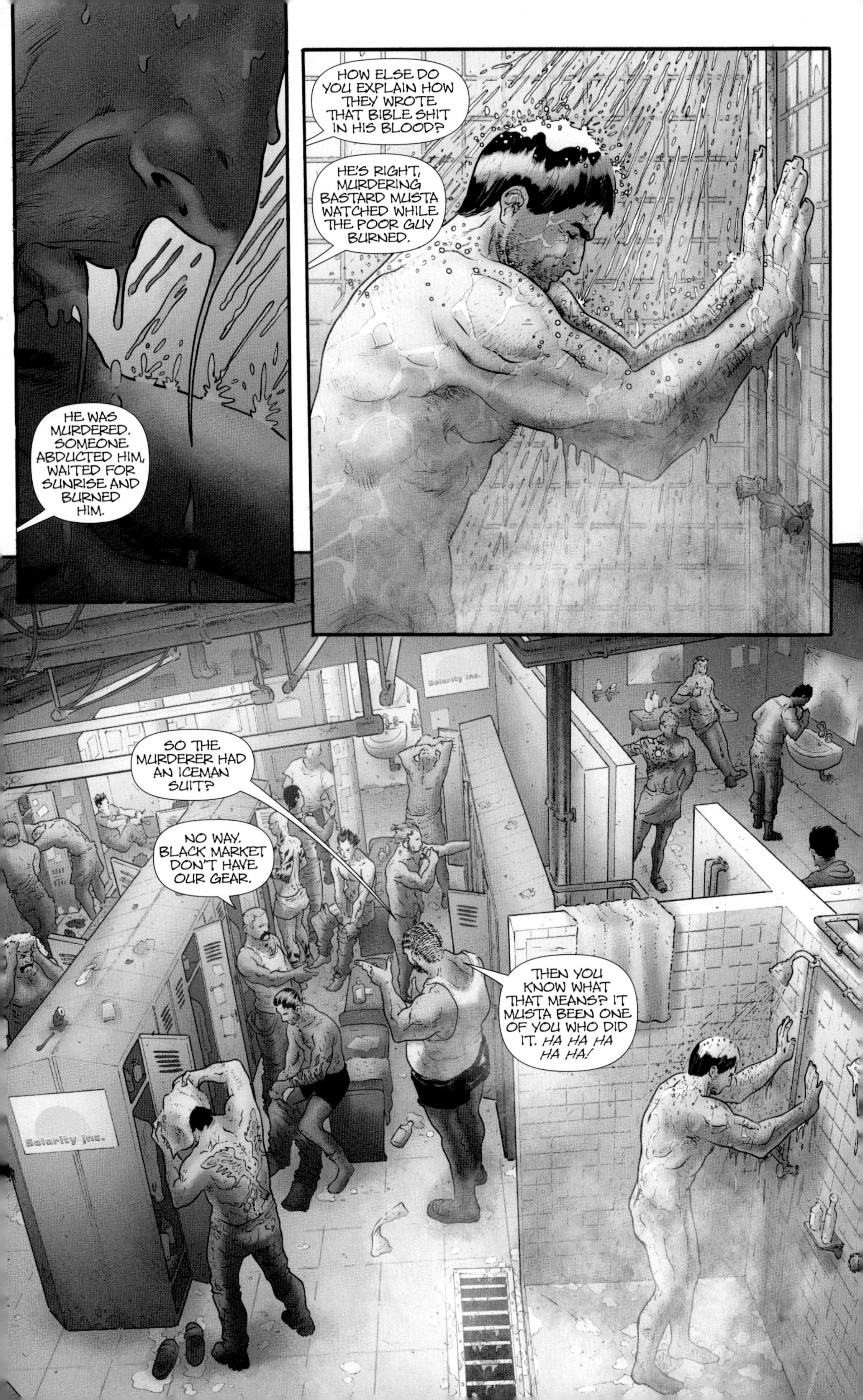
HE WAS MURDERED. SOMEONE ABDUCTED HIM, WAITED FOR SUNRISE AND BURNED HIM.
HOW ELSE DO YOU EXPLAIN HOW THEY WROTE THAT BIBLE SHIT IN HIS BLOOD?
HE'S RIGHT, MURDERING BASTARD MUSTA WATCHED WHILE THE POOR GUY BURNED.
Solarity Inc.
SO THE MURDERER HAD AN ICEMAN SUIT?
NO WAY. BLACK MARKET DON'T HAVE OUR GEAR.
THEN YOU KNOW WHAT THAT MEANS? IT MUSTA BEEN ONE OF YOU WHO DID IT. *HA HA HA HA HA!*
Solarity Inc.

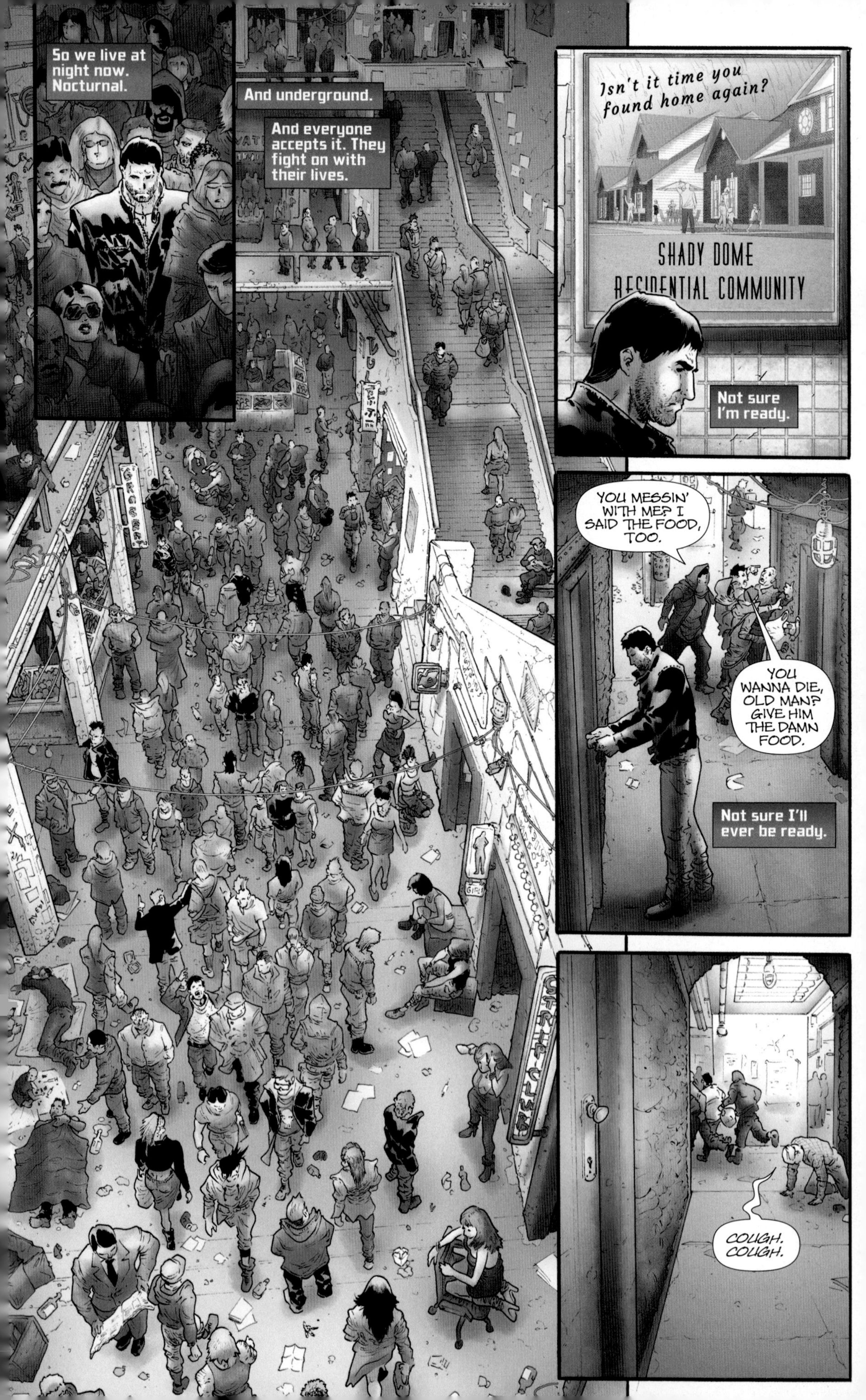
So we live at night now. Nocturnal.
And underground.
And everyone accepts it. They fight on with their lives.
Isn't it time you found home again?
SHADY DOME
RESIDENTIAL COMMUNITY
Not sure I'm ready.
YOU MESSIN' WITH ME? I SAID THE FOOD, TOO.
YOU WANNA DIE, OLD MAN? GIVE HIM THE DAMN FOOD.
Not sure I'll ever be ready.
COUGH. COUGH.

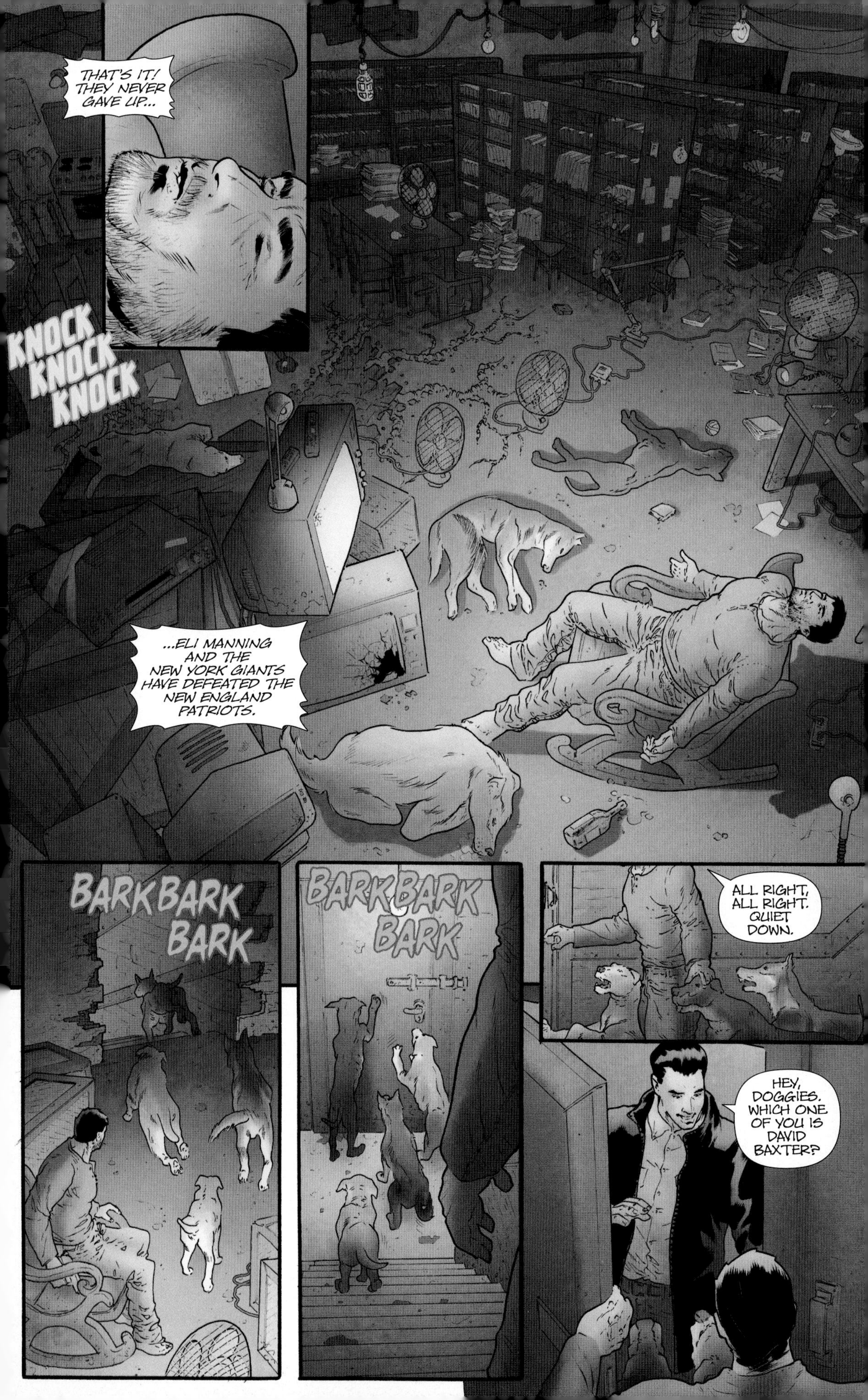
THAT'S IT! THEY NEVER GAVE UP...
KNOCK KNOCK KNOCK
...ELI MANNING AND THE NEW YORK GIANTS HAVE DEFEATED THE NEW ENGLAND PATRIOTS.
BARK BARK BARK
BARK BARK BARK
ALL RIGHT, ALL RIGHT. QUIET DOWN.
HEY, DOGGIES. WHICH ONE OF YOU IS DAVID BAXTER?

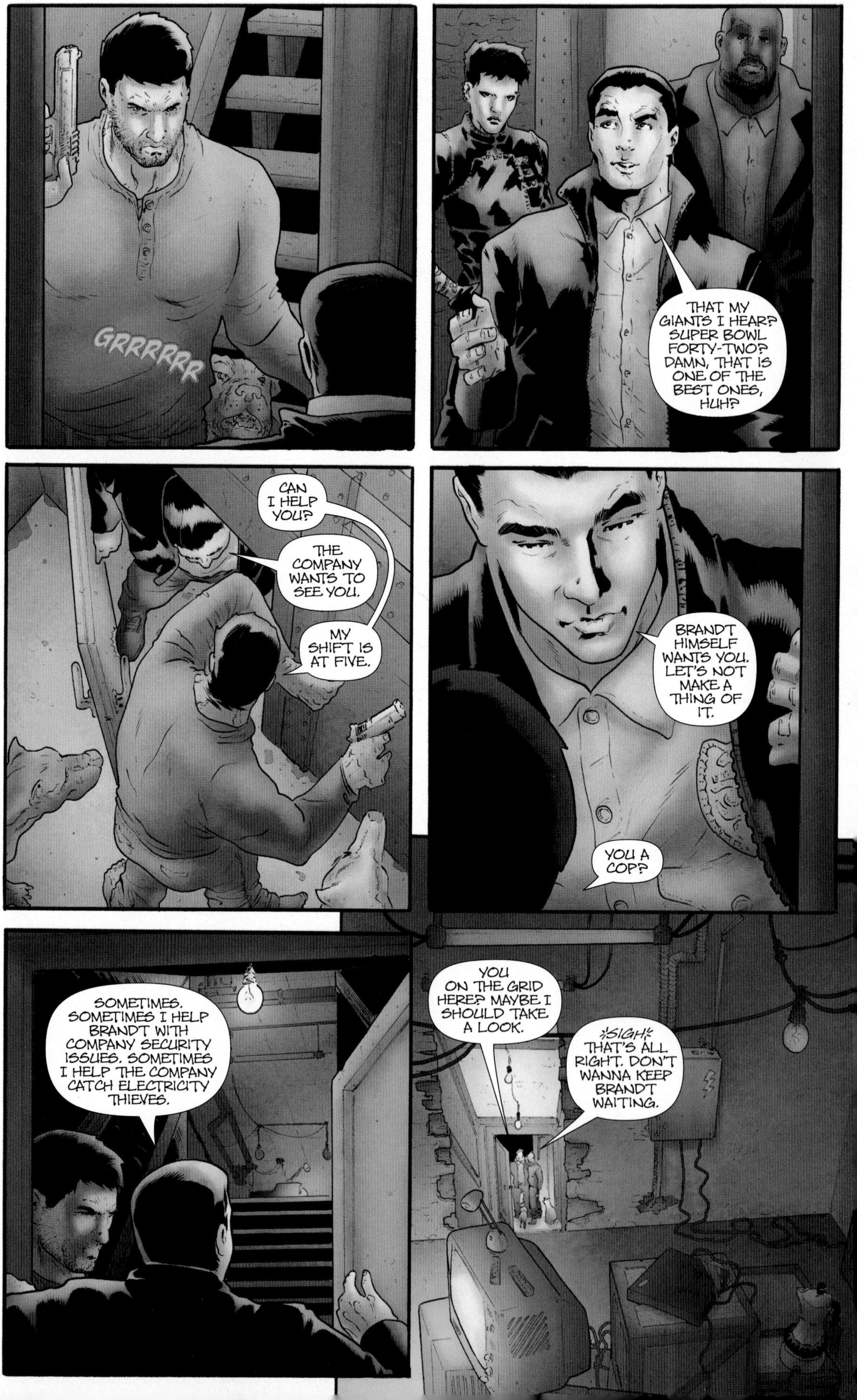
GRRRRRR
THAT MY GIANTS I HEAR? SUPER BOWL FORTY-TWO? DAMN, THAT IS ONE OF THE BEST ONES, HUH?
CAN I HELP YOU?
THE COMPANY WANTS TO SEE YOU.
MY SHIFT IS AT FIVE.
BRANDT HIMSELF WANTS YOU. LET'S NOT MAKE A THING OF IT.
YOU A COP?
SOMETIMES. SOMETIMES I HELP BRANDT WITH COMPANY SECURITY ISSUES. SOMETIMES I HELP THE COMPANY CATCH ELECTRICITY THIEVES.
YOU ON THE GRID HERE? MAYBE I SHOULD TAKE A LOOK.
SIGH THAT'S ALL RIGHT. DON'T WANNA KEEP BRANDT WAITING.

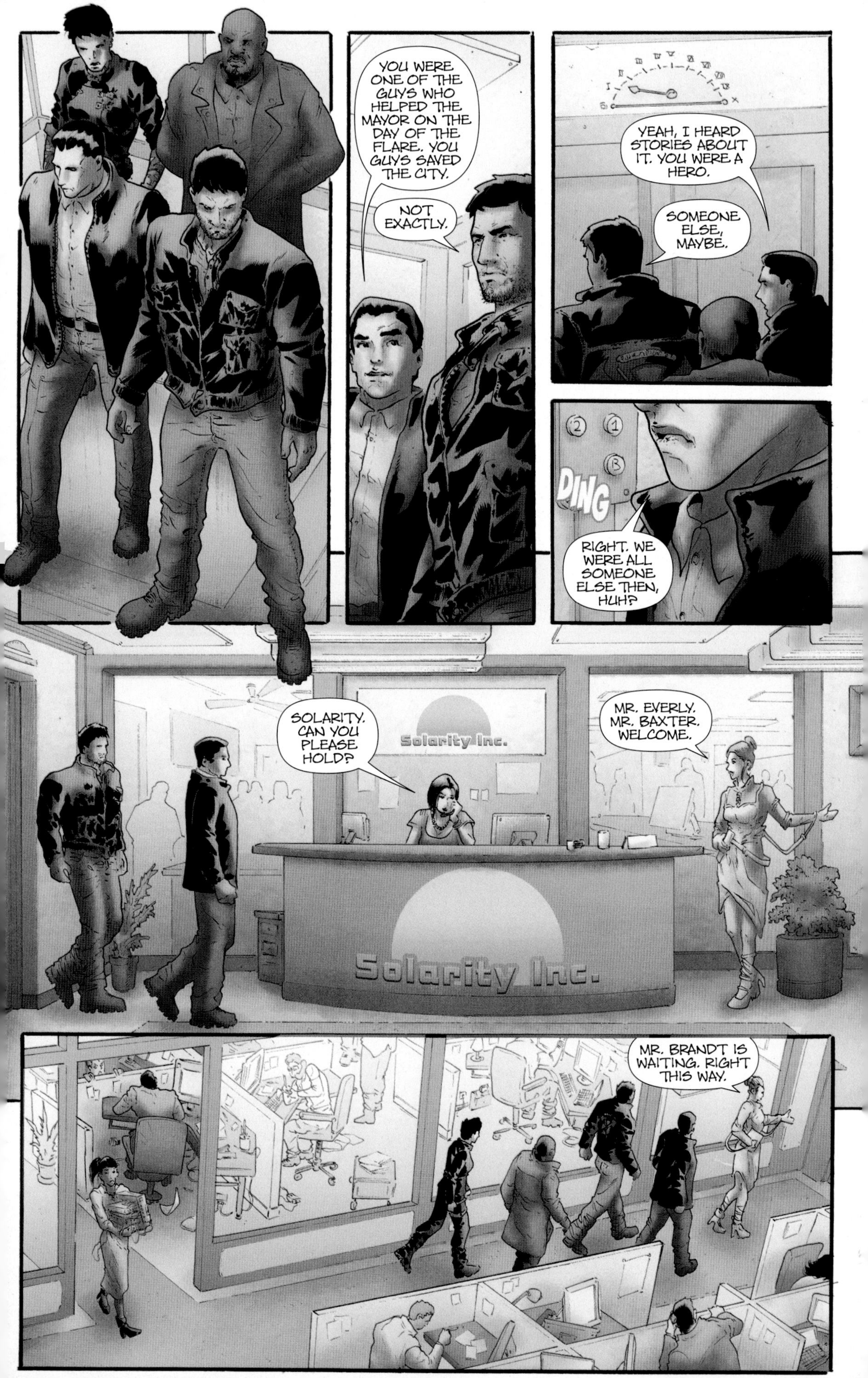
YOU WERE ONE OF THE GUYS WHO HELPED THE MAYOR ON THE DAY OF THE FLARE. YOU GUYS SAVED THE CITY.
NOT EXACTLY.
YEAH, I HEARD STORIES ABOUT IT. YOU WERE A HERO.
SOMEONE ELSE, MAYBE.
DING
RIGHT. WE WERE ALL SOMEONE ELSE THEN, HUH?
Solarity Inc.
SOLARITY. CAN YOU PLEASE HOLD?
MR. EVERLY. MR. BAXTER. WELCOME.
Solarity Inc.
MR. BRANDT IS WAITING. RIGHT THIS WAY.

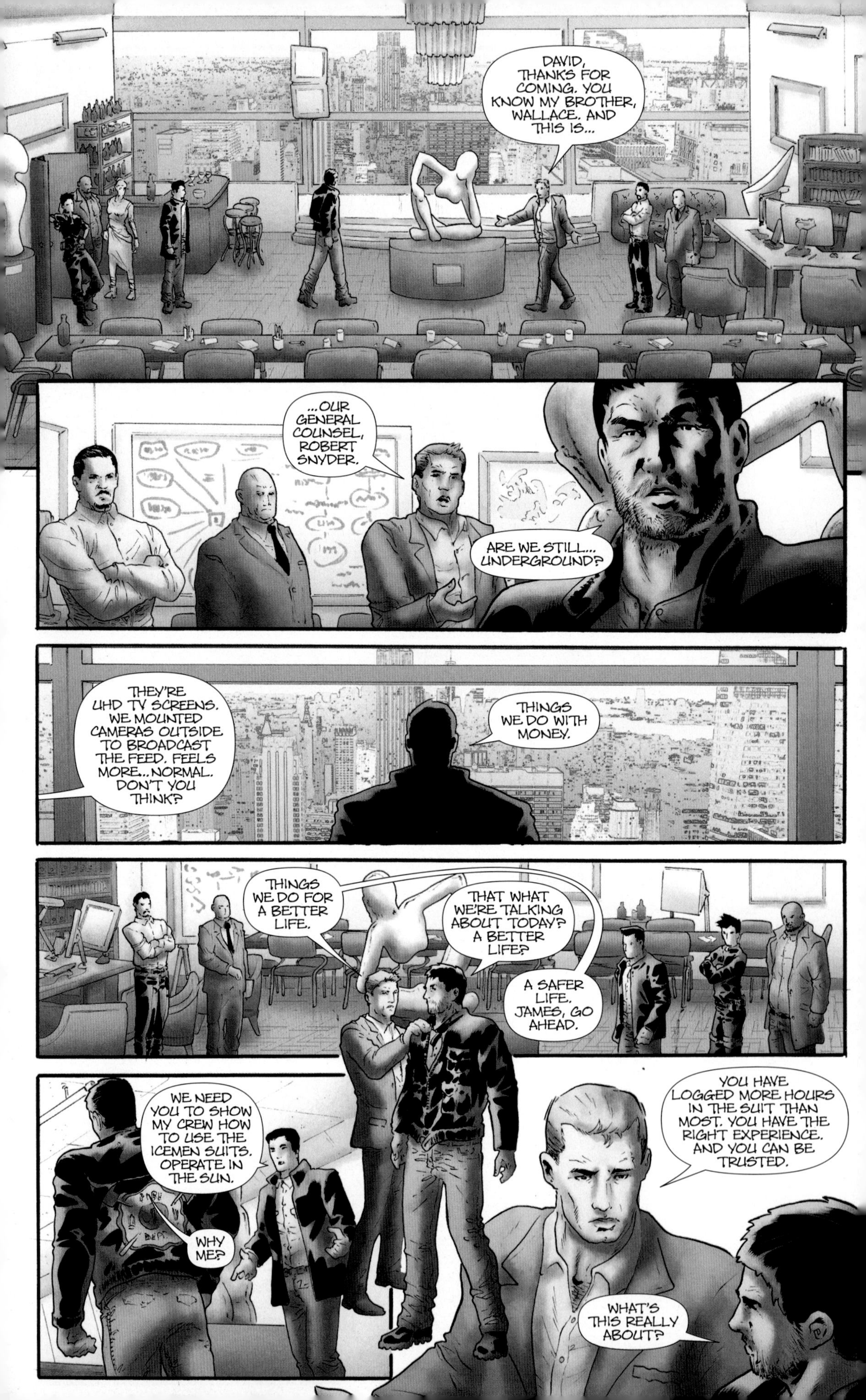
DAVID, THANKS FOR COMING. YOU KNOW MY BROTHER, WALLACE. AND THIS IS...
...OUR GENERAL COUNSEL, ROBERT SNYDER.
ARE WE STILL... UNDERGROUND?
THEY'RE UHD TV SCREENS. WE MOUNTED CAMERAS OUTSIDE TO BROADCAST THE FEED. FEELS MORE...NORMAL. DON'T YOU THINK?
THINGS WE DO WITH MONEY.
THINGS WE DO FOR A BETTER LIFE.
THAT WHAT WE'RE TALKING ABOUT TODAY? A BETTER LIFE?
A SAFER LIFE. JAMES, GO AHEAD.
WE NEED YOU TO SHOW MY CREW HOW TO USE THE ICEMEN SUITS. OPERATE IN THE SUN.
WHY ME?
YOU HAVE LOGGED MORE HOURS IN THE SUIT THAN MOST. YOU HAVE THE RIGHT EXPERIENCE. AND YOU CAN BE TRUSTED.
WHAT'S THIS REALLY ABOUT?

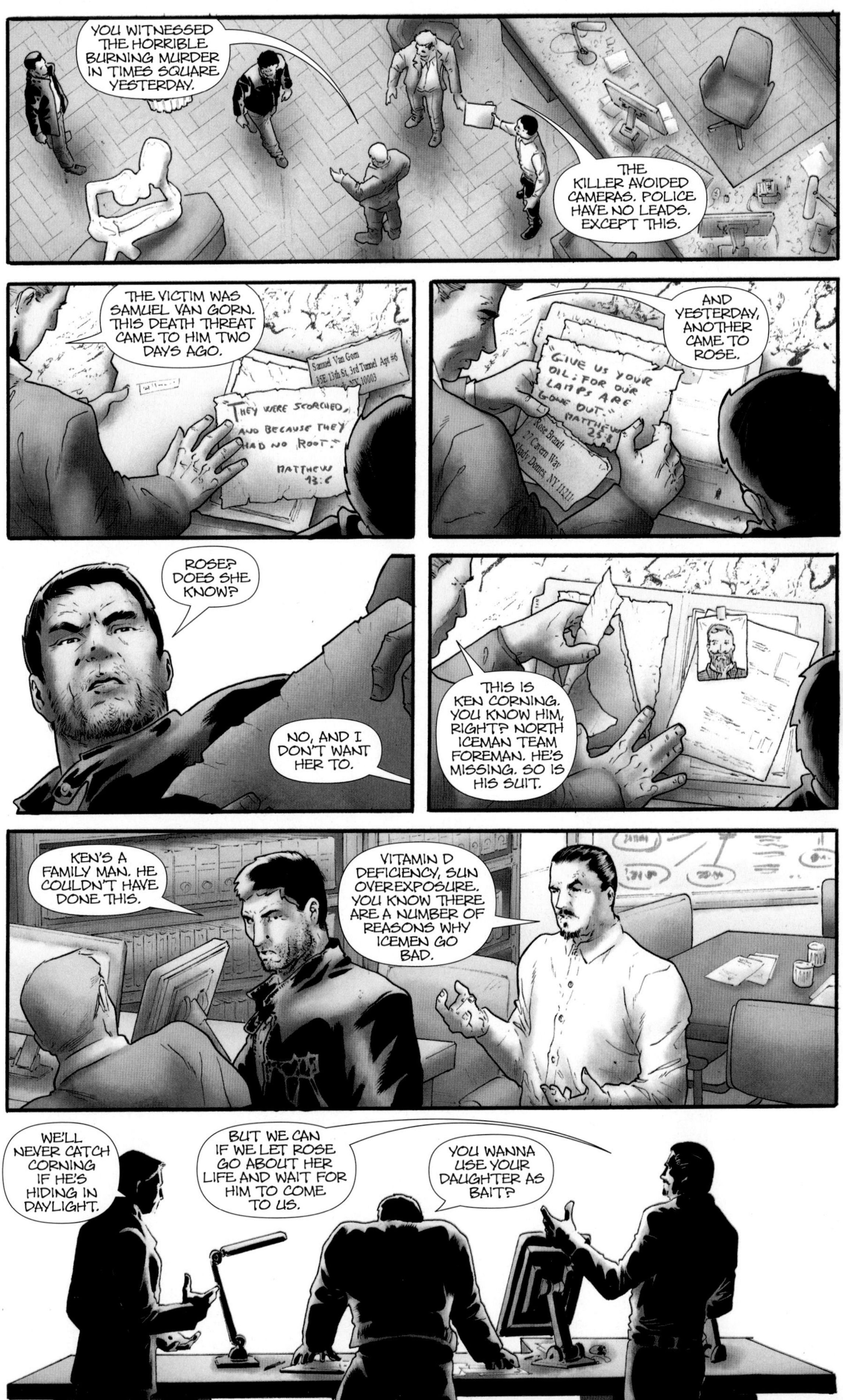
YOU WITNESSED THE HORRIBLE BURNING MURDER IN TIMES SQUARE YESTERDAY.
THE KILLER AVOIDED CAMERAS. POLICE HAVE NO LEADS. EXCEPT THIS.
THE VICTIM WAS SAMUEL VAN GORN. THIS DEATH THREAT CAME TO HIM TWO DAYS AGO.
Samuel Van Gorn
35E 13th St, 3rd Tunnel Apt #6
NY 10003
"THEY WERE SCORCHED, AND BECAUSE THEY HAD NO ROOT." MATTHEW 13:6
AND YESTERDAY, ANOTHER CAME TO ROSE.
"GIVE US YOUR OIL; FOR OUR LAMPS ARE GONE OUT." MATTHEW 25:8
Rose Brandt
27 Cavern Way
Shady Domes, NY 11211
ROSE? DOES SHE KNOW?
NO, AND I DON'T WANT HER TO.
THIS IS KEN CORNING. YOU KNOW HIM, RIGHT? NORTH ICEMAN TEAM FOREMAN. HE'S MISSING. SO IS HIS SUIT.
KEN'S A FAMILY MAN. HE COULDN'T HAVE DONE THIS.
VITAMIN D DEFICIENCY, SUN OVEREXPOSURE. YOU KNOW THERE ARE A NUMBER OF REASONS WHY ICEMEN GO BAD.
WE'LL NEVER CATCH CORNING IF HE'S HIDING IN DAYLIGHT.
BUT WE CAN IF WE LET ROSE GO ABOUT HER LIFE AND WAIT FOR HIM TO COME TO US.
YOU WANNA USE YOUR DAUGHTER AS BAIT?

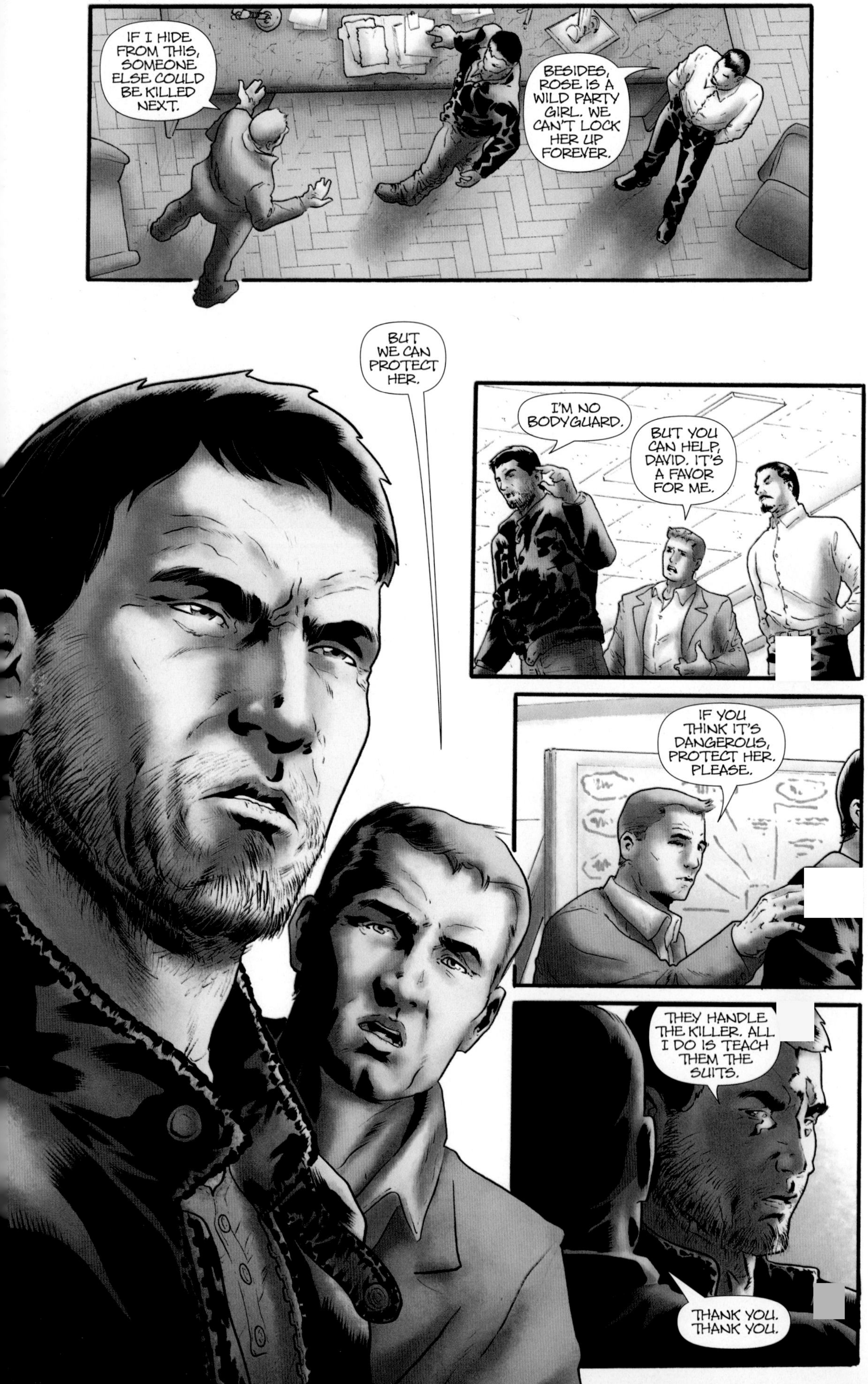
IF I HIDE FROM THIS, SOMEONE ELSE COULD BE KILLED NEXT.
BESIDES, ROSE IS A WILD PARTY GIRL. WE CAN'T LOCK HER UP FOREVER.
BUT WE CAN PROTECT HER.
I'M NO BODYGUARD.
BUT YOU CAN HELP, DAVID. IT'S A FAVOR FOR ME.
IF YOU THINK IT'S DANGEROUS, PROTECT HER. PLEASE.
THEY HANDLE THE KILLER. ALL I DO IS TEACH THEM THE SUITS.
THANK YOU. THANK YOU.

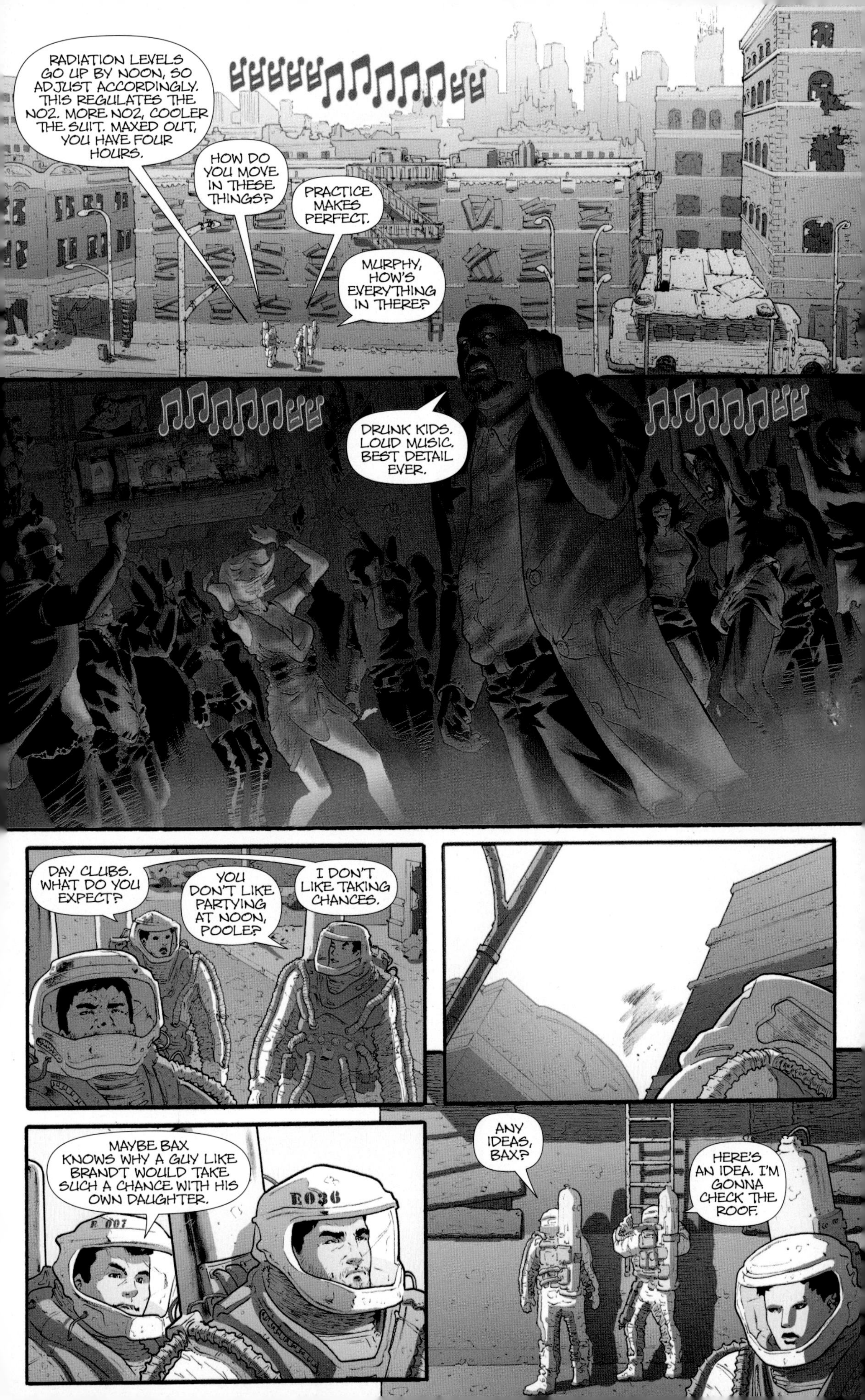
RADIATION LEVELS GO UP BY NOON, SO ADJUST ACCORDINGLY. THIS REGULATES THE NO2. MORE NO2, COOLER THE SUIT. MAXED OUT, YOU HAVE FOUR HOURS.
HOW DO YOU MOVE IN THESE THINGS?
PRACTICE MAKES PERFECT.
MURPHY, HOW'S EVERYTHING IN THERE?
DRUNK KIDS. LOUD MUSIC. BEST DETAIL EVER.
DAY CLUBS. WHAT DO YOU EXPECT?
YOU DON'T LIKE PARTYING AT NOON, POOLE?
I DON'T LIKE TAKING CHANCES.
MAYBE BAX KNOWS WHY A GUY LIKE BRANDT WOULD TAKE SUCH A CHANCE WITH HIS OWN DAUGHTER.
E 007
E036
ANY IDEAS, BAX?
HERE'S AN IDEA. I'M GONNA CHECK THE ROOF.

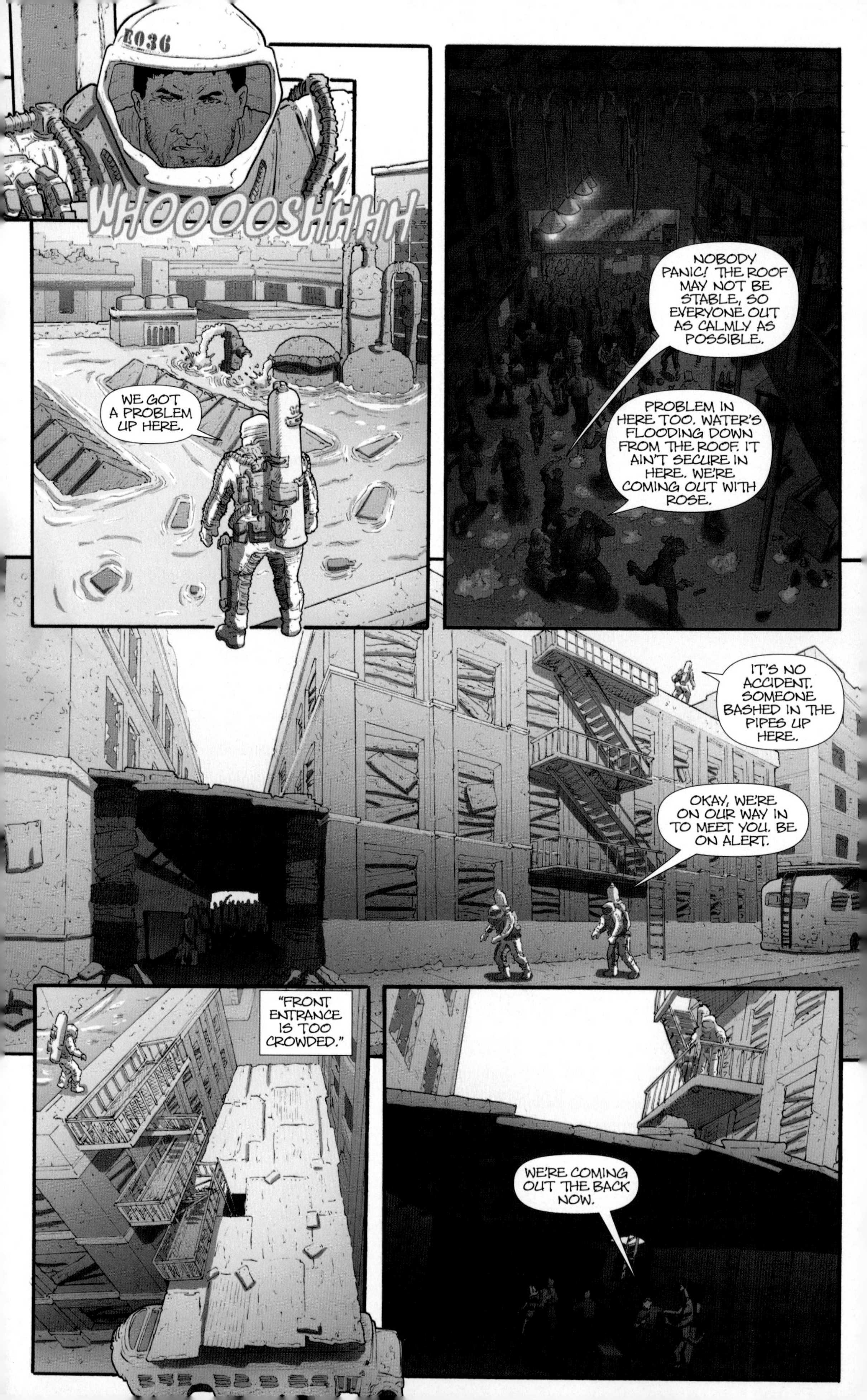
R036
WHOOOOOSHHHH
WE GOT A PROBLEM UP HERE.
NOBODY PANIC! THE ROOF MAY NOT BE STABLE, SO EVERYONE OUT AS CALMLY AS POSSIBLE.
PROBLEM IN HERE TOO. WATER'S FLOODING DOWN FROM THE ROOF. IT AIN'T SECURE IN HERE. WE'RE COMING OUT WITH ROSE.
IT'S NO ACCIDENT. SOMEONE BASHED IN THE PIPES UP HERE.
OKAY, WE'RE ON OUR WAY IN TO MEET YOU. BE ON ALERT.
"FRONT ENTRANCE IS TOO CROWDED."
WE'RE COMING OUT THE BACK NOW.

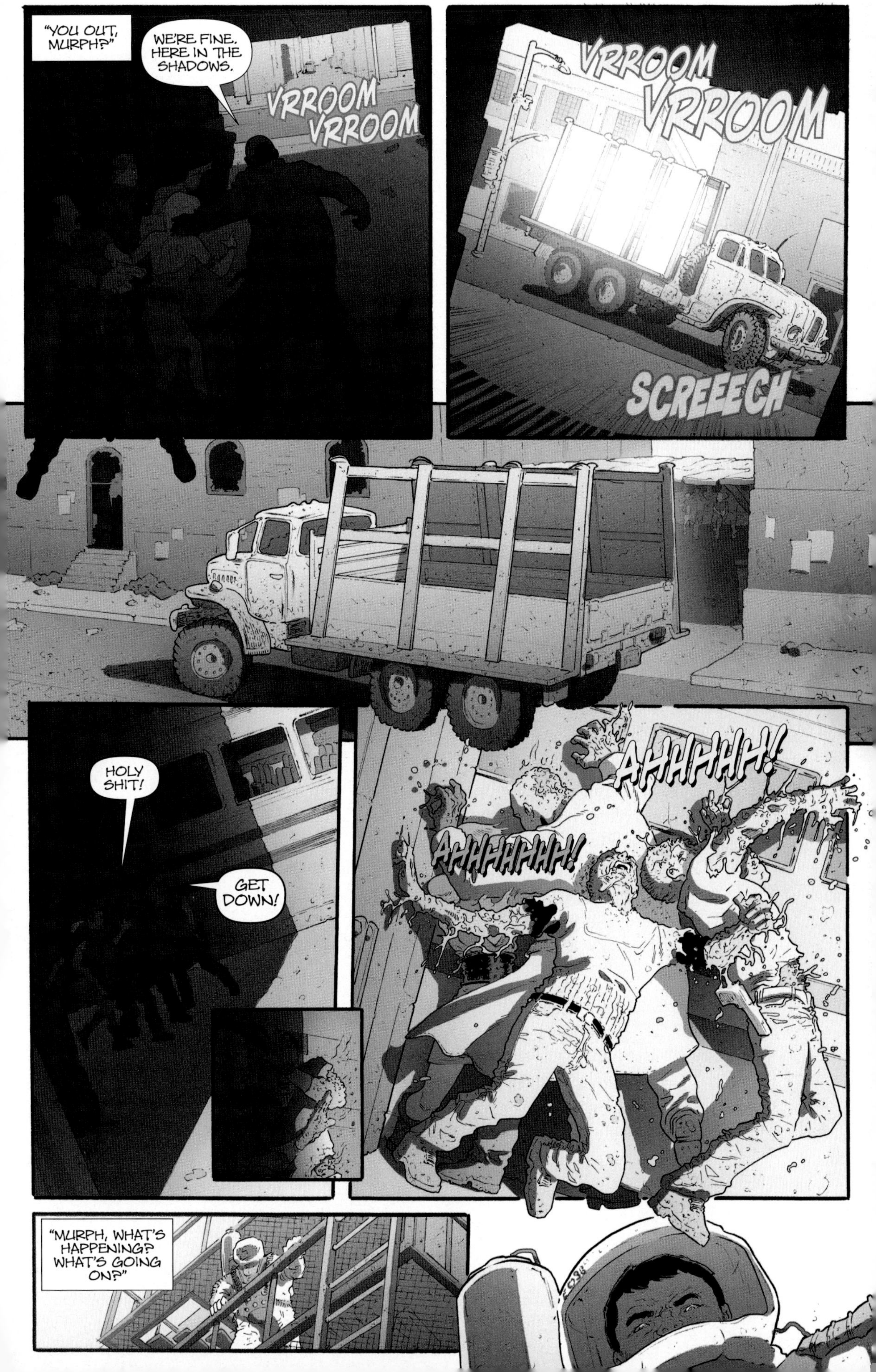
"YOU OUT, MURPH?"
WE'RE FINE. HERE IN THE SHADOWS.
VRROOM VRROOM
VRROOM VRROOM
SCREEECH
HOLY SHIT!
GET DOWN!
AHHHHH!
AHHHHHHH!
"MURPH, WHAT'S HAPPENING? WHAT'S GOING ON?"

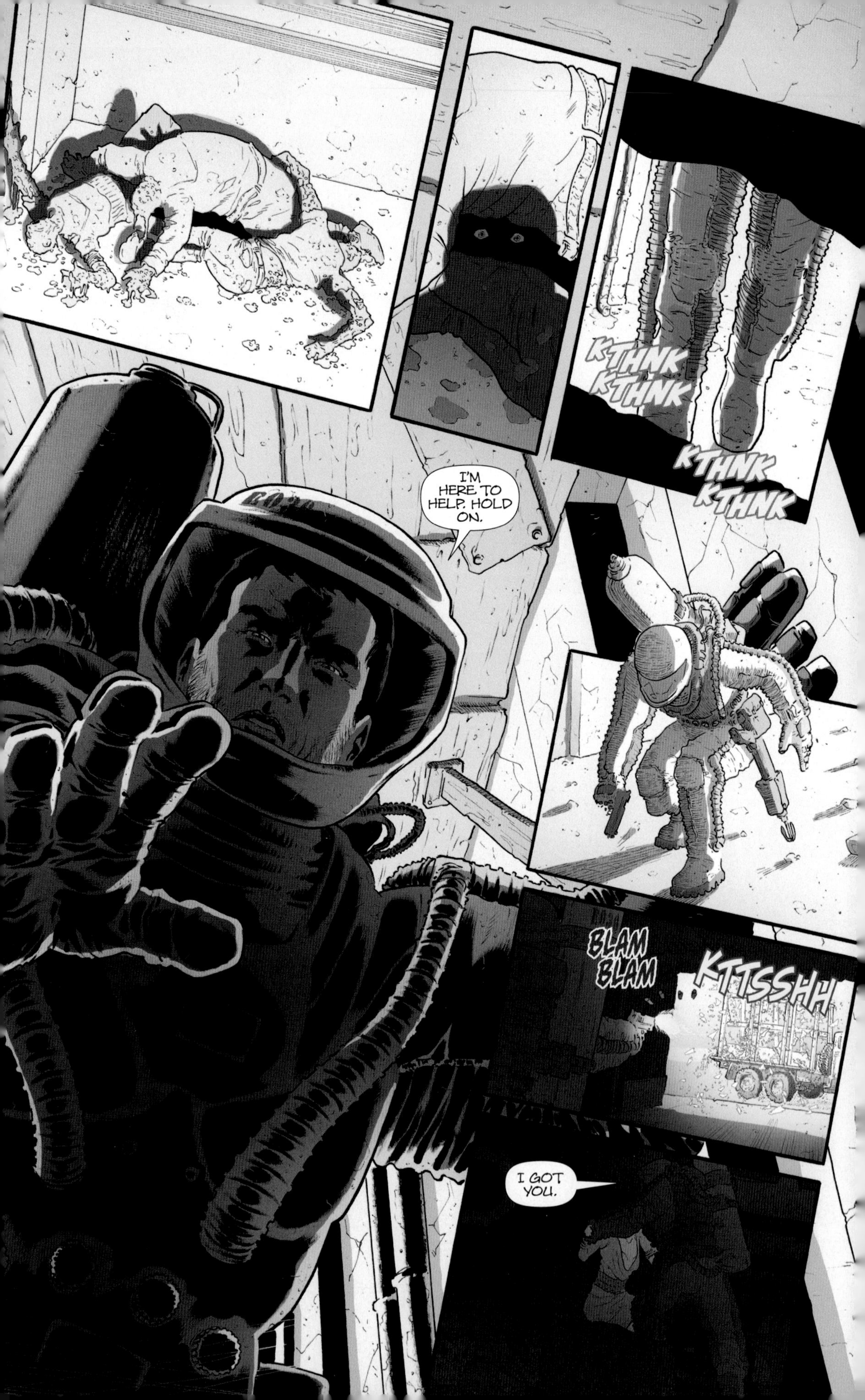
KTHNK
KTHNK
KTHNK
KTHNK
I'M HERE TO HELP. HOLD ON.
BLAM
BLAM
KTTSSHH
I GOT YOU.

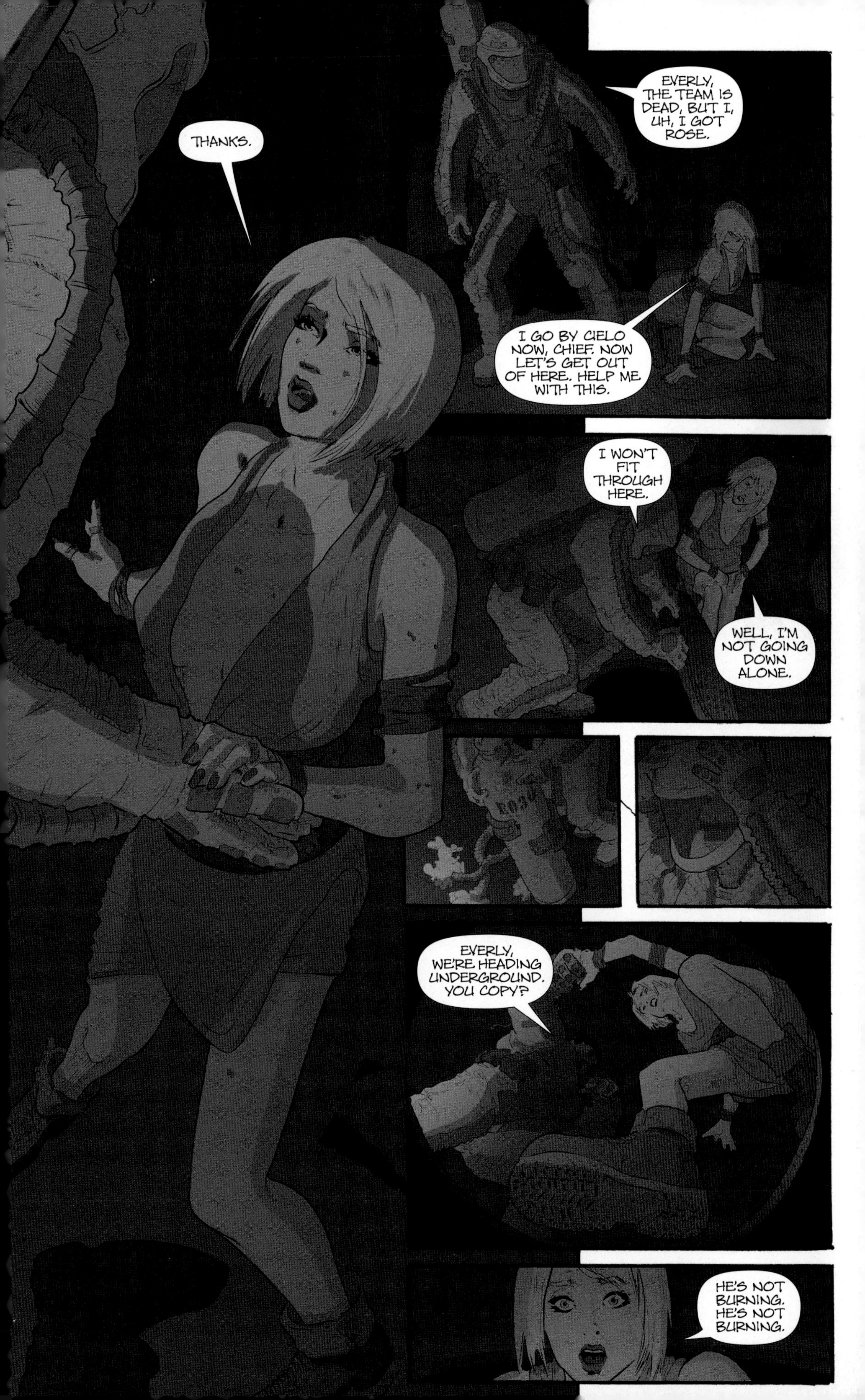
THANKS.
EVERLY, THE TEAM IS DEAD, BUT I, UH, I GOT ROSE.
I GO BY CIELO NOW, CHIEF. NOW LET'S GET OUT OF HERE. HELP ME WITH THIS.
I WON'T FIT THROUGH HERE.
WELL, I'M NOT GOING DOWN ALONE.
EVERLY, WE'RE HEADING UNDERGROUND. YOU COPY?
HE'S NOT BURNING. HE'S NOT BURNING.

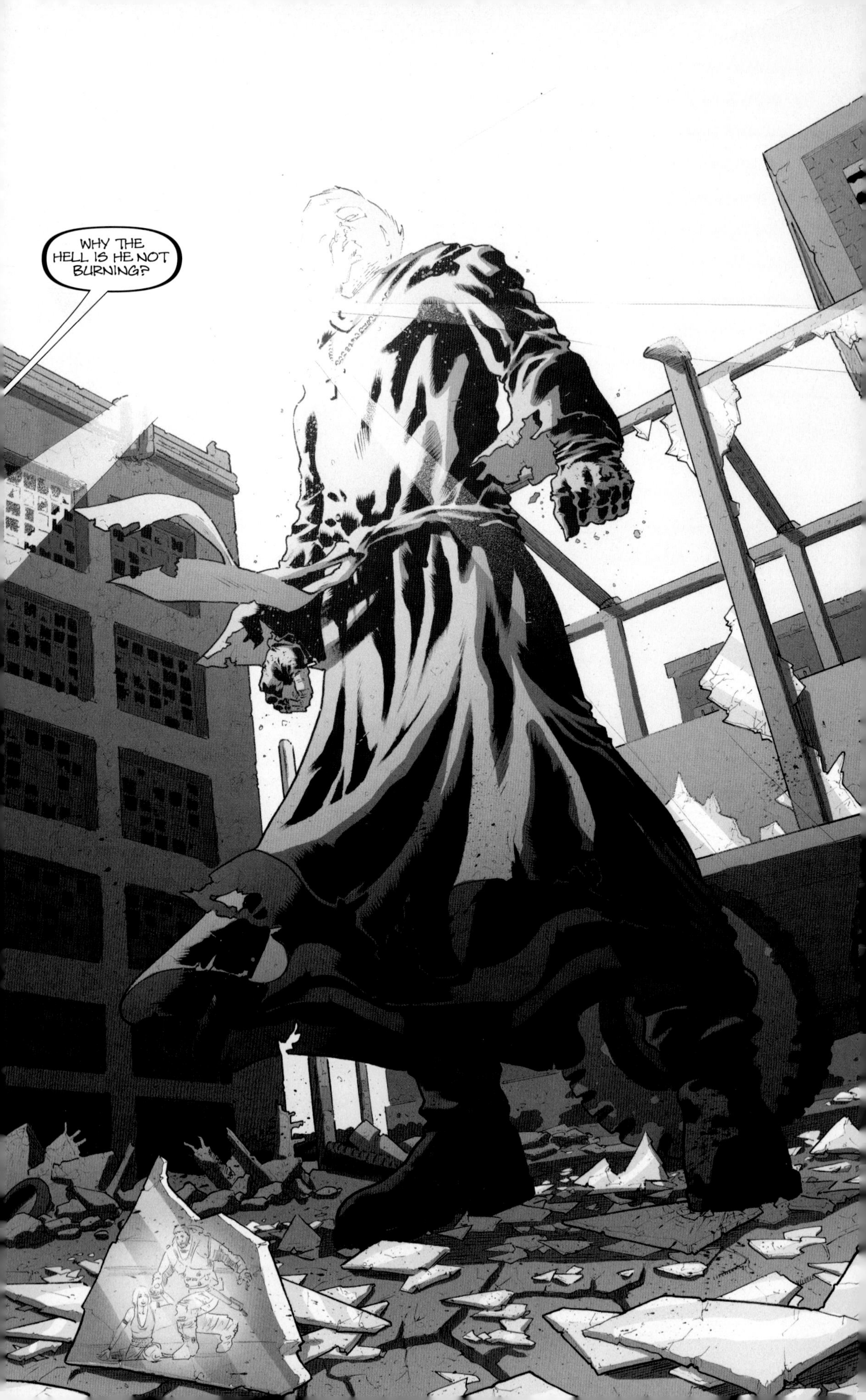
WHY THE HELL IS HE NOT BURNING?

CHAPTER TWO

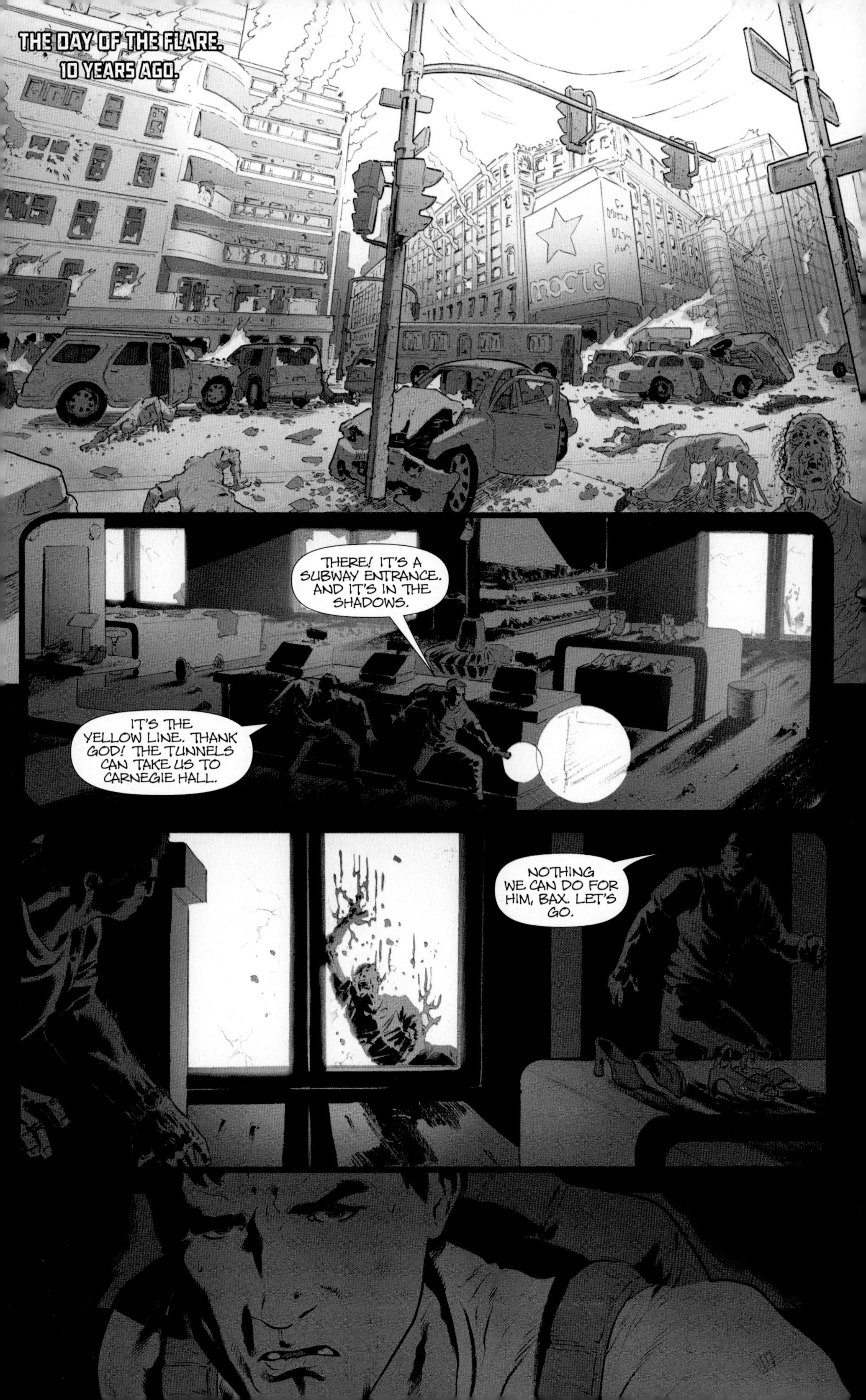
THE DAY OF THE FLARE.
10 YEARS AGO.
THERE! IT'S A SUBWAY ENTRANCE. AND IT'S IN THE SHADOWS.
IT'S THE YELLOW LINE. THANK GOD! THE TUNNELS CAN TAKE US TO CARNEGIE HALL.
NOTHING WE CAN DO FOR HIM, BAX. LET'S GO.

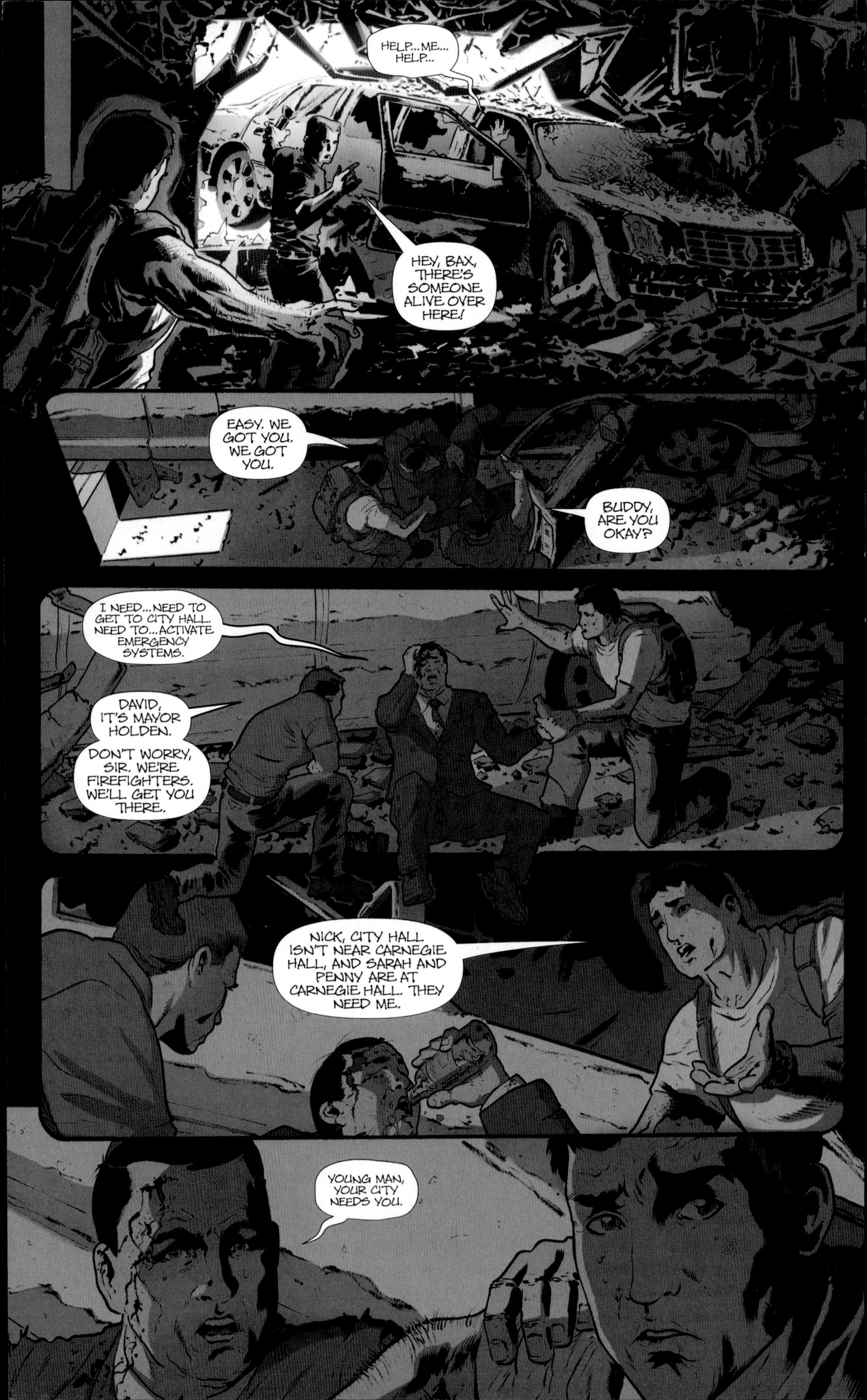
HELP...ME... HELP...
HEY, BAX, THERE'S SOMEONE ALIVE OVER HERE!
EASY. WE GOT YOU. WE GOT YOU.
BUDDY, ARE YOU OKAY?
I NEED...NEED TO GET TO CITY HALL. NEED TO...ACTIVATE EMERGENCY SYSTEMS.
DAVID, IT'S MAYOR HOLDEN.
DON'T WORRY, SIR. WE'RE FIREFIGHTERS. WE'LL GET YOU THERE.
NICK, CITY HALL ISN'T NEAR CARNEGIE HALL, AND SARAH AND PENNY ARE AT CARNEGIE HALL. THEY NEED ME.
YOUNG MAN, YOUR CITY NEEDS YOU.

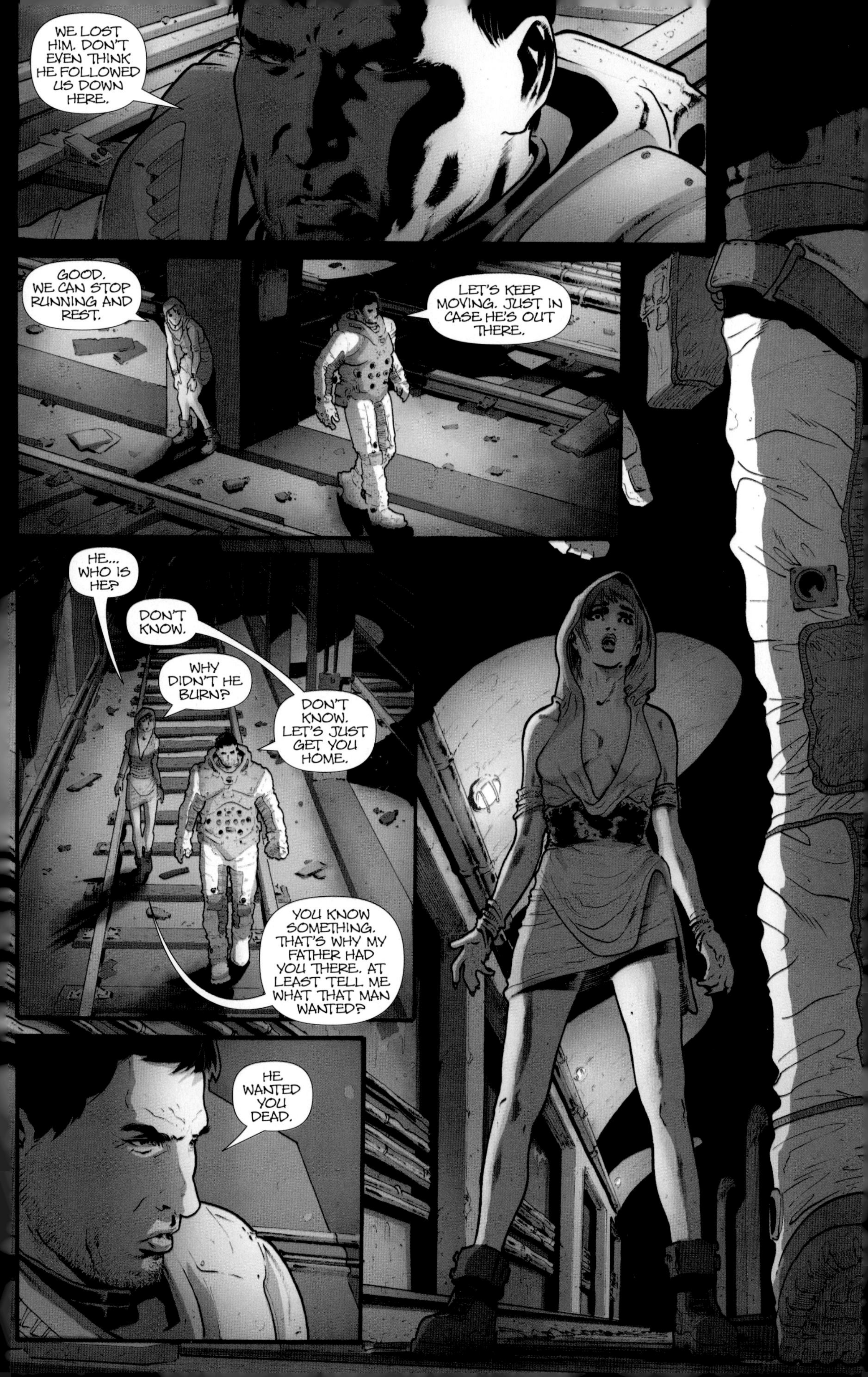
WE LOST HIM. DON'T EVEN THINK HE FOLLOWED US DOWN HERE.
GOOD. WE CAN STOP RUNNING AND REST.
LET'S KEEP MOVING. JUST IN CASE HE'S OUT THERE.
HE... WHO IS HE?
DON'T KNOW.
WHY DIDN'T HE BURN?
DON'T KNOW. LET'S JUST GET YOU HOME.
YOU KNOW SOMETHING. THAT'S WHY MY FATHER HAD YOU THERE. AT LEAST TELL ME WHAT THAT MAN WANTED?
HE WANTED YOU DEAD.

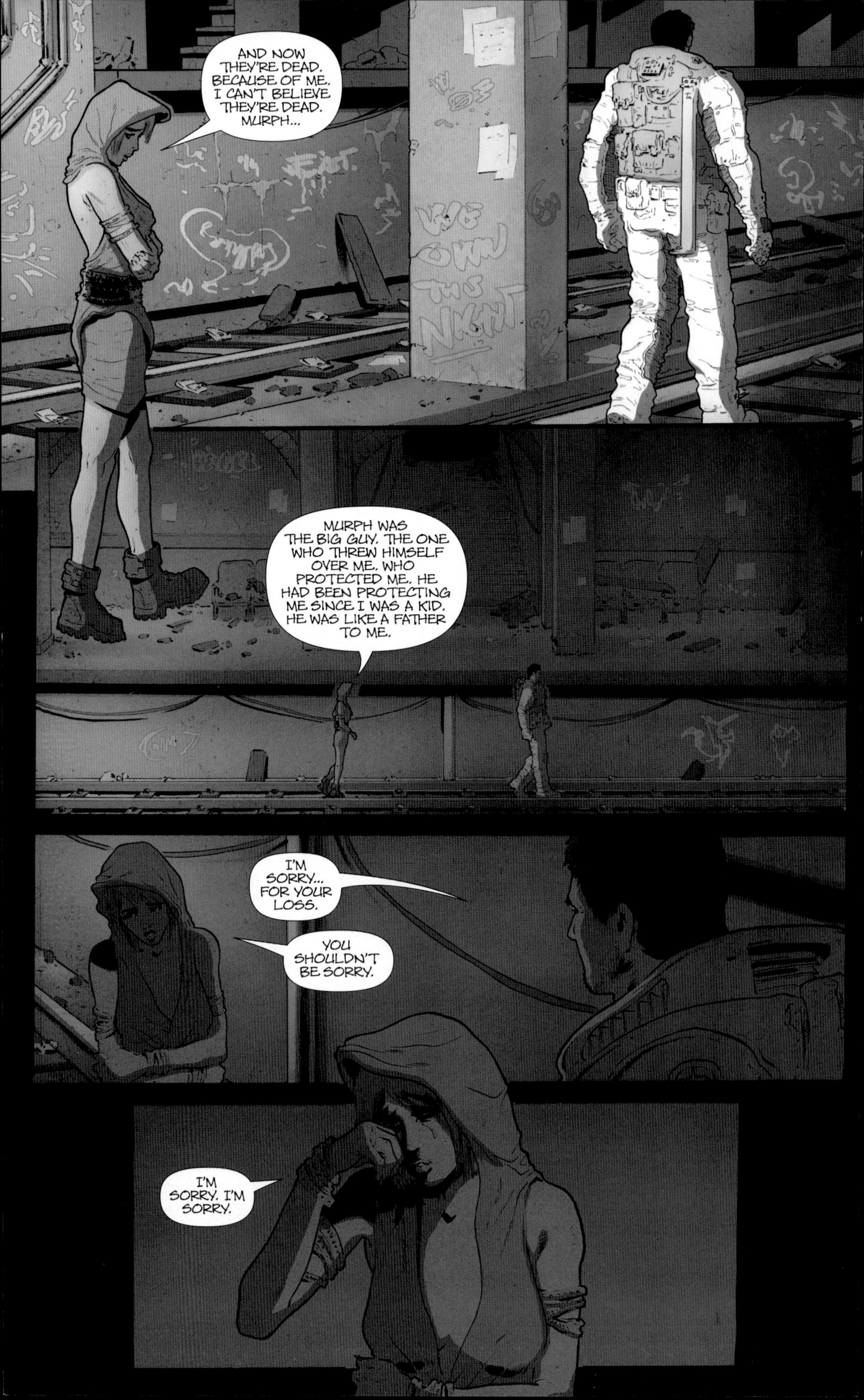
AND NOW THEY'RE DEAD. BECAUSE OF ME. I CAN'T BELIEVE THEY'RE DEAD. MURPH...
MURPH WAS THE BIG GUY. THE ONE WHO THREW HIMSELF OVER ME. WHO PROTECTED ME. HE HAD BEEN PROTECTING ME SINCE I WAS A KID. HE WAS LIKE A FATHER TO ME.
I'M SORRY... FOR YOUR LOSS.
YOU SHOULDN'T BE SORRY.
I'M SORRY. I'M SORRY.

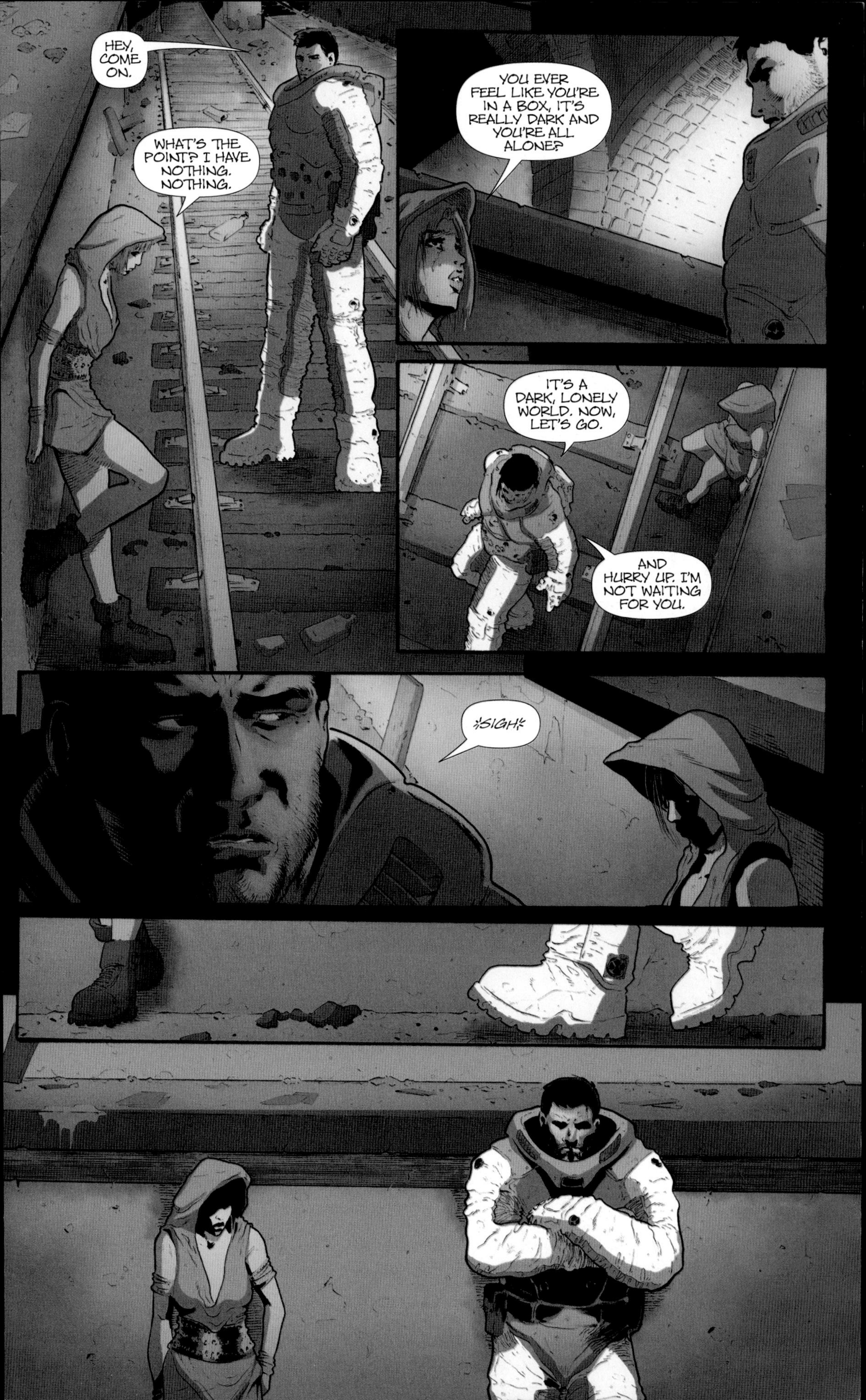
HEY, COME ON.
WHAT'S THE POINT? I HAVE NOTHING. NOTHING.
YOU EVER FEEL LIKE YOU'RE IN A BOX, IT'S REALLY DARK AND YOU'RE ALL ALONE?
IT'S A DARK, LONELY WORLD. NOW, LET'S GO.
AND HURRY UP. I'M NOT WAITING FOR YOU.
SIGH

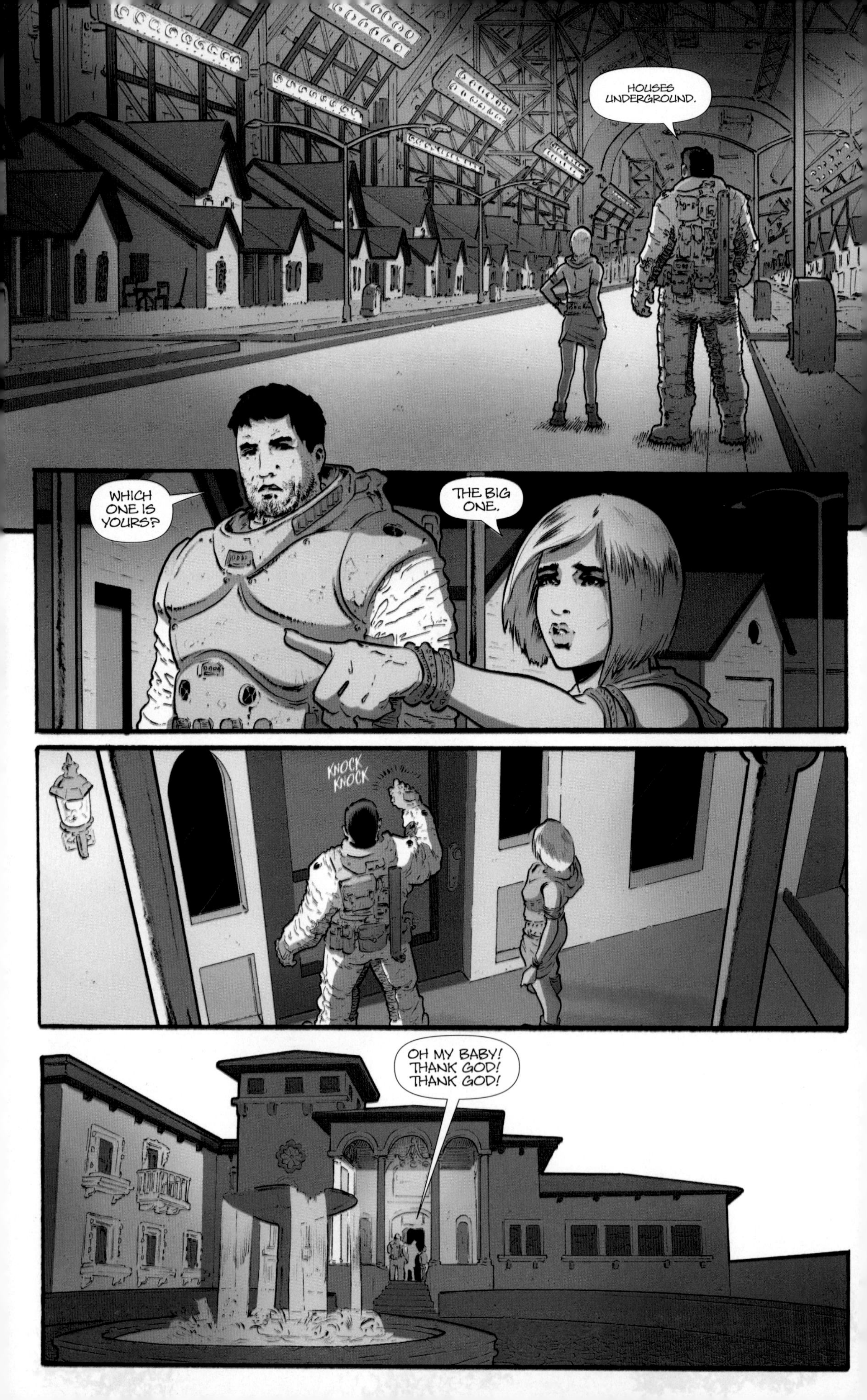
HOUSES UNDERGROUND.
WHICH ONE IS YOURS?
THE BIG ONE.
KNOCK KNOCK
OH MY BABY! THANK GOD! THANK GOD!

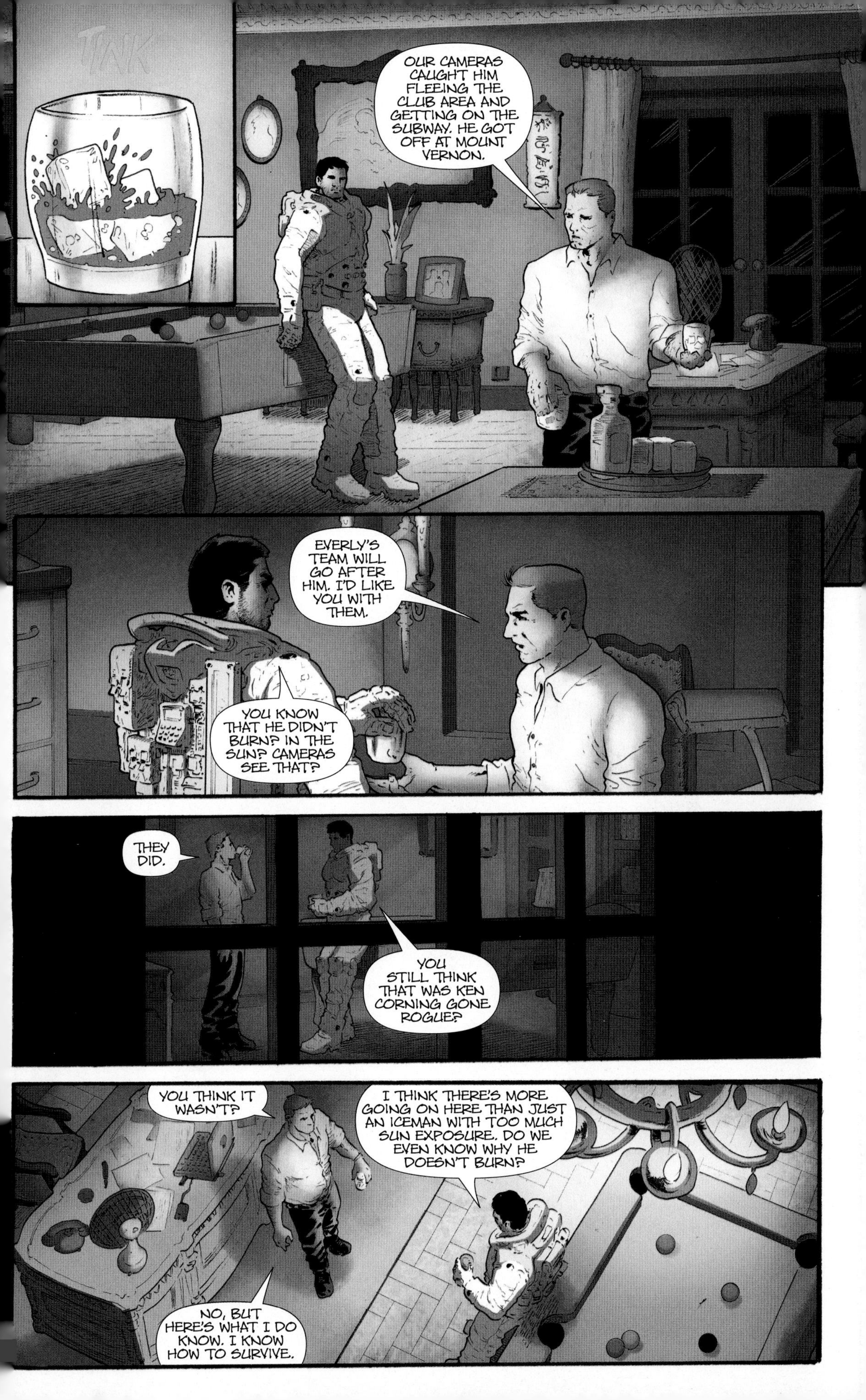
TINK
OUR CAMERAS CAUGHT HIM FLEEING THE CLUB AREA AND GETTING ON THE SUBWAY. HE GOT OFF AT MOUNT VERNON.
EVERLY'S TEAM WILL GO AFTER HIM. I'D LIKE YOU WITH THEM.
YOU KNOW THAT HE DIDN'T BURN? IN THE SUN? CAMERAS SEE THAT?
THEY DID.
YOU STILL THINK THAT WAS KEN CORNING GONE ROGUE?
YOU THINK IT WASN'T?
I THINK THERE'S MORE GOING ON HERE THAN JUST AN ICEMAN WITH TOO MUCH SUN EXPOSURE. DO WE EVEN KNOW WHY HE DOESN'T BURN?
NO, BUT HERE'S WHAT I DO KNOW. I KNOW HOW TO SURVIVE.

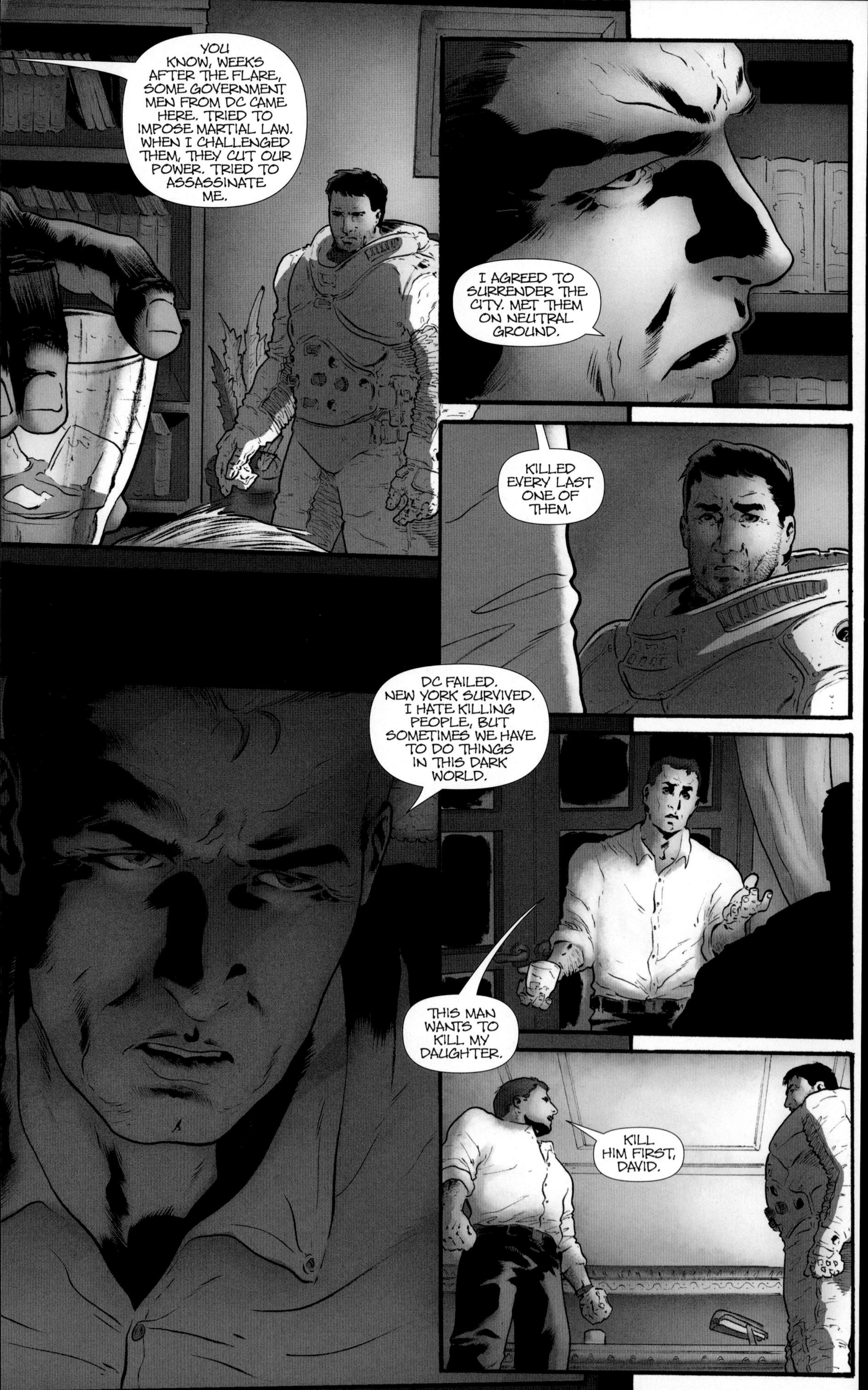
YOU KNOW, WEEKS AFTER THE FLARE, SOME GOVERNMENT MEN FROM DC CAME HERE. TRIED TO IMPOSE MARTIAL LAW. WHEN I CHALLENGED THEM, THEY CUT OUR POWER. TRIED TO ASSASSINATE ME.
I AGREED TO SURRENDER THE CITY. MET THEM ON NEUTRAL GROUND.
KILLED EVERY LAST ONE OF THEM.
DC FAILED. NEW YORK SURVIVED. I HATE KILLING PEOPLE, BUT SOMETIMES WE HAVE TO DO THINGS IN THIS DARK WORLD.
THIS MAN WANTS TO KILL MY DAUGHTER.
KILL HIM FIRST, DAVID.

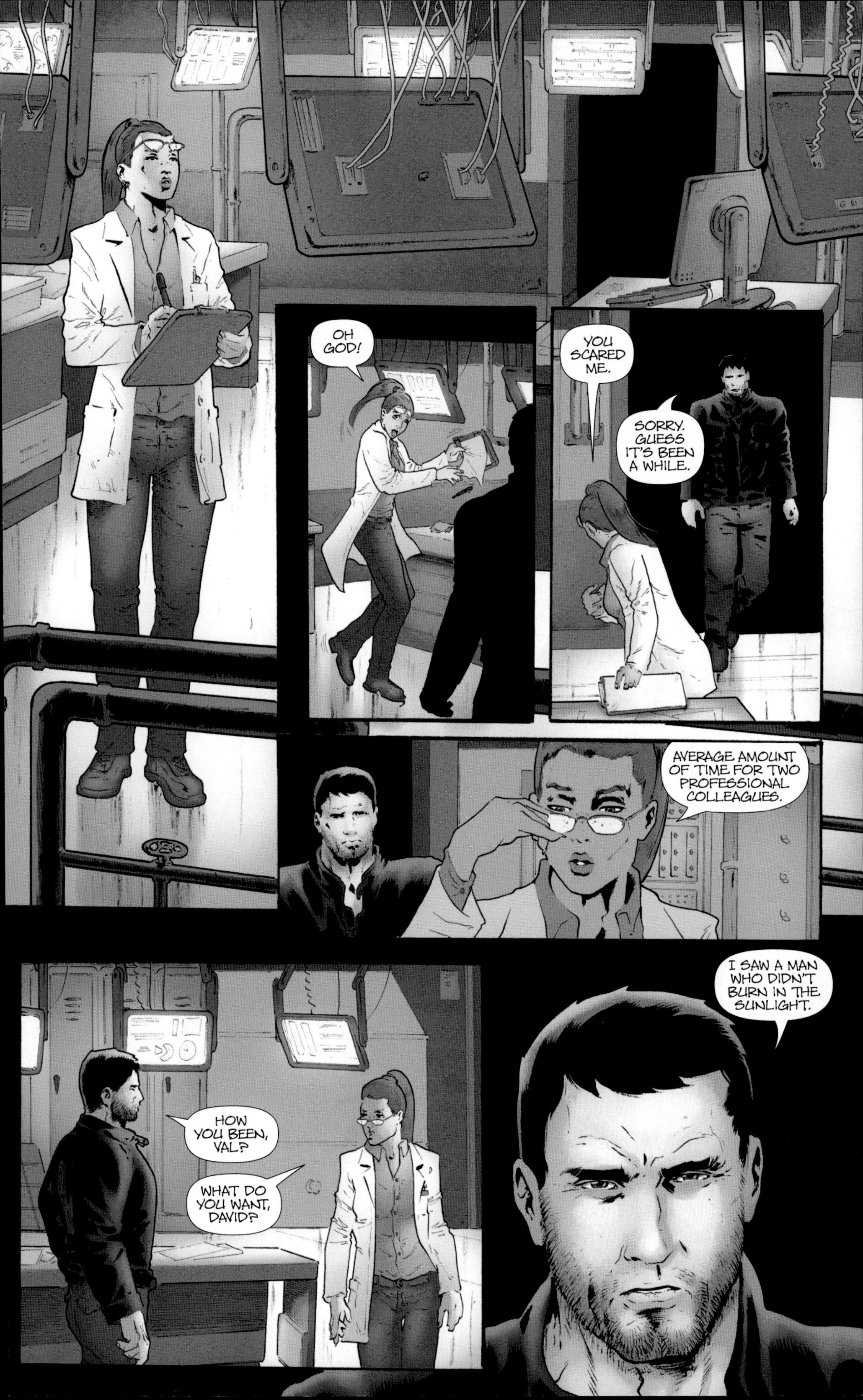
OH GOD!
YOU SCARED ME.
SORRY. GUESS IT'S BEEN A WHILE.
AVERAGE AMOUNT OF TIME FOR TWO PROFESSIONAL COLLEAGUES.
HOW YOU BEEN, VAL?
WHAT DO YOU WANT, DAVID?
I SAW A MAN WHO DIDN'T BURN IN THE SUNLIGHT.

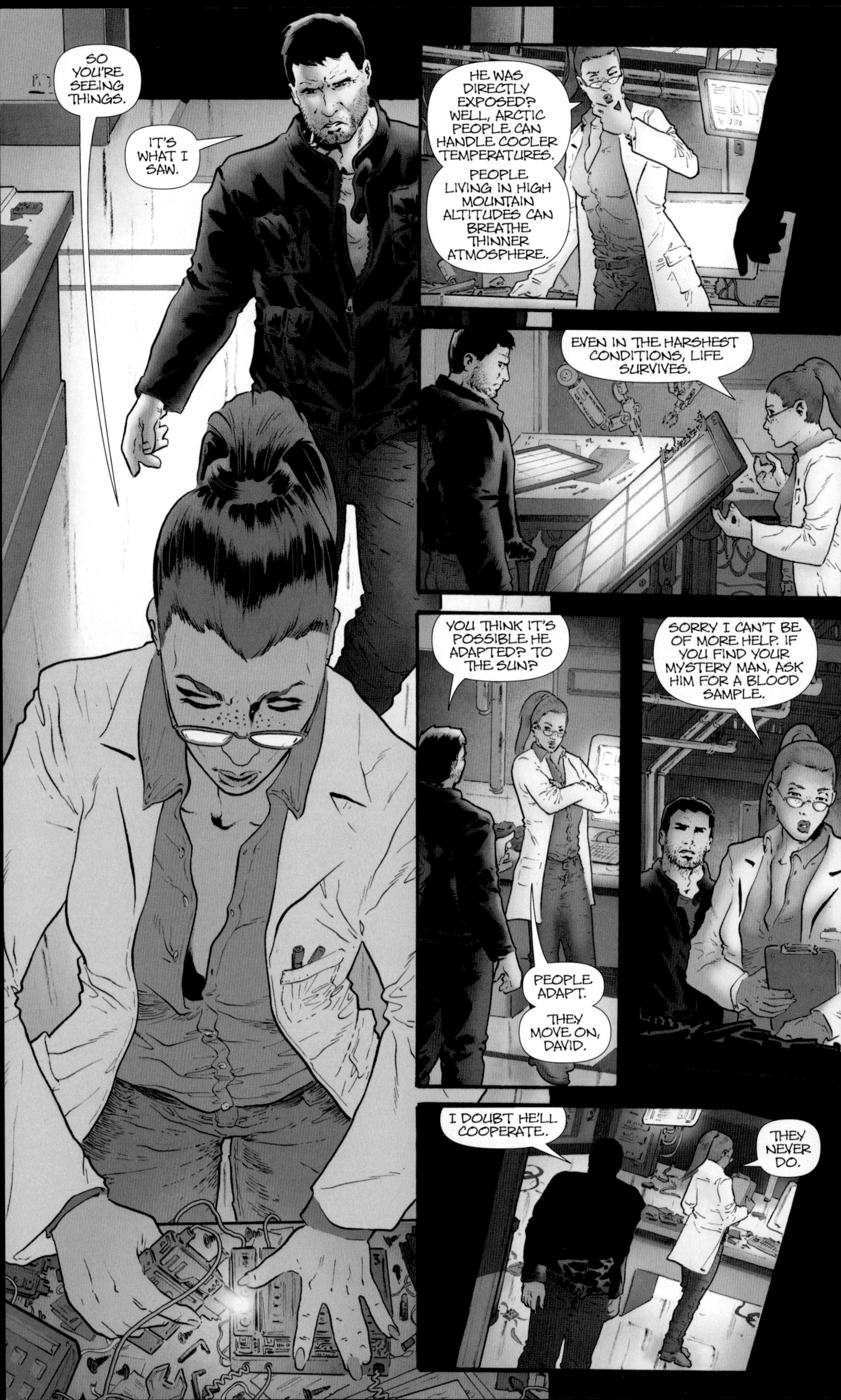
SO YOU'RE SEEING THINGS.
IT'S WHAT I SAW.
HE WAS DIRECTLY EXPOSED? WELL, ARCTIC PEOPLE CAN HANDLE COOLER TEMPERATURES.
PEOPLE LIVING IN HIGH MOUNTAIN ALTITUDES CAN BREATHE THINNER ATMOSPHERE.
EVEN IN THE HARSHEST CONDITIONS, LIFE SURVIVES.
YOU THINK IT'S POSSIBLE HE ADAPTED? TO THE SUN?
PEOPLE ADAPT.
THEY MOVE ON, DAVID.
SORRY I CAN'T BE OF MORE HELP. IF YOU FIND YOUR MYSTERY MAN, ASK HIM FOR A BLOOD SAMPLE.
I DOUBT HE'LL COOPERATE.
THEY NEVER DO.

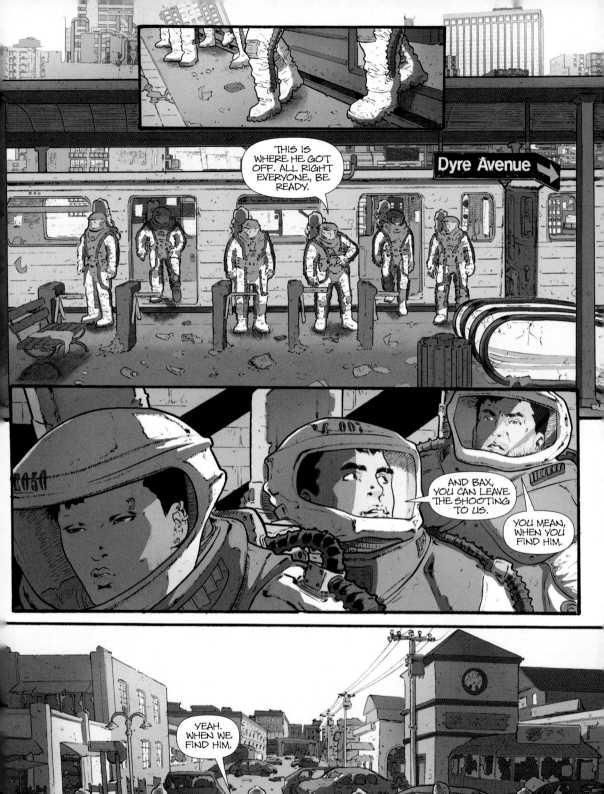

Dyre Avenue

THIS IS WHERE HE GOT OFF. ALL RIGHT EVERYONE, BE READY.

AND BAX, YOU CAN LEAVE THE SHOOTING TO US.

YOU MEAN, WHEN YOU FIND HIM.

YEAH. WHEN WE FIND HIM.

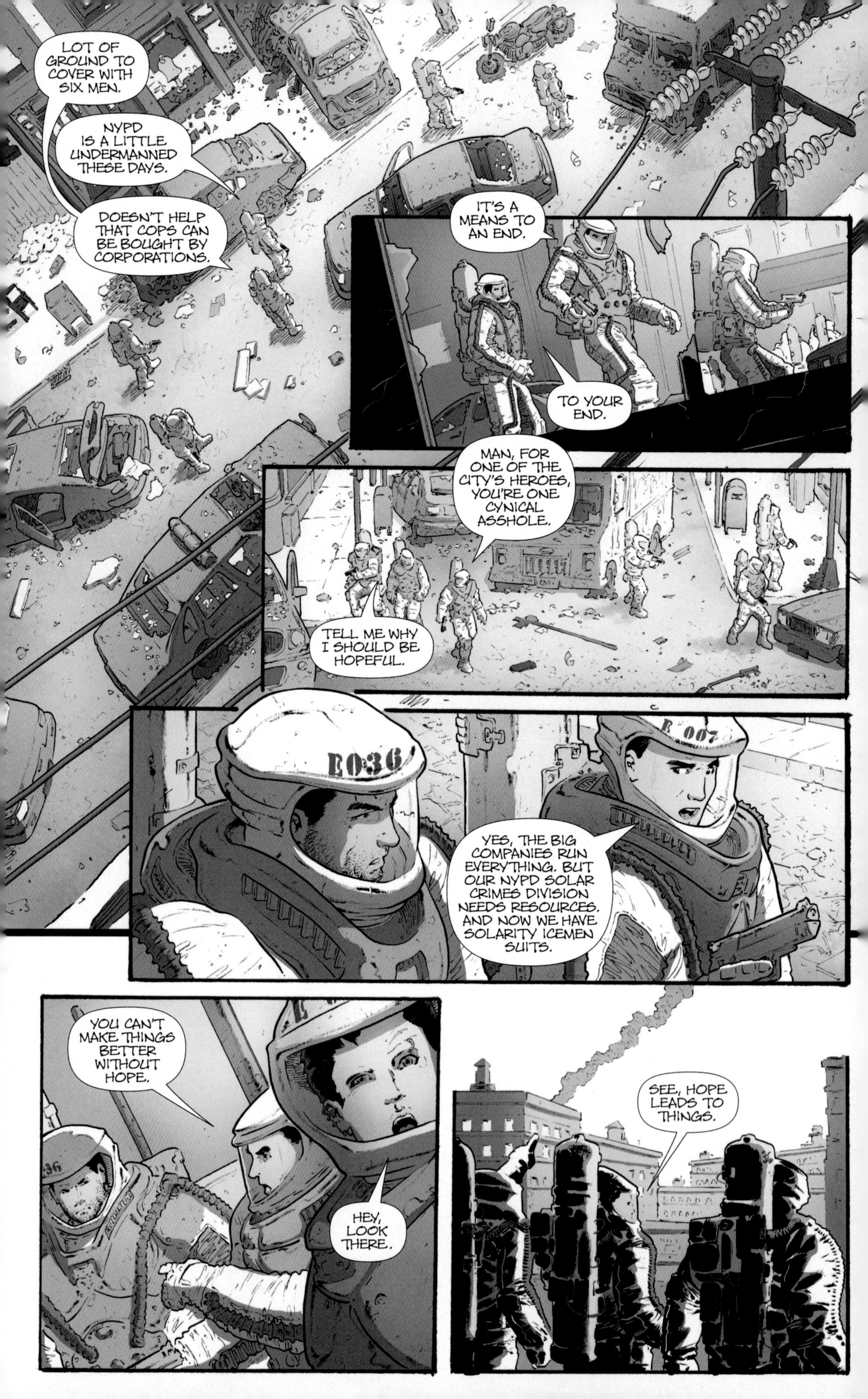
LOT OF GROUND TO COVER WITH SIX MEN.
NYPD IS A LITTLE UNDERMANNED THESE DAYS.
DOESN'T HELP THAT COPS CAN BE BOUGHT BY CORPORATIONS.
IT'S A MEANS TO AN END.
TO YOUR END.
MAN, FOR ONE OF THE CITY'S HEROES, YOU'RE ONE CYNICAL ASSHOLE.
TELL ME WHY I SHOULD BE HOPEFUL.
E036
E 007
YES, THE BIG COMPANIES RUN EVERYTHING. BUT OUR NYPD SOLAR CRIMES DIVISION NEEDS RESOURCES. AND NOW WE HAVE SOLARITY ICEMEN SUITS.
YOU CAN'T MAKE THINGS BETTER WITHOUT HOPE.
HEY, LOOK THERE.
SEE, HOPE LEADS TO THINGS.

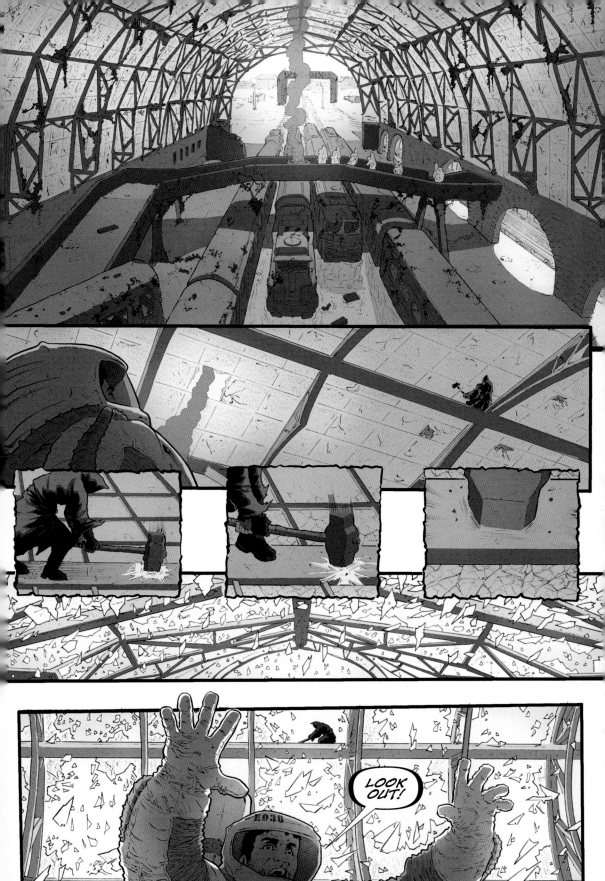

LOOK
OUT!

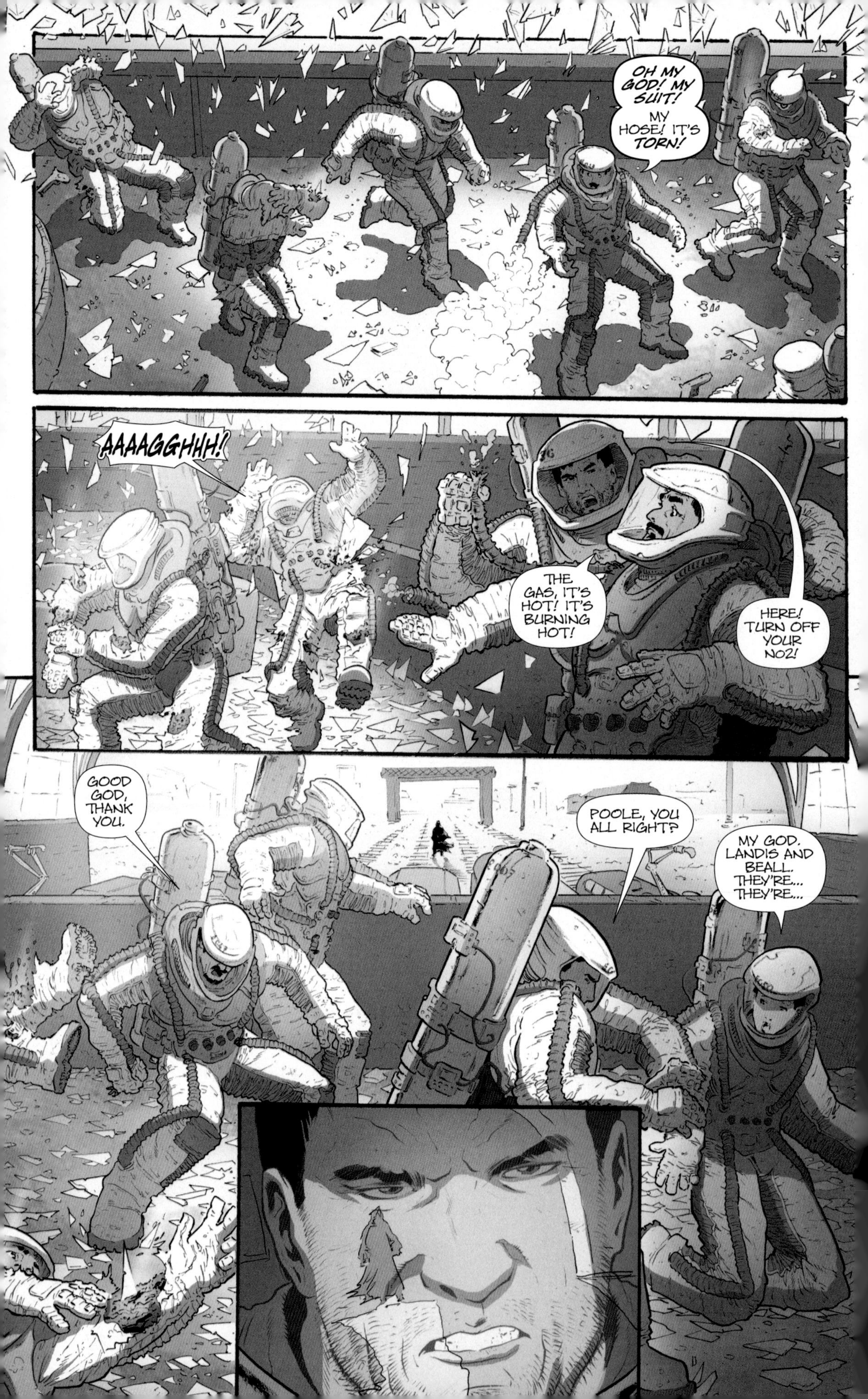
OH MY GOD! MY SUIT!
MY HOSE! IT'S TORN!
AAAAGGHHH!
THE GAS, IT'S HOT! IT'S BURNING HOT!
HERE! TURN OFF YOUR NO2!
GOOD GOD, THANK YOU.
POOLE, YOU ALL RIGHT?
MY GOD. LANDIS AND BEALL. THEY'RE... THEY'RE...

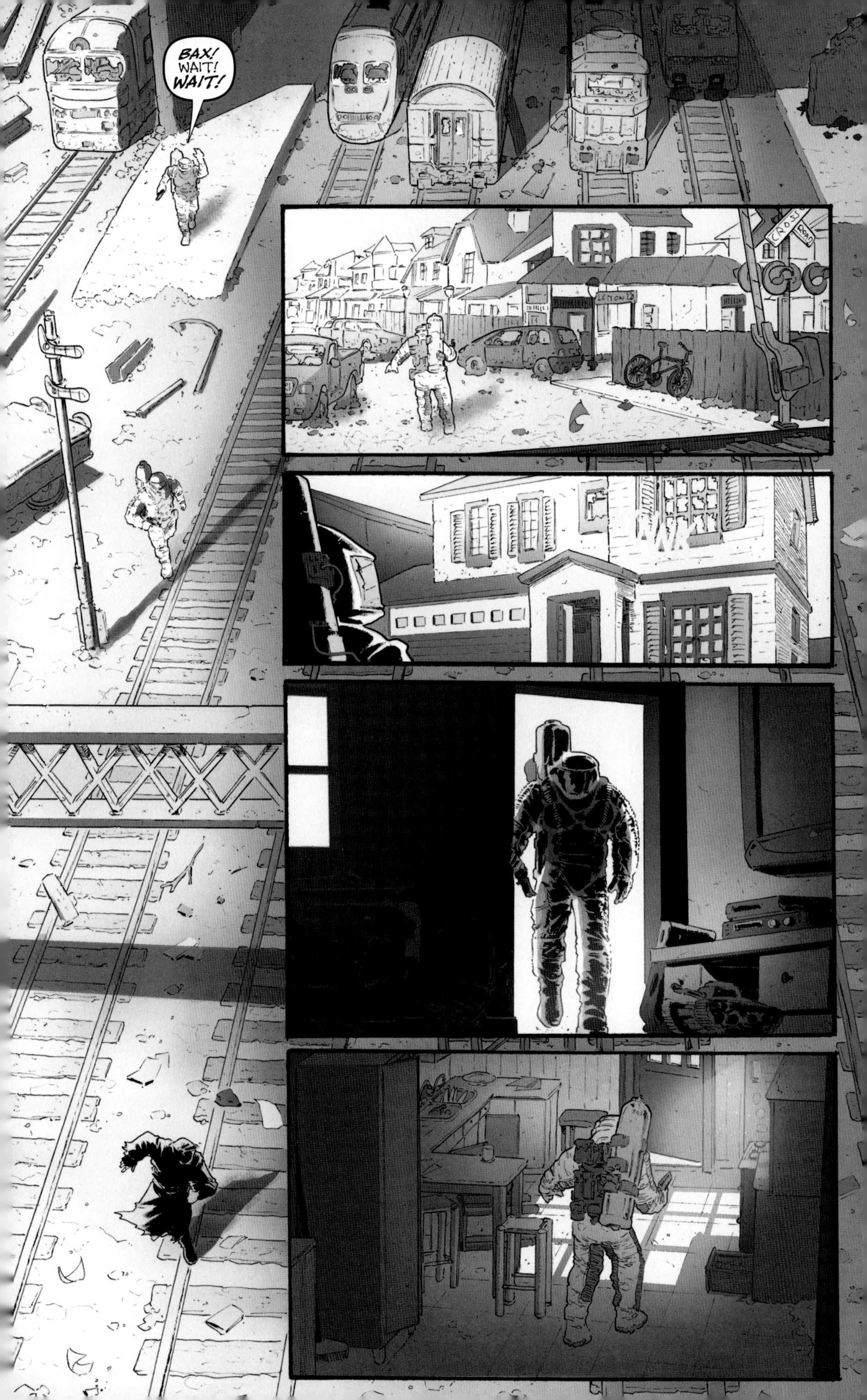
BAX! WAIT! WAIT!
CROSS ROAD
LEMON

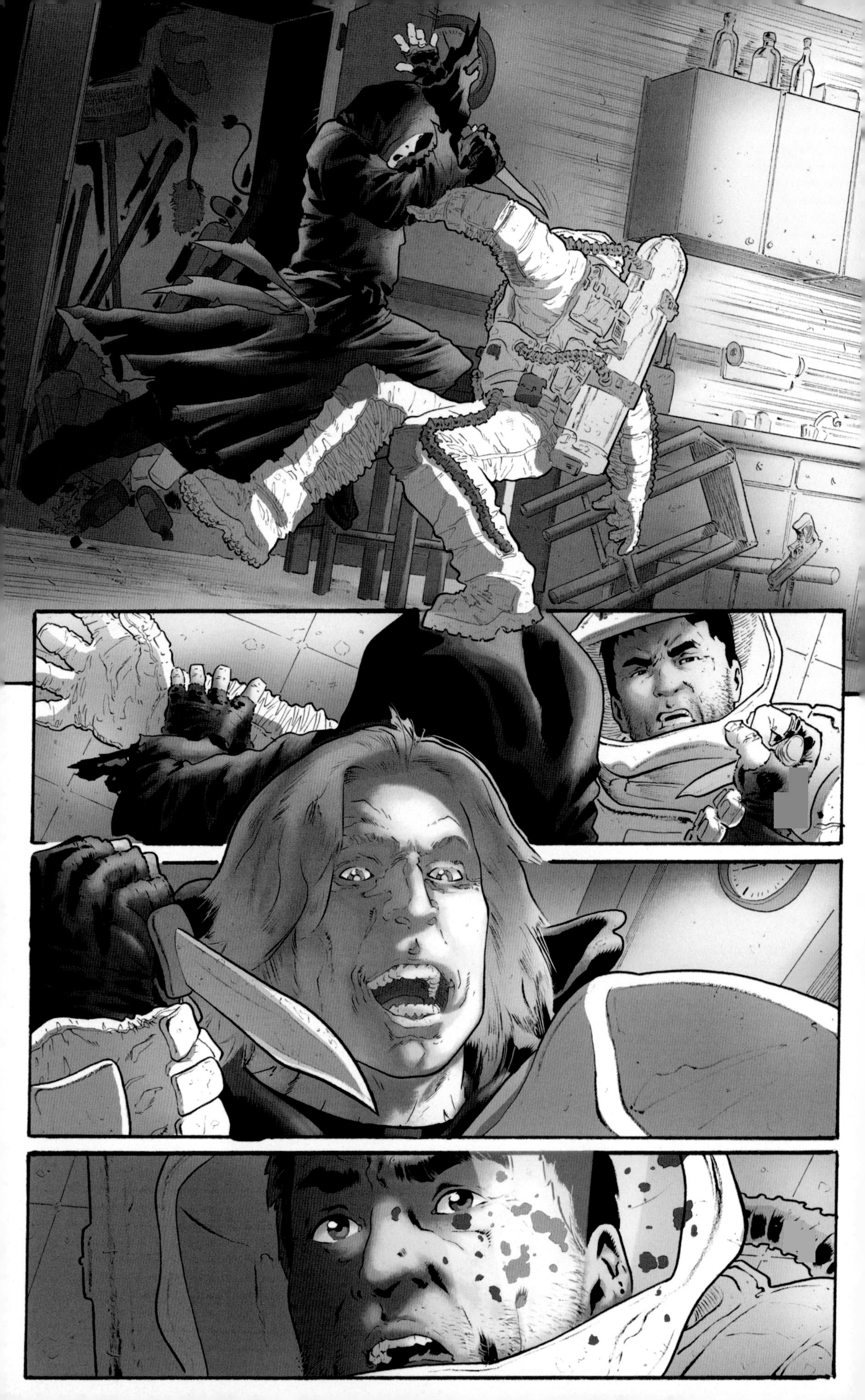

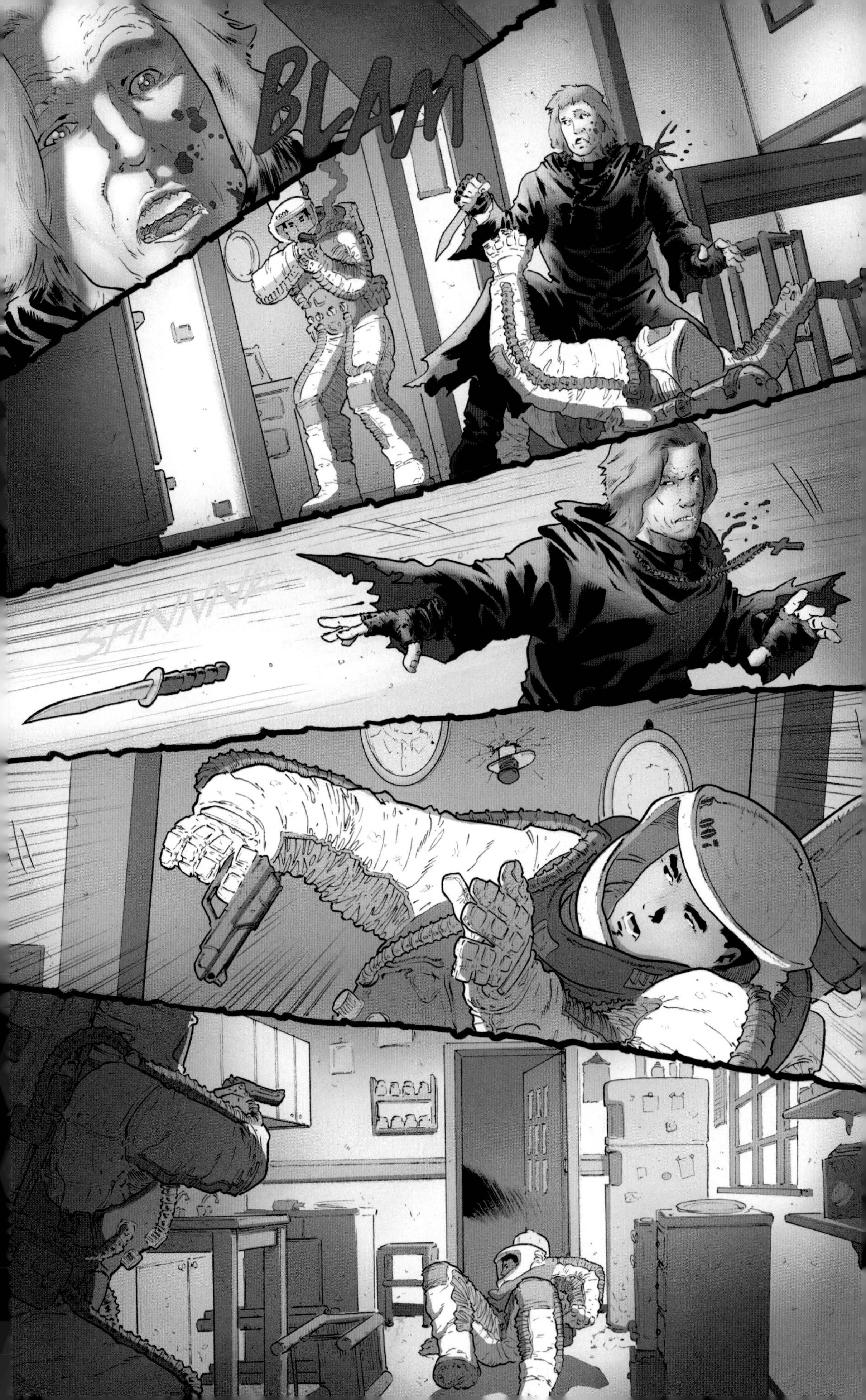
BLAM
SHNNNK

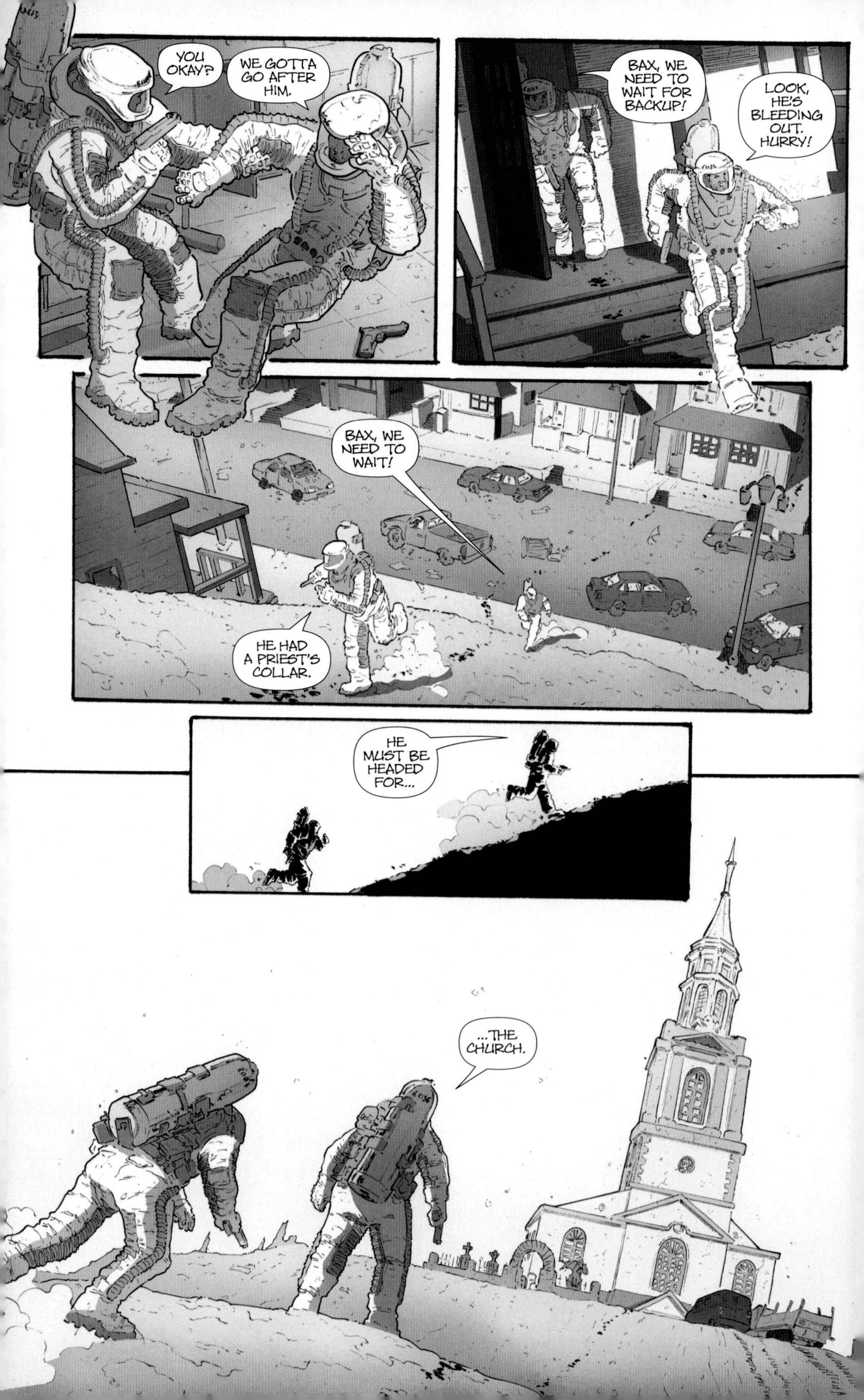
YOU OKAY?
WE GOTTA GO AFTER HIM.
BAX, WE NEED TO WAIT FOR BACKUP!
LOOK, HE'S BLEEDING OUT. HURRY!
BAX, WE NEED TO WAIT!
HE HAD A PRIEST'S COLLAR.
HE MUST BE HEADED FOR...
...THE CHURCH.

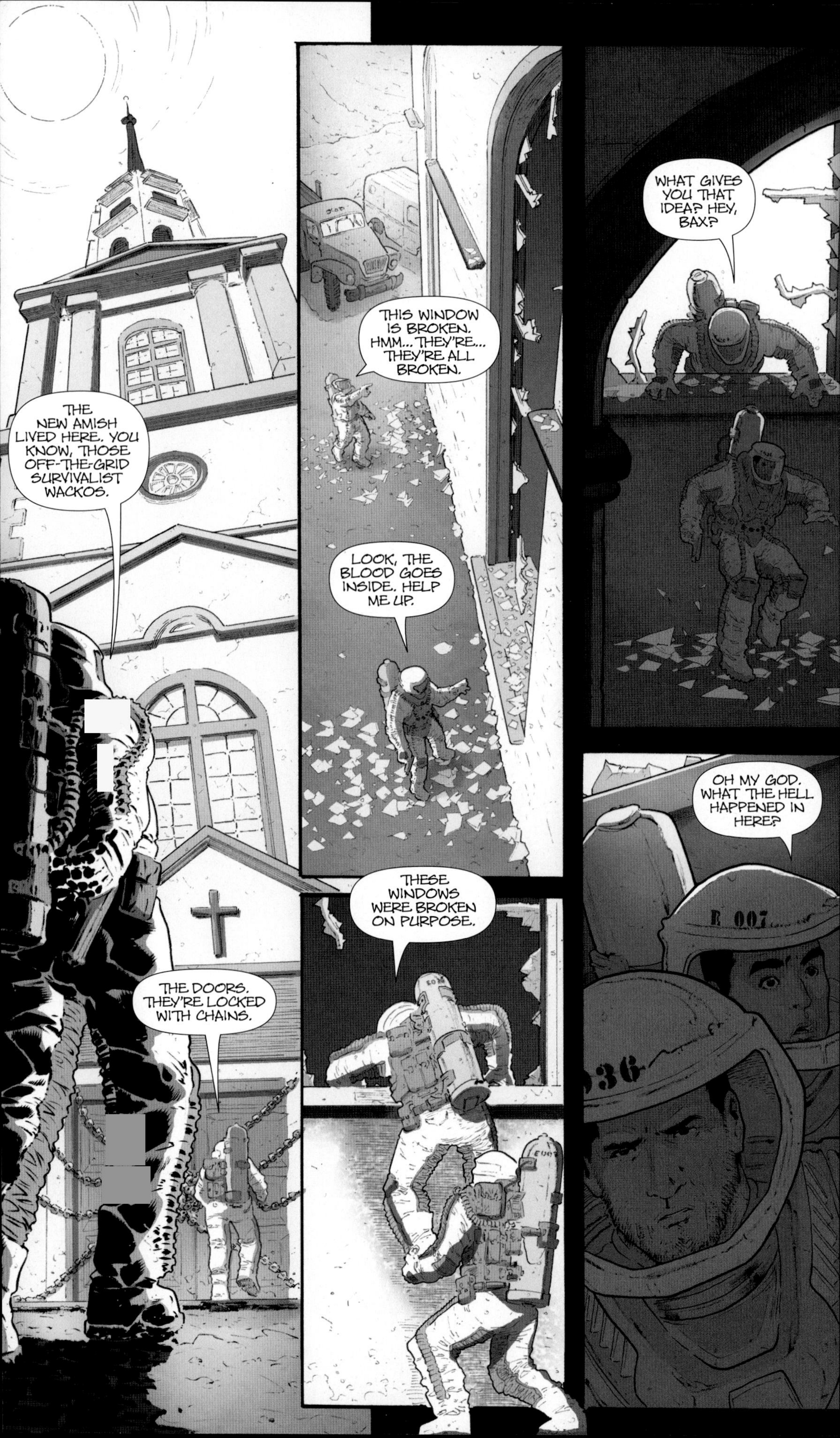
THE NEW AMISH LIVED HERE. YOU KNOW, THOSE OFF-THE-GRID SURVIVALIST WACKOS.
THE DOORS. THEY'RE LOCKED WITH CHAINS.
THIS WINDOW IS BROKEN. HMM... THEY'RE... THEY'RE ALL BROKEN.
LOOK, THE BLOOD GOES INSIDE. HELP ME UP.
THESE WINDOWS WERE BROKEN ON PURPOSE.
WHAT GIVES YOU THAT IDEA? HEY, BAX?
OH MY GOD. WHAT THE HELL HAPPENED IN HERE?

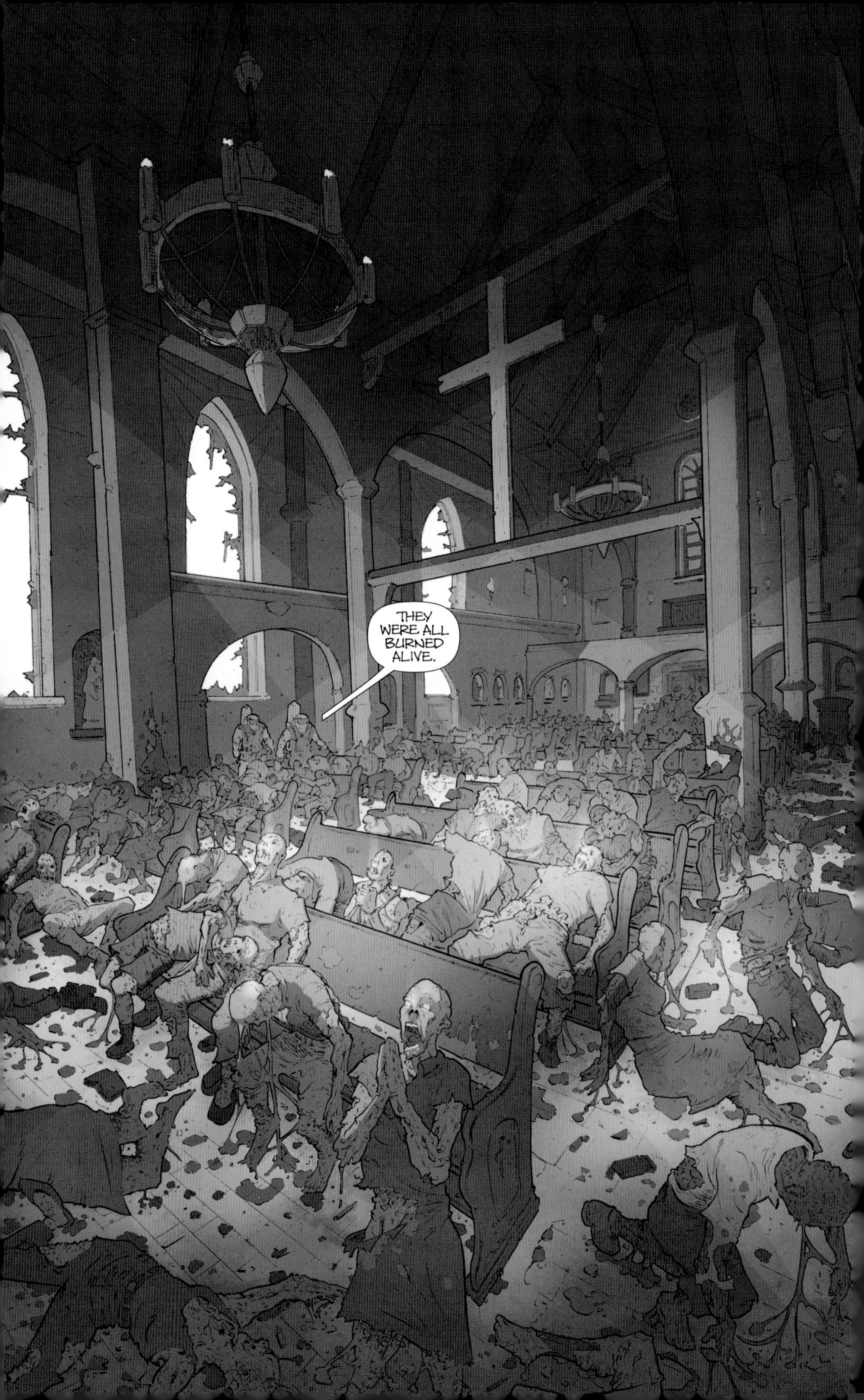
THEY WERE ALL BURNED ALIVE.

CHAPTER THREE

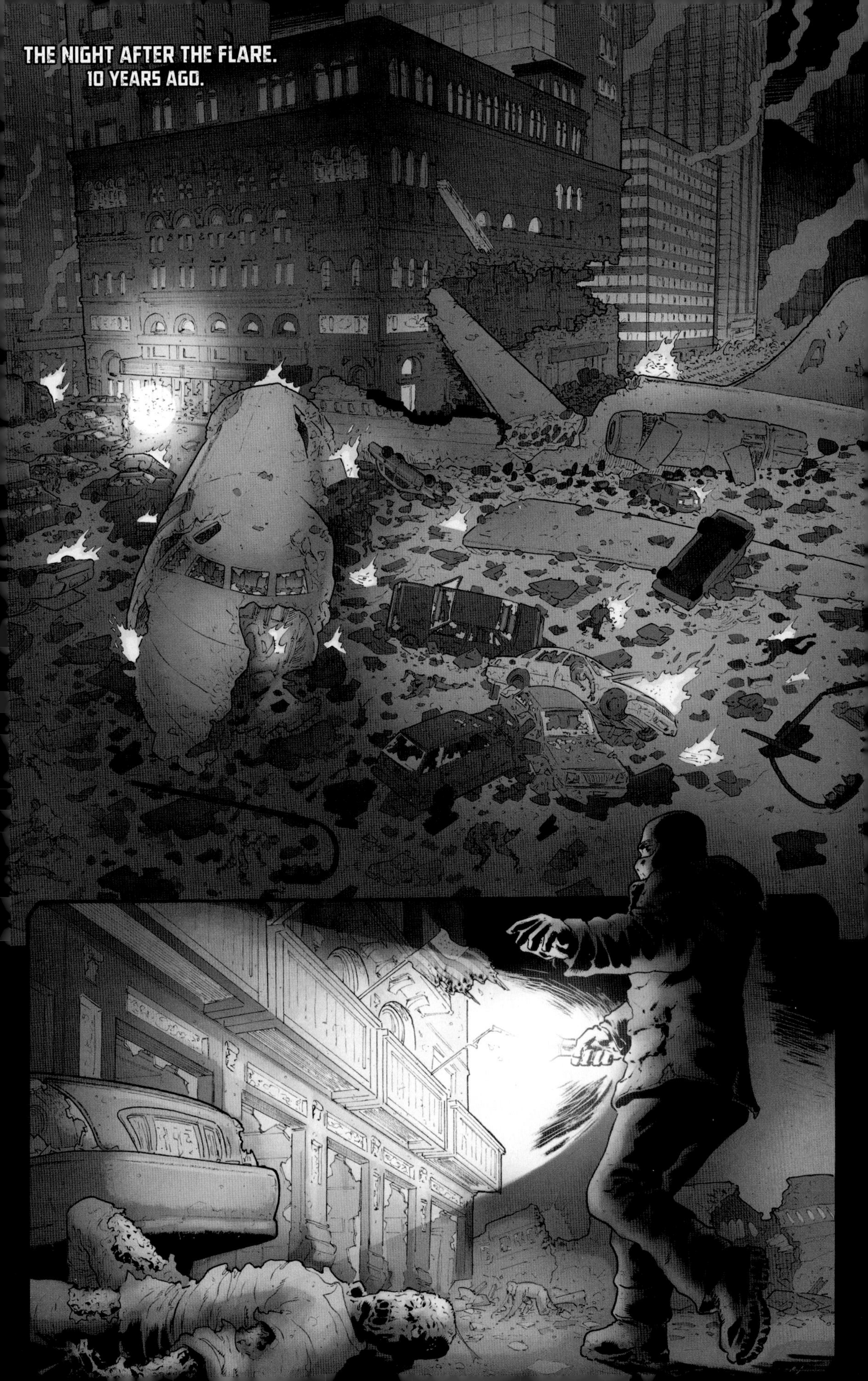
THE NIGHT AFTER THE FLARE.
10 YEARS AGO.

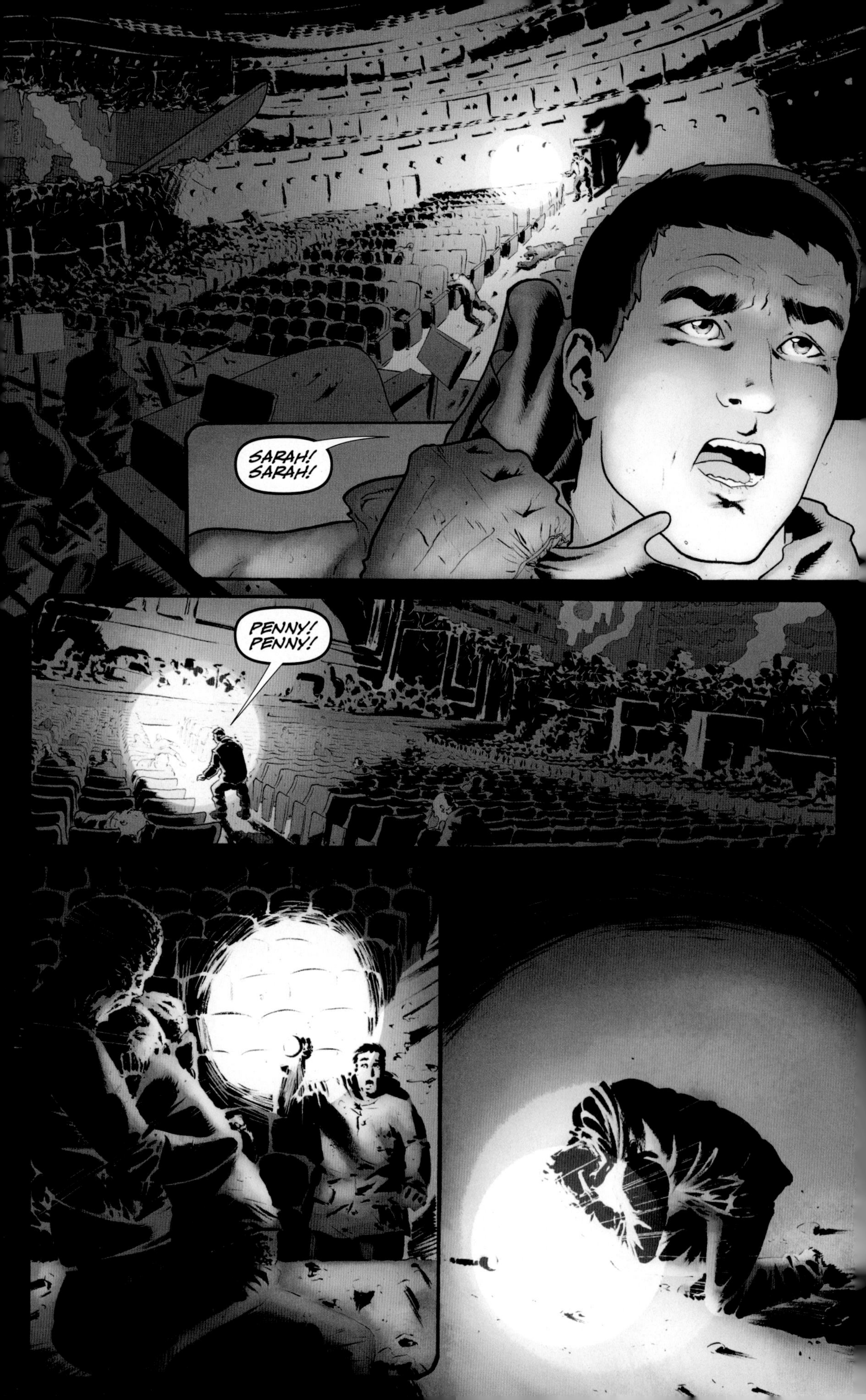
SARAH!
SARAH!
PENNY!
PENNY!

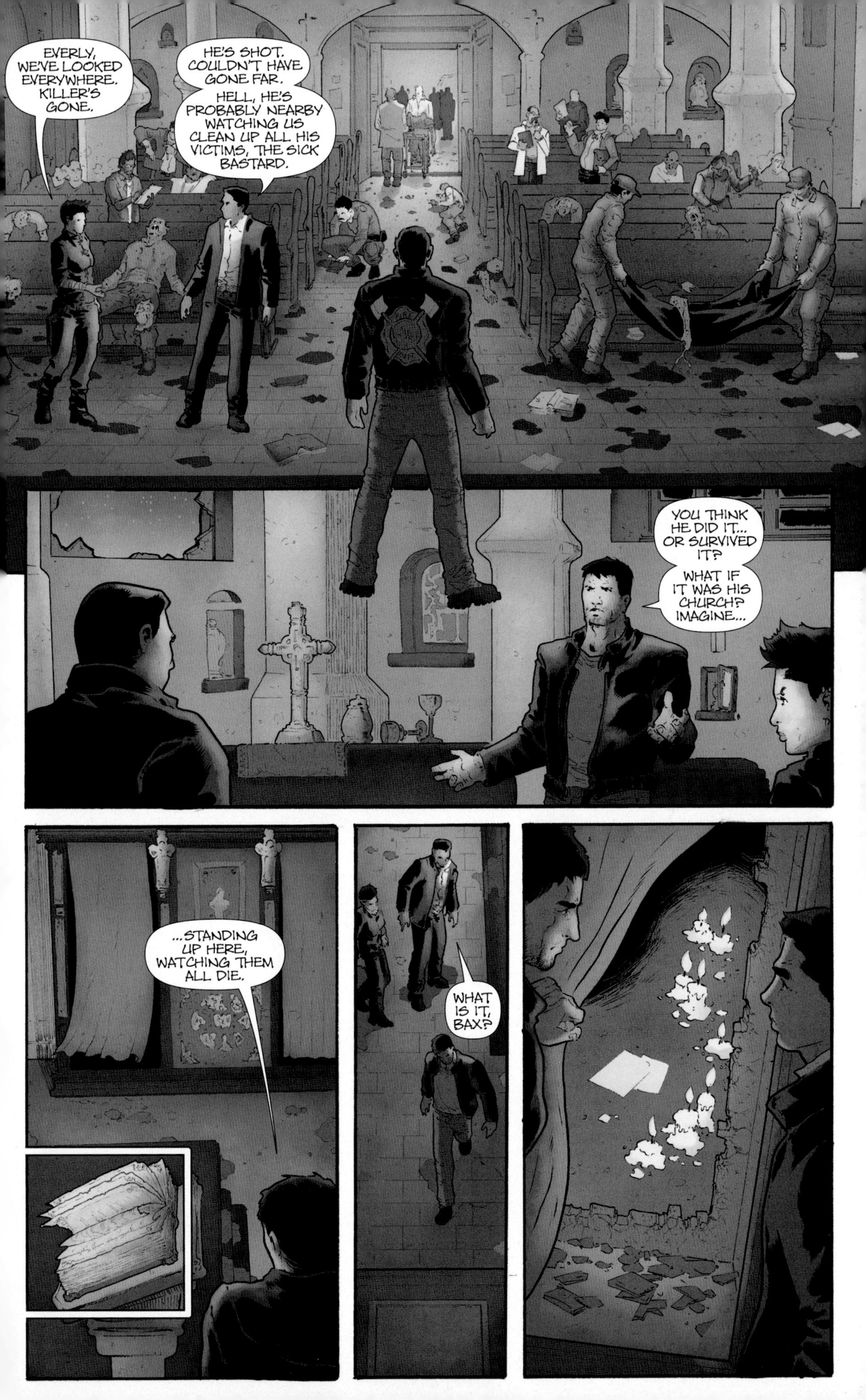
EVERLY, WE'VE LOOKED EVERYWHERE. KILLER'S GONE.
HE'S SHOT. COULDN'T HAVE GONE FAR.
HELL, HE'S PROBABLY NEARBY WATCHING US CLEAN UP ALL HIS VICTIMS, THE SICK BASTARD.
YOU THINK HE DID IT... OR SURVIVED IT?
WHAT IF IT WAS HIS CHURCH? IMAGINE...
...STANDING UP HERE, WATCHING THEM ALL DIE.
WHAT IS IT, BAX?

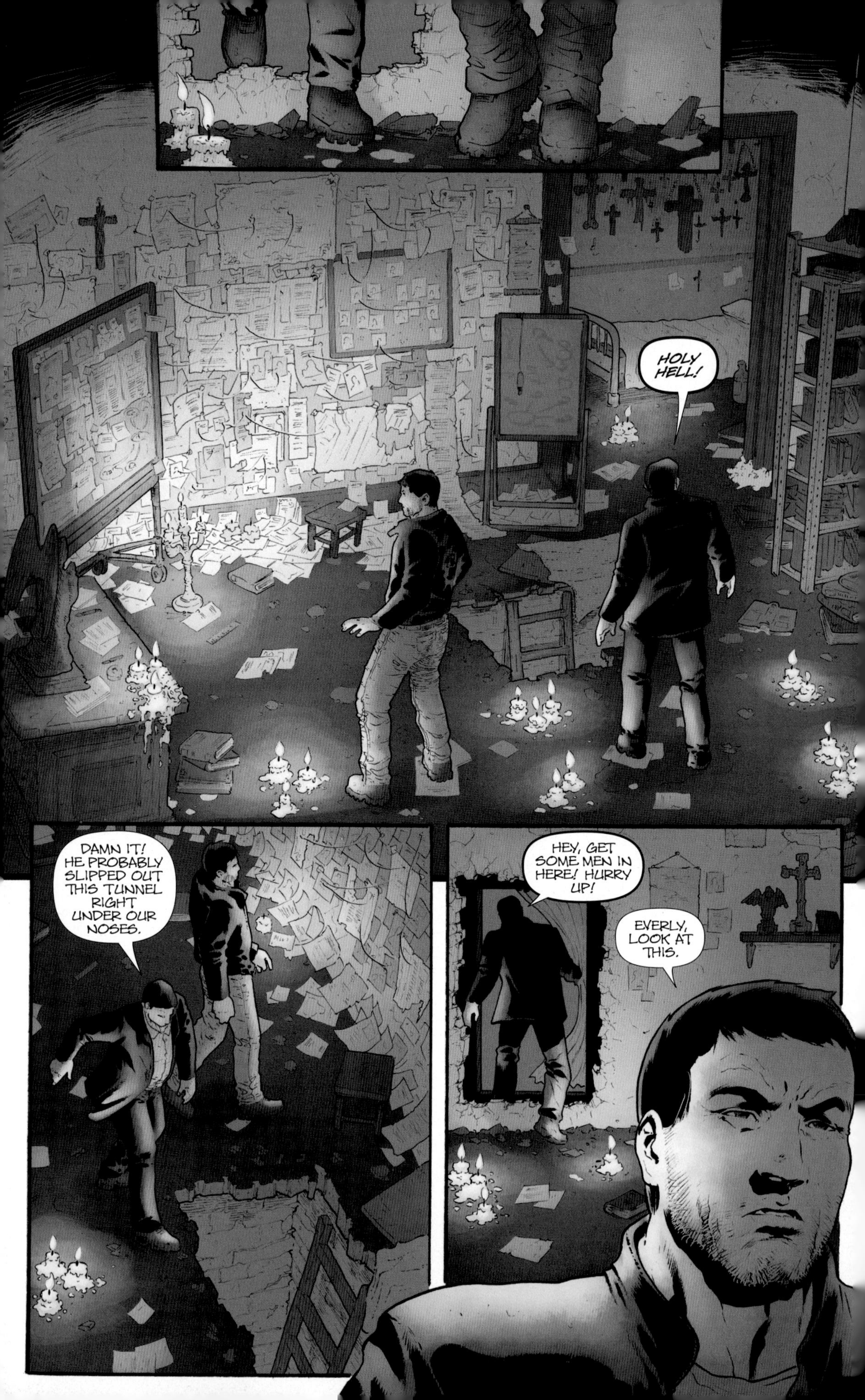
HOLY HELL!
DAMN IT! HE PROBABLY SLIPPED OUT THIS TUNNEL RIGHT UNDER OUR NOSES.
HEY, GET SOME MEN IN HERE! HURRY UP!
EVERLY, LOOK AT THIS.

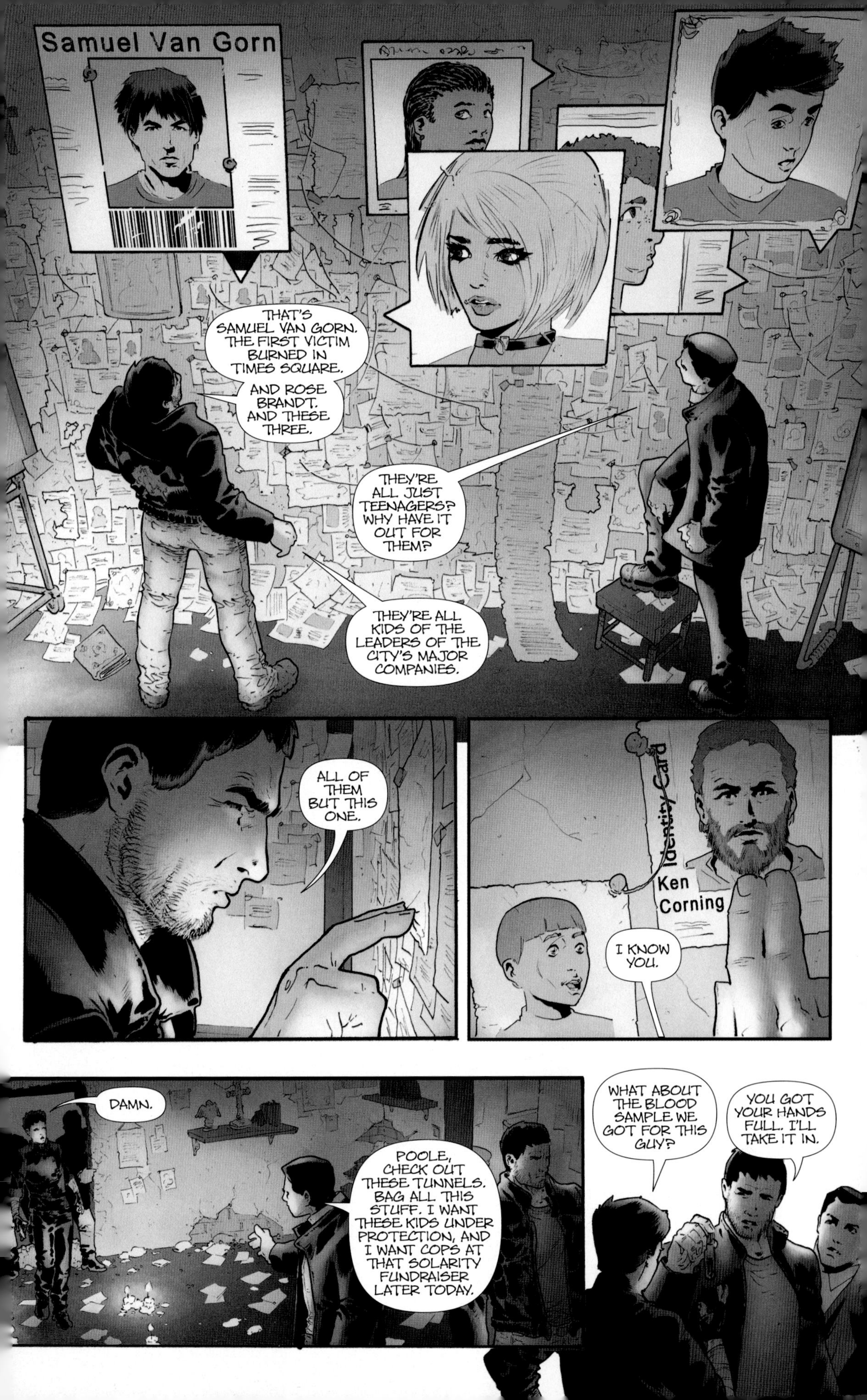
Samuel Van Gorn
THAT'S SAMUEL VAN GORN. THE FIRST VICTIM BURNED IN TIMES SQUARE.
AND ROSE BRANDT. AND THESE THREE.
THEY'RE ALL JUST TEENAGERS? WHY HAVE IT OUT FOR THEM?
THEY'RE ALL KIDS OF THE LEADERS OF THE CITY'S MAJOR COMPANIES.
ALL OF THEM BUT THIS ONE.
Identity Card
Ken Corning
I KNOW YOU.
DAMN.
POOLE, CHECK OUT THESE TUNNELS. BAG ALL THIS STUFF. I WANT THESE KIDS UNDER PROTECTION, AND I WANT COPS AT THAT SOLARITY FUNDRAISER LATER TODAY.
WHAT ABOUT THE BLOOD SAMPLE WE GOT FOR THIS GUY?
YOU GOT YOUR HANDS FULL. I'LL TAKE IT IN.

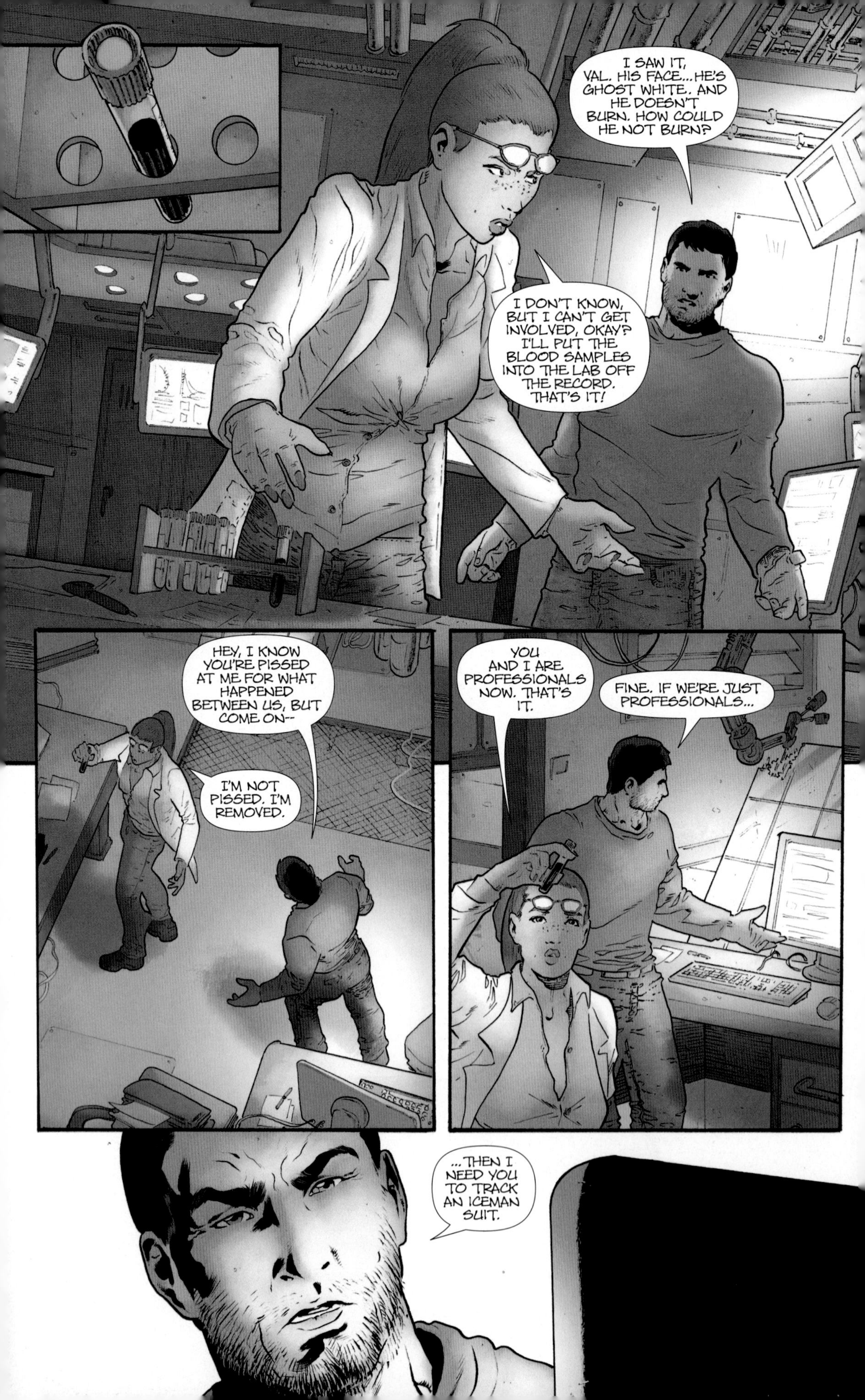
I SAW IT, VAL. HIS FACE... HE'S GHOST WHITE. AND HE DOESN'T BURN. HOW COULD HE NOT BURN?
I DON'T KNOW, BUT I CAN'T GET INVOLVED, OKAY? I'LL PUT THE BLOOD SAMPLES INTO THE LAB OFF THE RECORD. THAT'S IT!
HEY, I KNOW YOU'RE PISSED AT ME FOR WHAT HAPPENED BETWEEN US, BUT COME ON--
I'M NOT PISSED. I'M REMOVED.
YOU AND I ARE PROFESSIONALS NOW. THAT'S IT.
FINE. IF WE'RE JUST PROFESSIONALS...
...THEN I NEED YOU TO TRACK AN ICEMAN SUIT.

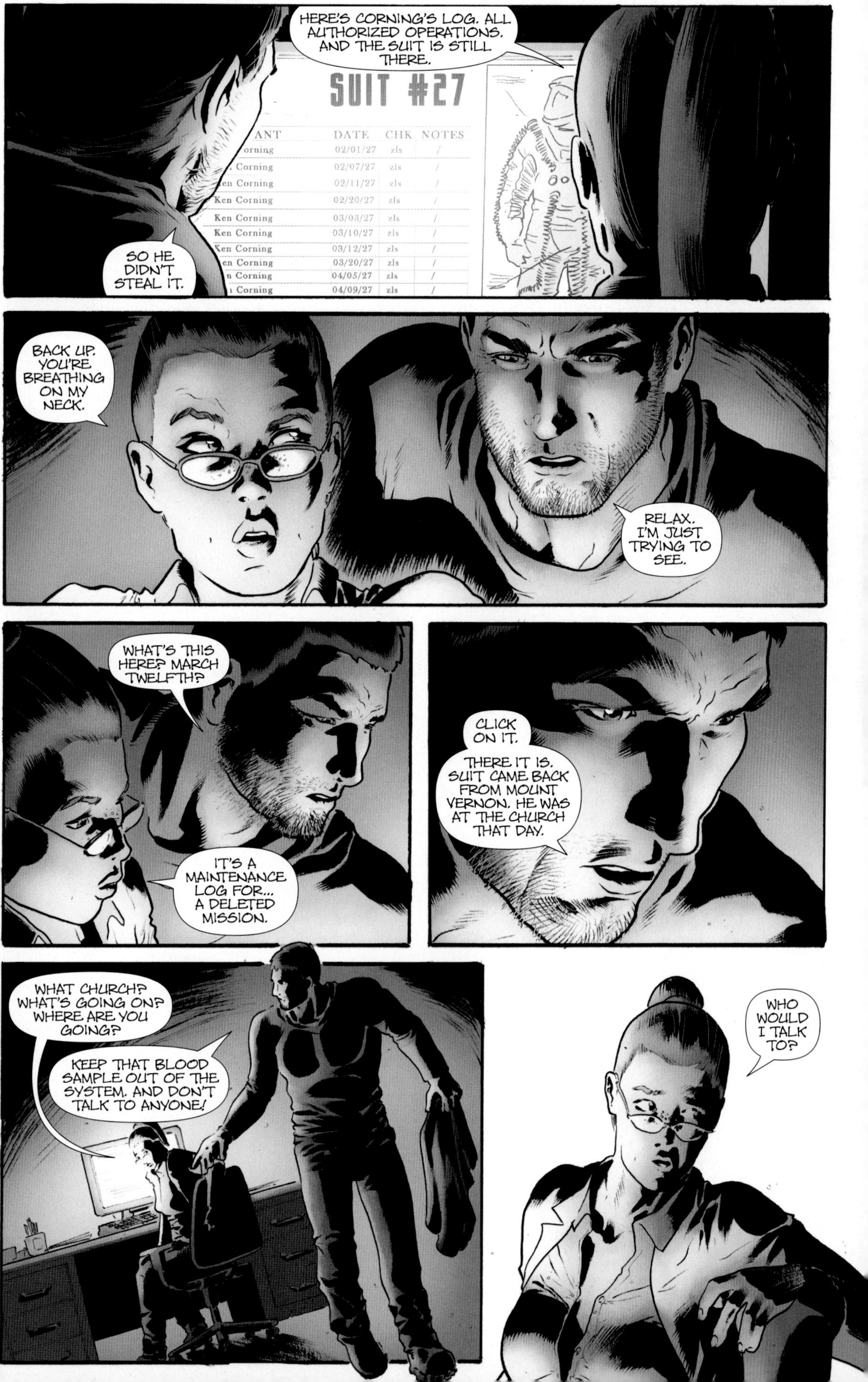
HERE'S CORNING'S LOG. ALL AUTHORIZED OPERATIONS. AND THE SUIT IS STILL THERE.
SUIT #27
DATE CHK NOTES
Ken Corning 02/20/27 zls
Ken Corning 03/03/27 zls
Ken Corning 03/10/27 zls
SO HE DIDN'T STEAL IT.
BACK UP. YOU'RE BREATHING ON MY NECK.
RELAX. I'M JUST TRYING TO SEE.
WHAT'S THIS HERE? MARCH TWELFTH?
IT'S A MAINTENANCE LOG FOR... A DELETED MISSION.
CLICK ON IT.
THERE IT IS. SUIT CAME BACK FROM MOUNT VERNON. HE WAS AT THE CHURCH THAT DAY.
WHAT CHURCH? WHAT'S GOING ON? WHERE ARE YOU GOING?
KEEP THAT BLOOD SAMPLE OUT OF THE SYSTEM. AND DON'T TALK TO ANYONE!
WHO WOULD I TALK TO?

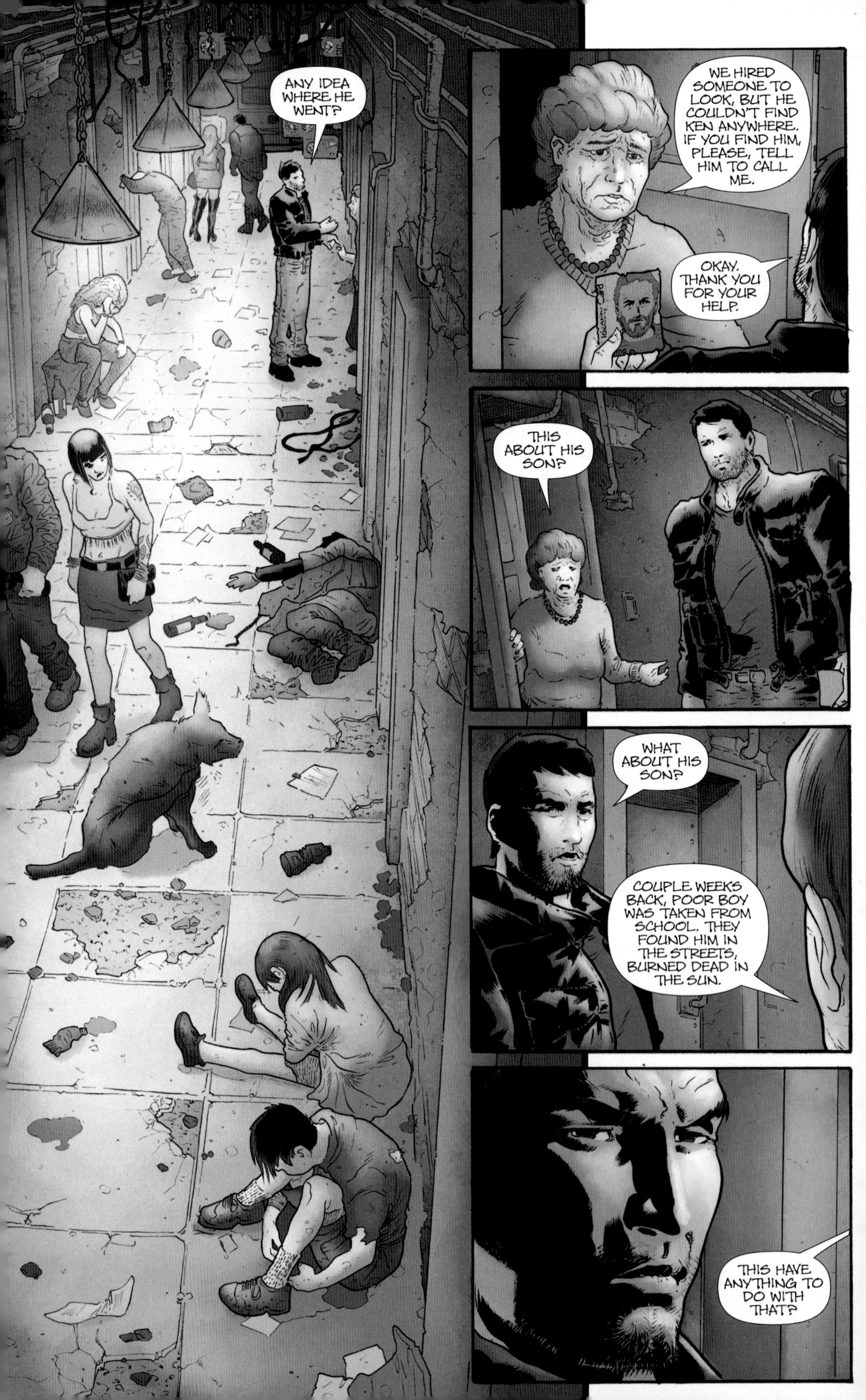
ANY IDEA WHERE HE WENT?
WE HIRED SOMEONE TO LOOK, BUT HE COULDN'T FIND KEN ANYWHERE. IF YOU FIND HIM, PLEASE, TELL HIM TO CALL ME.
OKAY. THANK YOU FOR YOUR HELP.
THIS ABOUT HIS SON?
WHAT ABOUT HIS SON?
COUPLE WEEKS BACK, POOR BOY WAS TAKEN FROM SCHOOL. THEY FOUND HIM IN THE STREETS, BURNED DEAD IN THE SUN.
THIS HAVE ANYTHING TO DO WITH THAT?

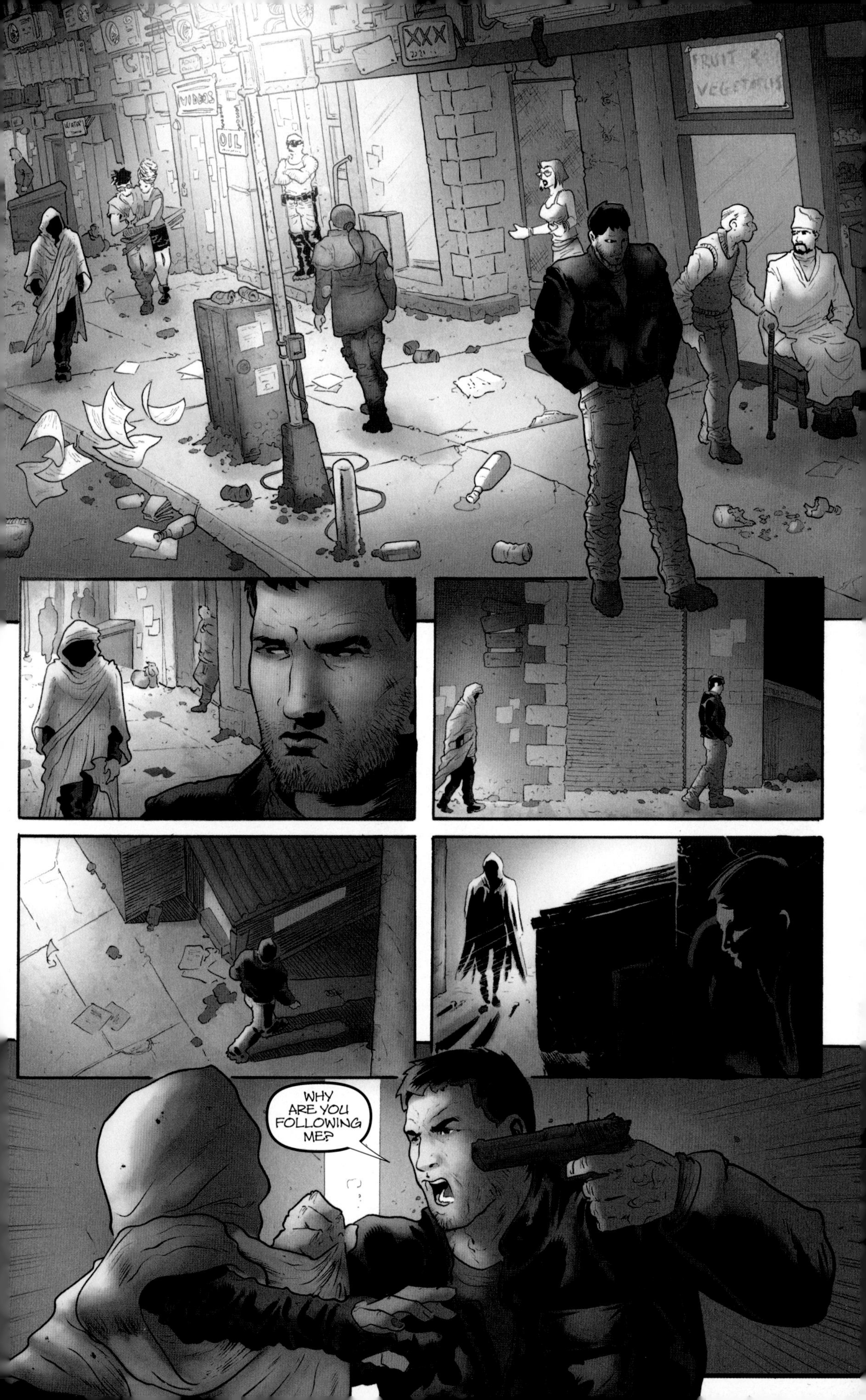
XXX
VIDEOS
OIL
WHY ARE YOU FOLLOWING ME?

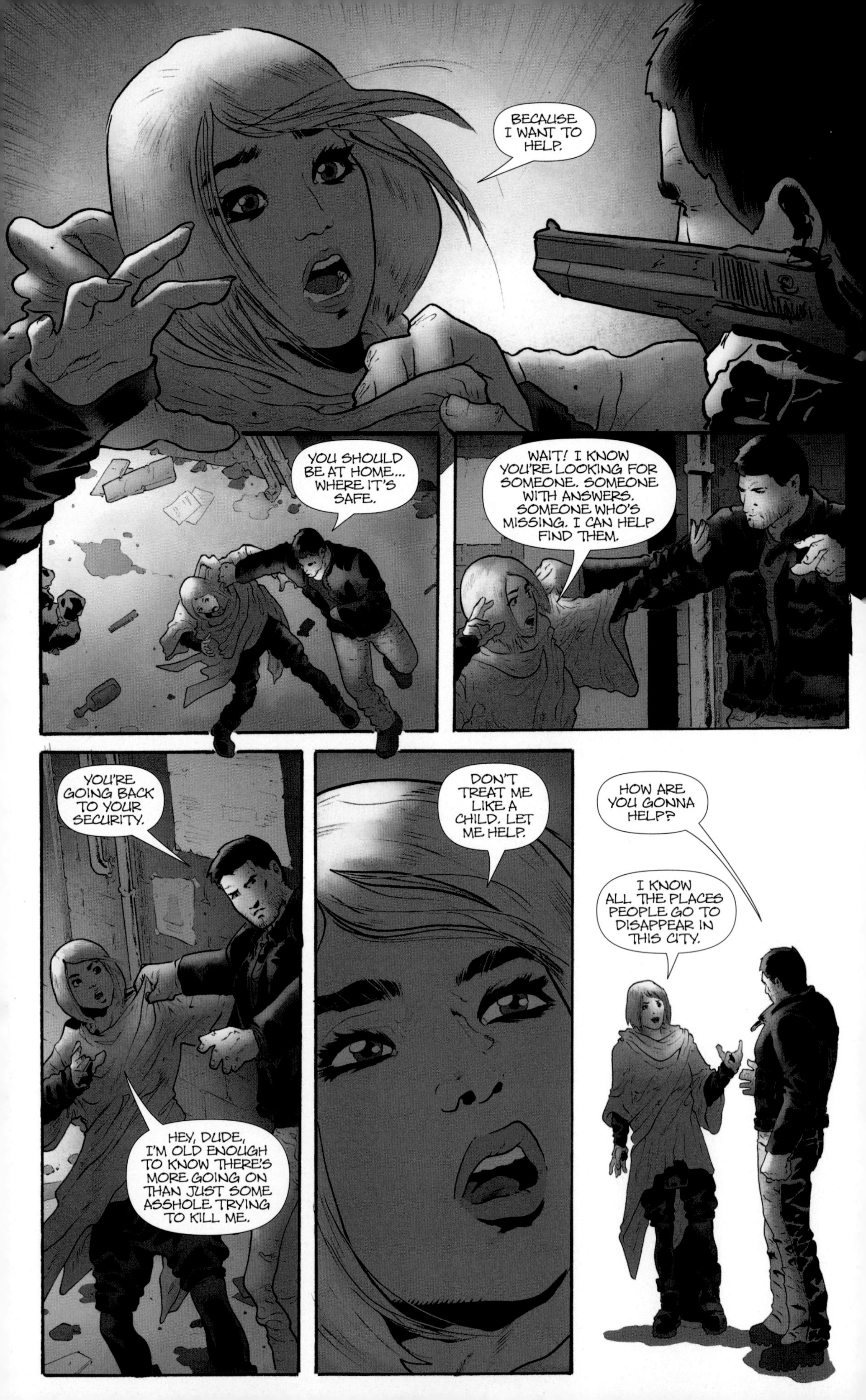
BECAUSE I WANT TO HELP.
YOU SHOULD BE AT HOME... WHERE IT'S SAFE.
WAIT! I KNOW YOU'RE LOOKING FOR SOMEONE. SOMEONE WITH ANSWERS. SOMEONE WHO'S MISSING. I CAN HELP FIND THEM.
YOU'RE GOING BACK TO YOUR SECURITY.
HEY, DUDE, I'M OLD ENOUGH TO KNOW THERE'S MORE GOING ON THAN JUST SOME ASSHOLE TRYING TO KILL ME.
DON'T TREAT ME LIKE A CHILD. LET ME HELP.
HOW ARE YOU GONNA HELP?
I KNOW ALL THE PLACES PEOPLE GO TO DISAPPEAR IN THIS CITY.

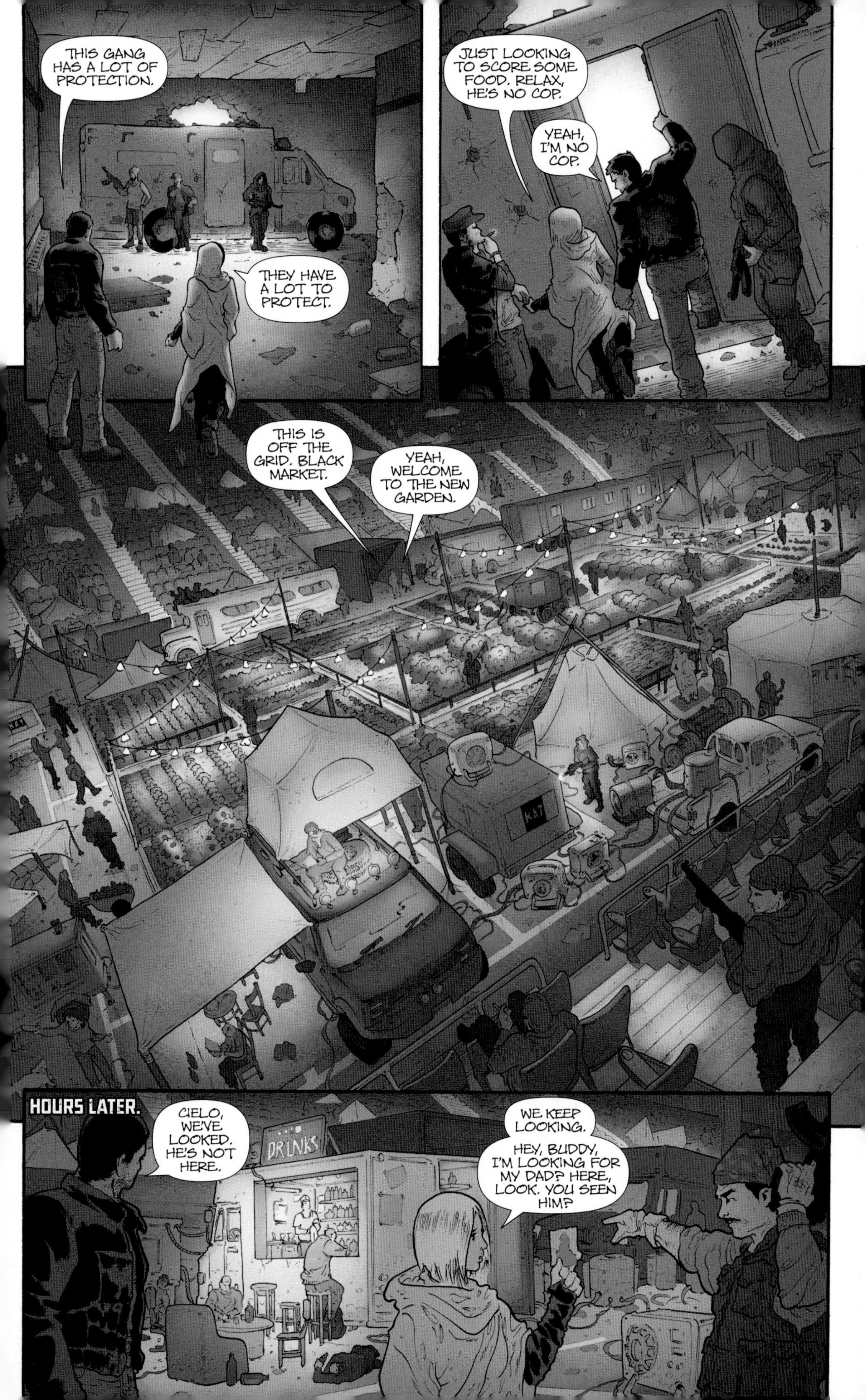
THIS GANG HAS A LOT OF PROTECTION.
THEY HAVE A LOT TO PROTECT.
JUST LOOKING TO SCORE SOME FOOD. RELAX, HE'S NO COP.
YEAH, I'M NO COP.
THIS IS OFF THE GRID. BLACK MARKET.
YEAH, WELCOME TO THE NEW GARDEN.
KAT
HOURS LATER.
CIELO, WE'VE LOOKED. HE'S NOT HERE.
DRINKS
WE KEEP LOOKING.
HEY, BUDDY, I'M LOOKING FOR MY DAD? HERE, LOOK. YOU SEEN HIM?

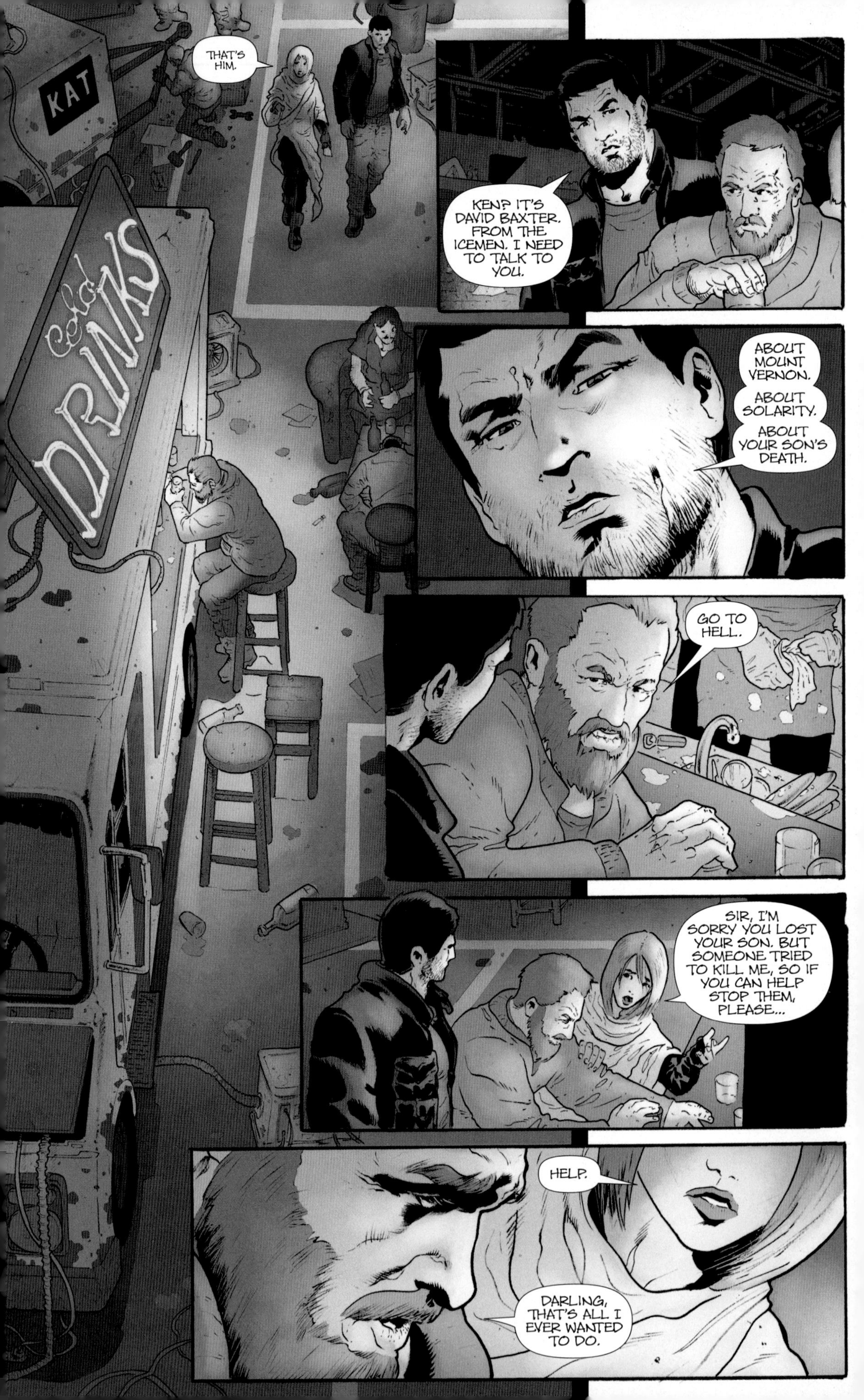
THAT'S HIM.
KAT
Cold DRINKS
KEN? IT'S DAVID BAXTER. FROM THE ICEMEN. I NEED TO TALK TO YOU.
ABOUT MOUNT VERNON.
ABOUT SOLARITY.
ABOUT YOUR SON'S DEATH.
GO TO HELL.
SIR, I'M SORRY YOU LOST YOUR SON. BUT SOMEONE TRIED TO KILL ME, SO IF YOU CAN HELP STOP THEM, PLEASE...
HELP.
DARLING, THAT'S ALL I EVER WANTED TO DO.

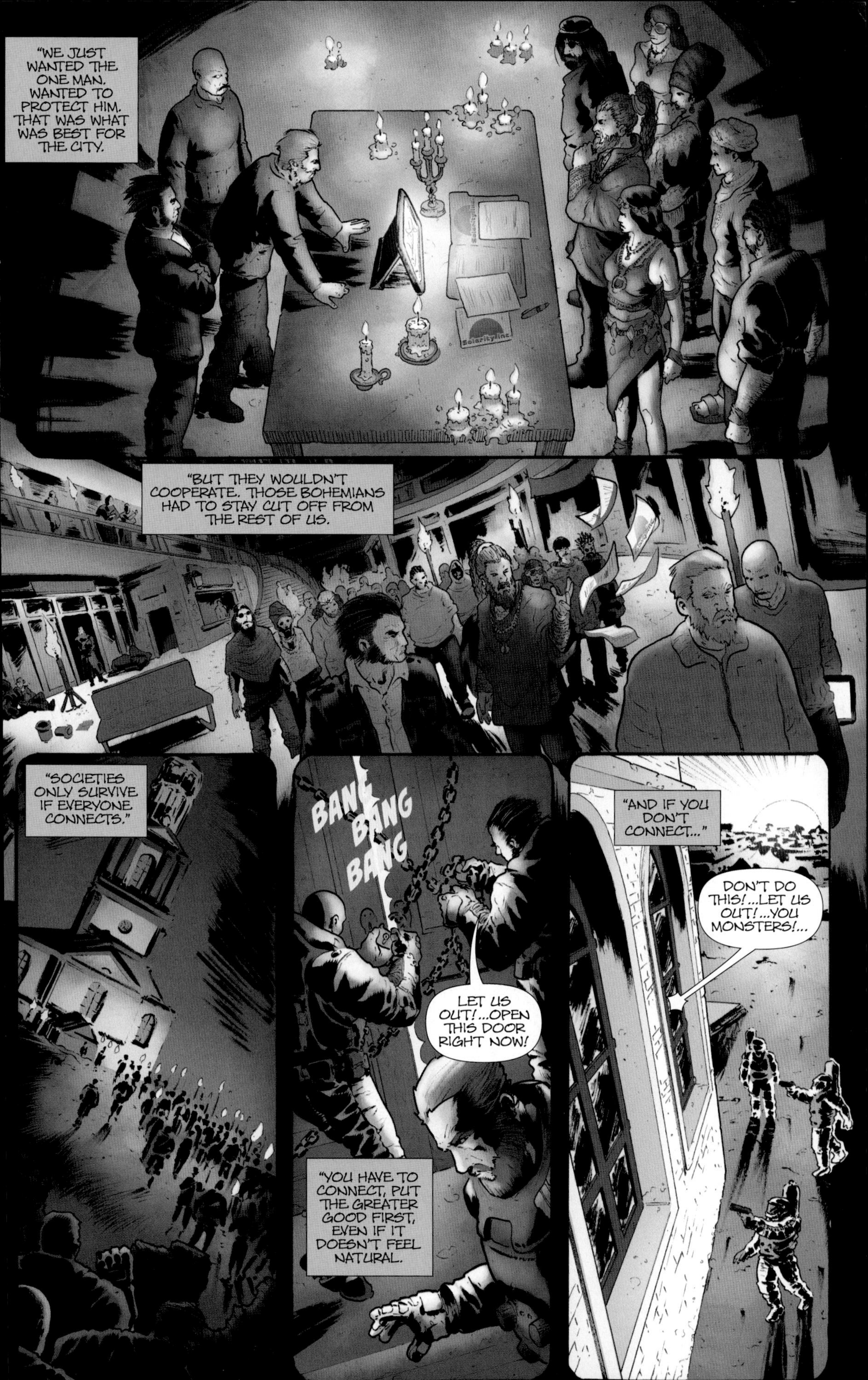
"WE JUST WANTED THE ONE MAN. WANTED TO PROTECT HIM. THAT WAS WHAT WAS BEST FOR THE CITY.
"BUT THEY WOULDN'T COOPERATE. THOSE BOHEMIANS HAD TO STAY CUT OFF FROM THE REST OF US.
"SOCIETIES ONLY SURVIVE IF EVERYONE CONNECTS."
BANG BANG BANG
LET US OUT!...OPEN THIS DOOR RIGHT NOW!
"YOU HAVE TO CONNECT, PUT THE GREATER GOOD FIRST, EVEN IF IT DOESN'T FEEL NATURAL.
"AND IF YOU DON'T CONNECT..."
DON'T DO THIS!...LET US OUT!...YOU MONSTERS!...

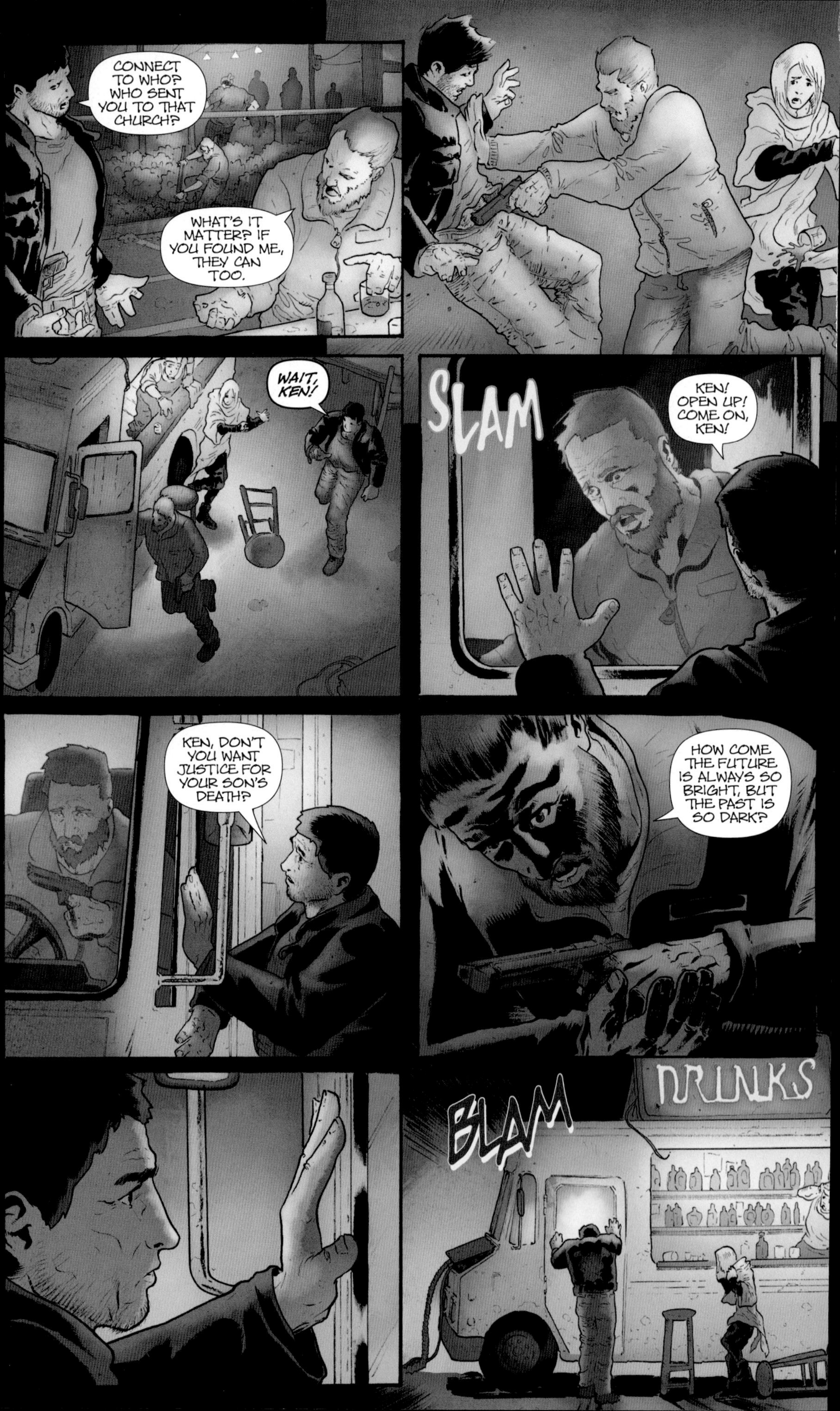
CONNECT TO WHO? WHO SENT YOU TO THAT CHURCH?
WHAT'S IT MATTER? IF YOU FOUND ME, THEY CAN TOO.
WAIT, KEN!
SLAM
KEN! OPEN UP! COME ON, KEN!
KEN, DON'T YOU WANT JUSTICE FOR YOUR SON'S DEATH?
HOW COME THE FUTURE IS ALWAYS SO BRIGHT, BUT THE PAST IS SO DARK?
DRINKS
BLAM

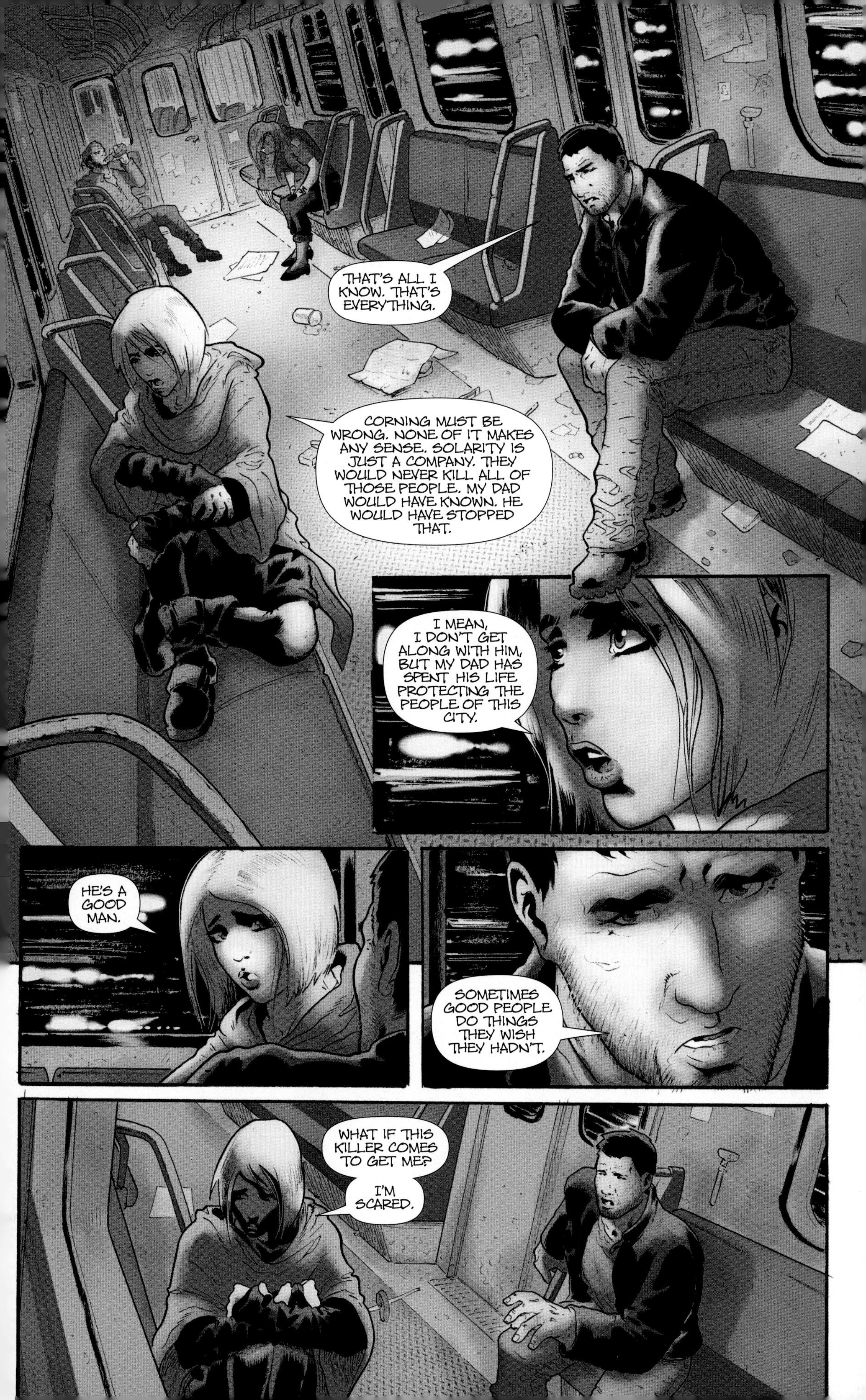
THAT'S ALL I KNOW. THAT'S EVERYTHING.
CORNING MUST BE WRONG. NONE OF IT MAKES ANY SENSE. SOLARITY IS JUST A COMPANY. THEY WOULD NEVER KILL ALL OF THOSE PEOPLE. MY DAD WOULD HAVE KNOWN. HE WOULD HAVE STOPPED THAT.
I MEAN, I DON'T GET ALONG WITH HIM, BUT MY DAD HAS SPENT HIS LIFE PROTECTING THE PEOPLE OF THIS CITY.
HE'S A GOOD MAN.
SOMETIMES GOOD PEOPLE DO THINGS THEY WISH THEY HADN'T.
WHAT IF THIS KILLER COMES TO GET ME?
I'M SCARED.

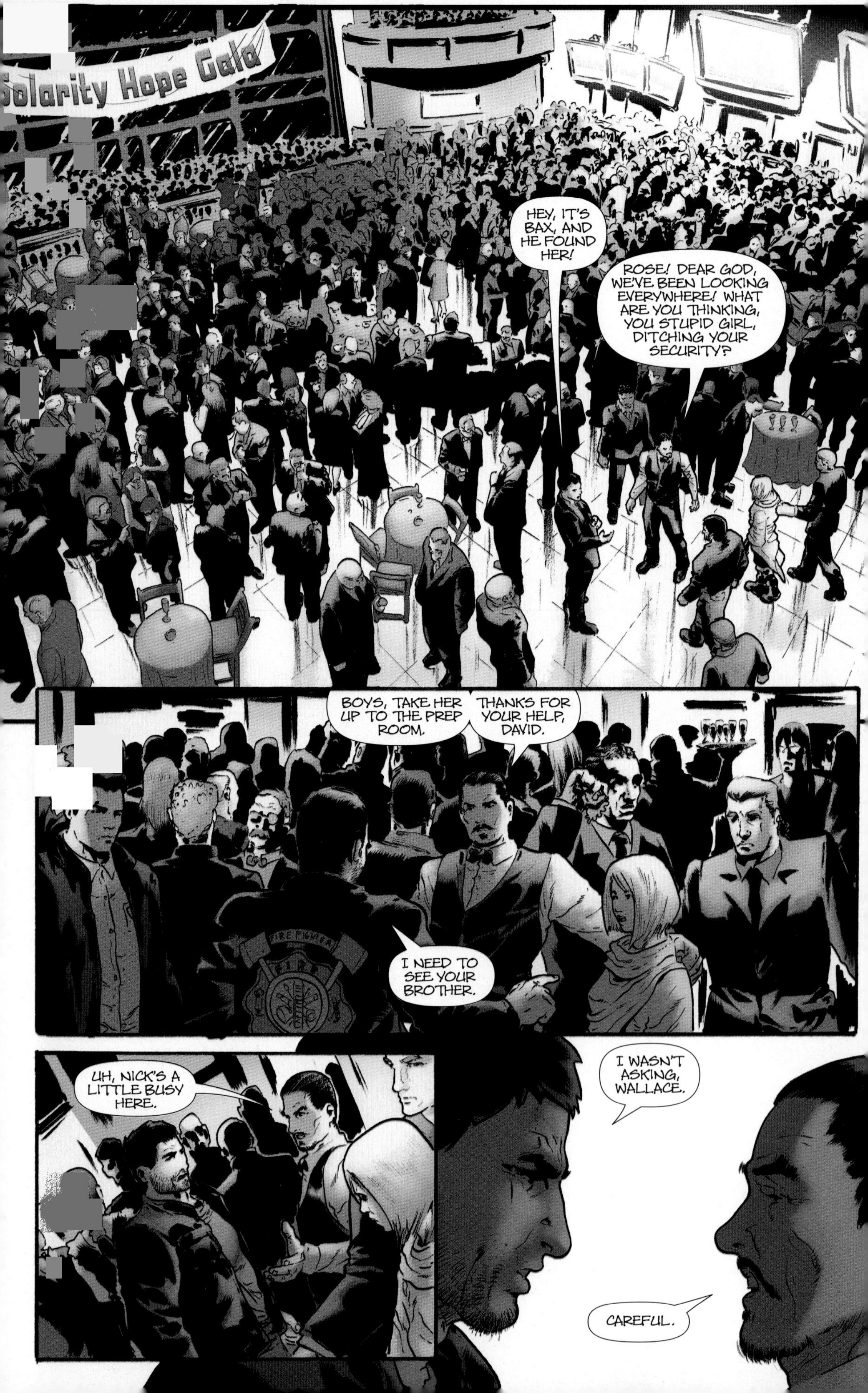
Solarity Hope Gala
HEY, IT'S BAX, AND HE FOUND HER!
ROSE! DEAR GOD, WE'VE BEEN LOOKING EVERYWHERE! WHAT ARE YOU THINKING, YOU STUPID GIRL, DITCHING YOUR SECURITY?
BOYS, TAKE HER UP TO THE PREP ROOM.
THANKS FOR YOUR HELP, DAVID.
FIRE FIGHTER
I NEED TO SEE YOUR BROTHER.
UH, NICK'S A LITTLE BUSY HERE.
I WASN'T ASKING, WALLACE.
CAREFUL.

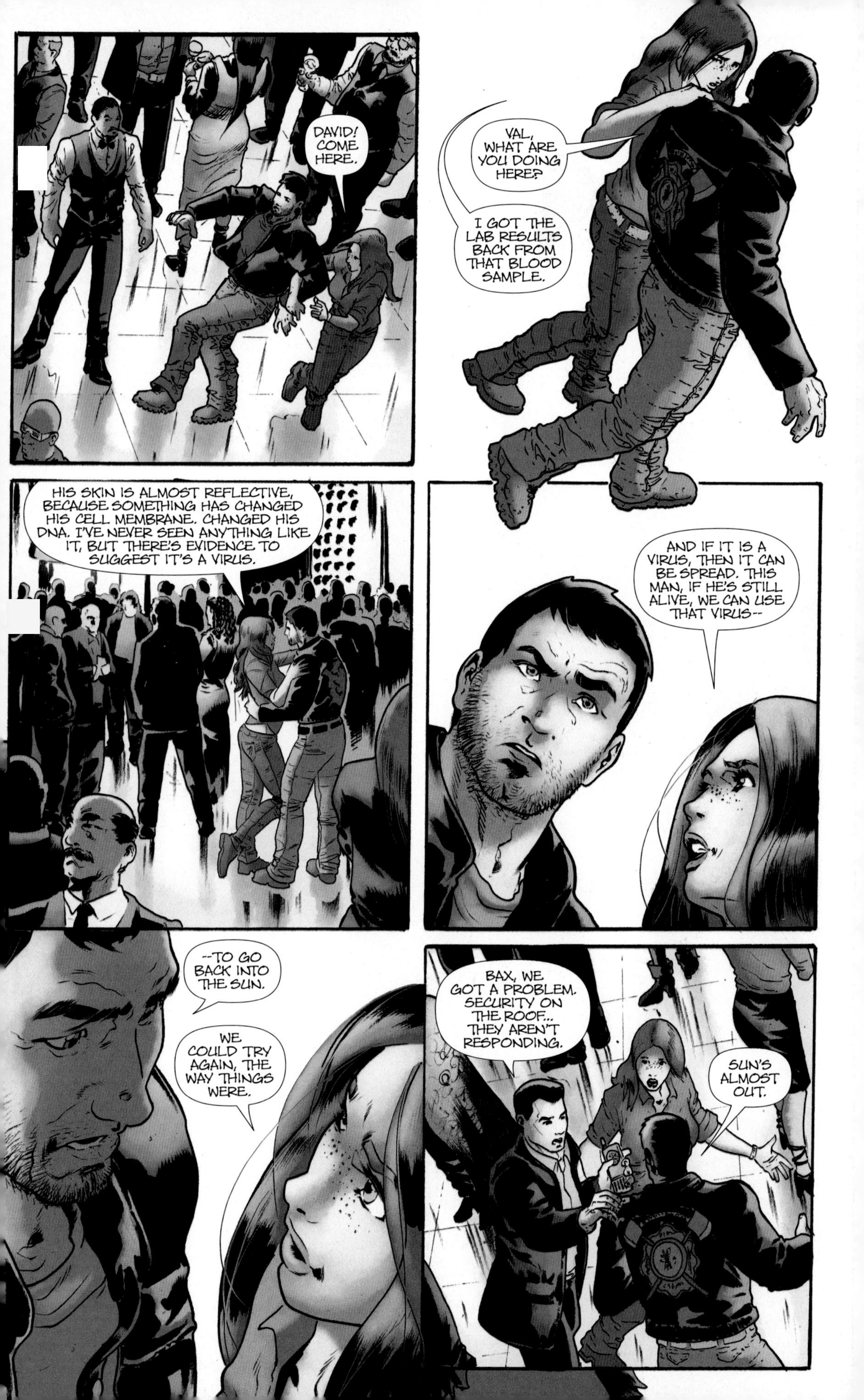
DAVID! COME HERE.
VAL, WHAT ARE YOU DOING HERE?
I GOT THE LAB RESULTS BACK FROM THAT BLOOD SAMPLE.
HIS SKIN IS ALMOST REFLECTIVE, BECAUSE SOMETHING HAS CHANGED HIS CELL MEMBRANE. CHANGED HIS DNA. I'VE NEVER SEEN ANYTHING LIKE IT, BUT THERE'S EVIDENCE TO SUGGEST IT'S A VIRUS.
AND IF IT IS A VIRUS, THEN IT CAN BE SPREAD. THIS MAN, IF HE'S STILL ALIVE, WE CAN USE THAT VIRUS--
--TO GO BACK INTO THE SUN.
WE COULD TRY AGAIN, THE WAY THINGS WERE.
BAX, WE GOT A PROBLEM. SECURITY ON THE ROOF... THEY AREN'T RESPONDING.
SUN'S ALMOST OUT.

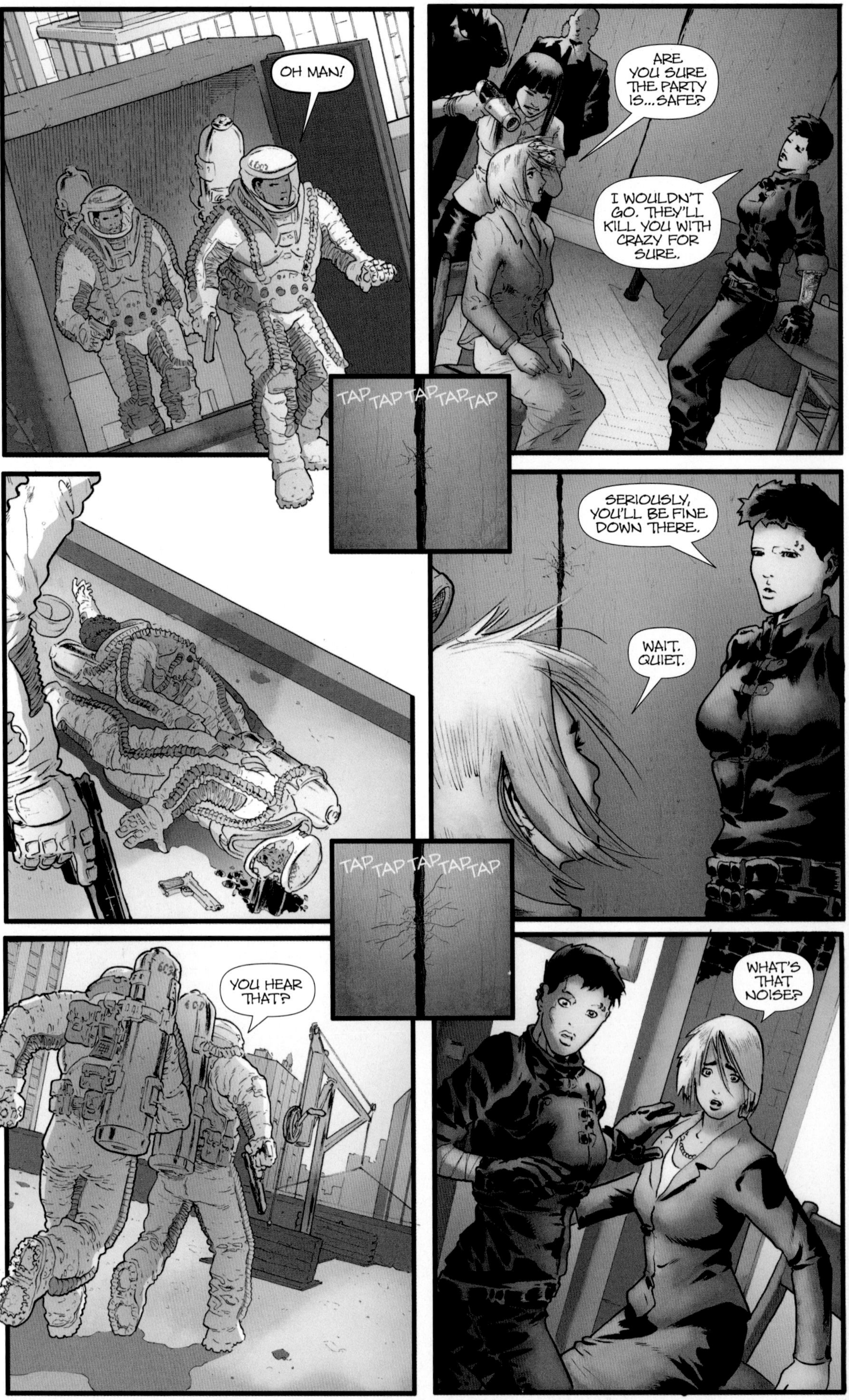
OH MAN!
ARE YOU SURE THE PARTY IS...SAFE?
I WOULDN'T GO. THEY'LL KILL YOU WITH CRAZY FOR SURE.
TAP TAP TAP TAP TAP
SERIOUSLY, YOU'LL BE FINE DOWN THERE.
WAIT. QUIET.
TAP TAP TAP TAP TAP
YOU HEAR THAT?
WHAT'S THAT NOISE?

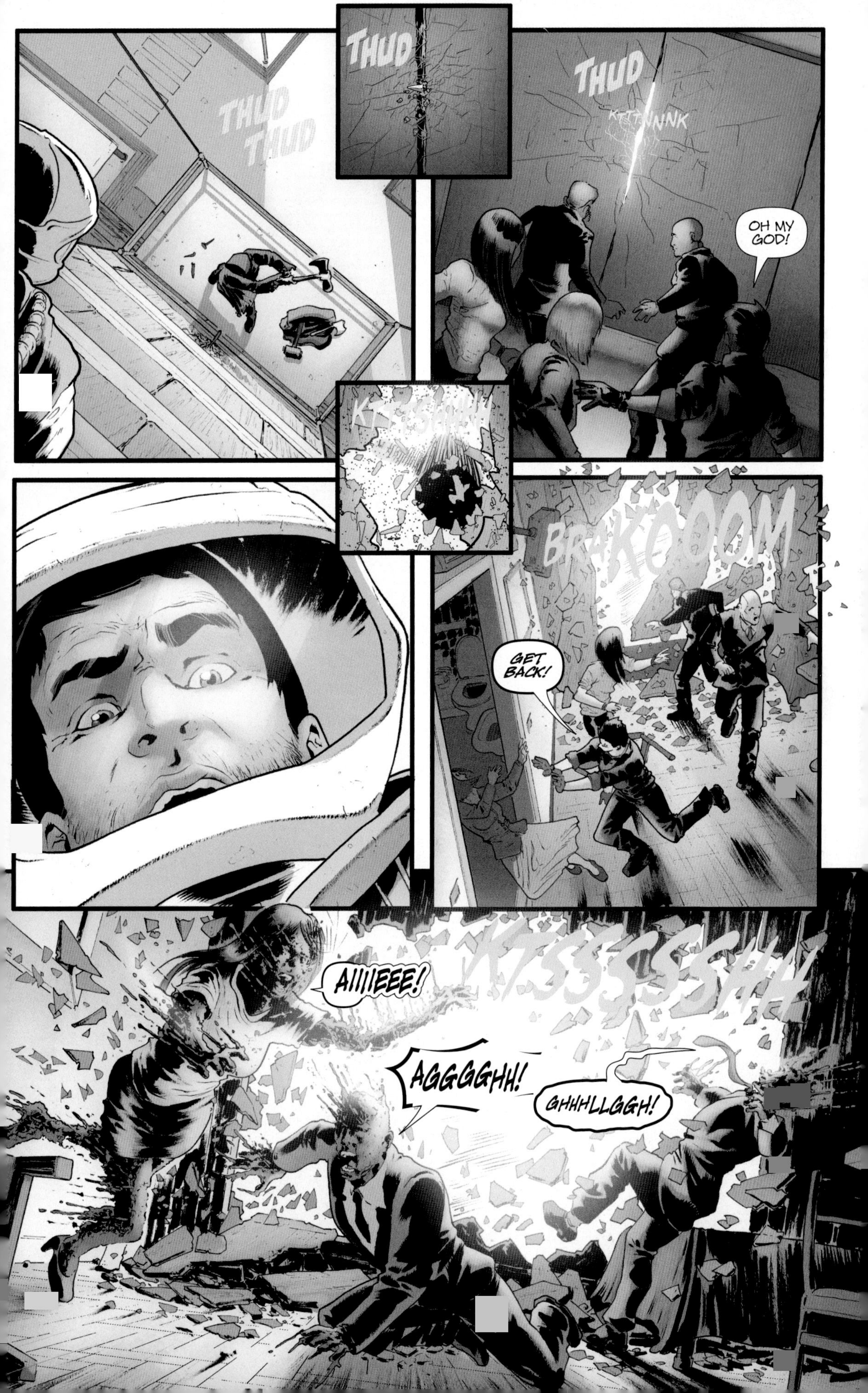
THUD
THUD
THUD
THUD
KTTTNNNK
OH MY GOD!
BRAKOOOM
GET BACK!
KTSSSSSHH
AIIIEEE!
AGGGGHH!
GHHHLLGGH!

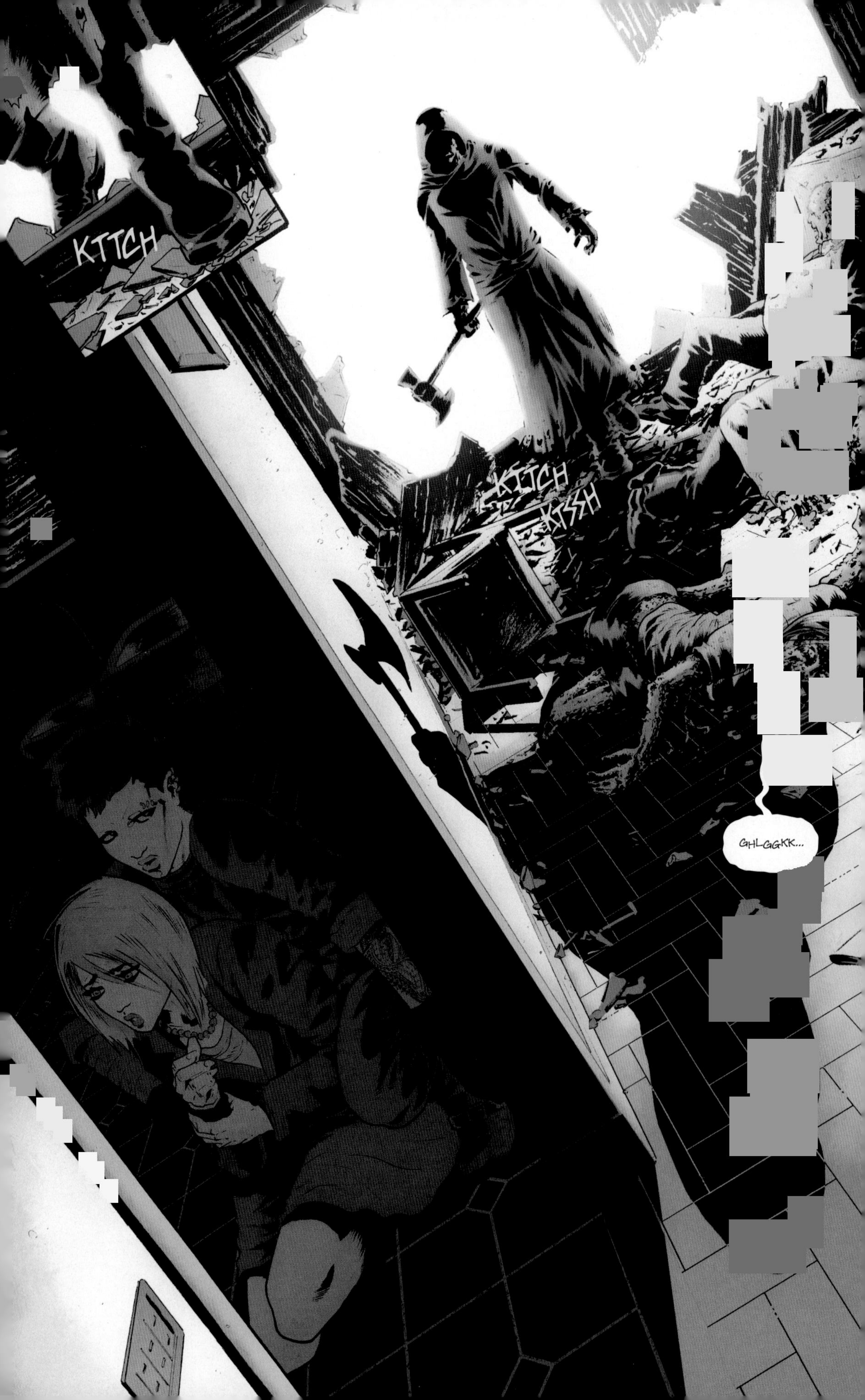
KTTCH
KTTCH
KTSSH
GHLGGKK...

CHAPTER FOUR

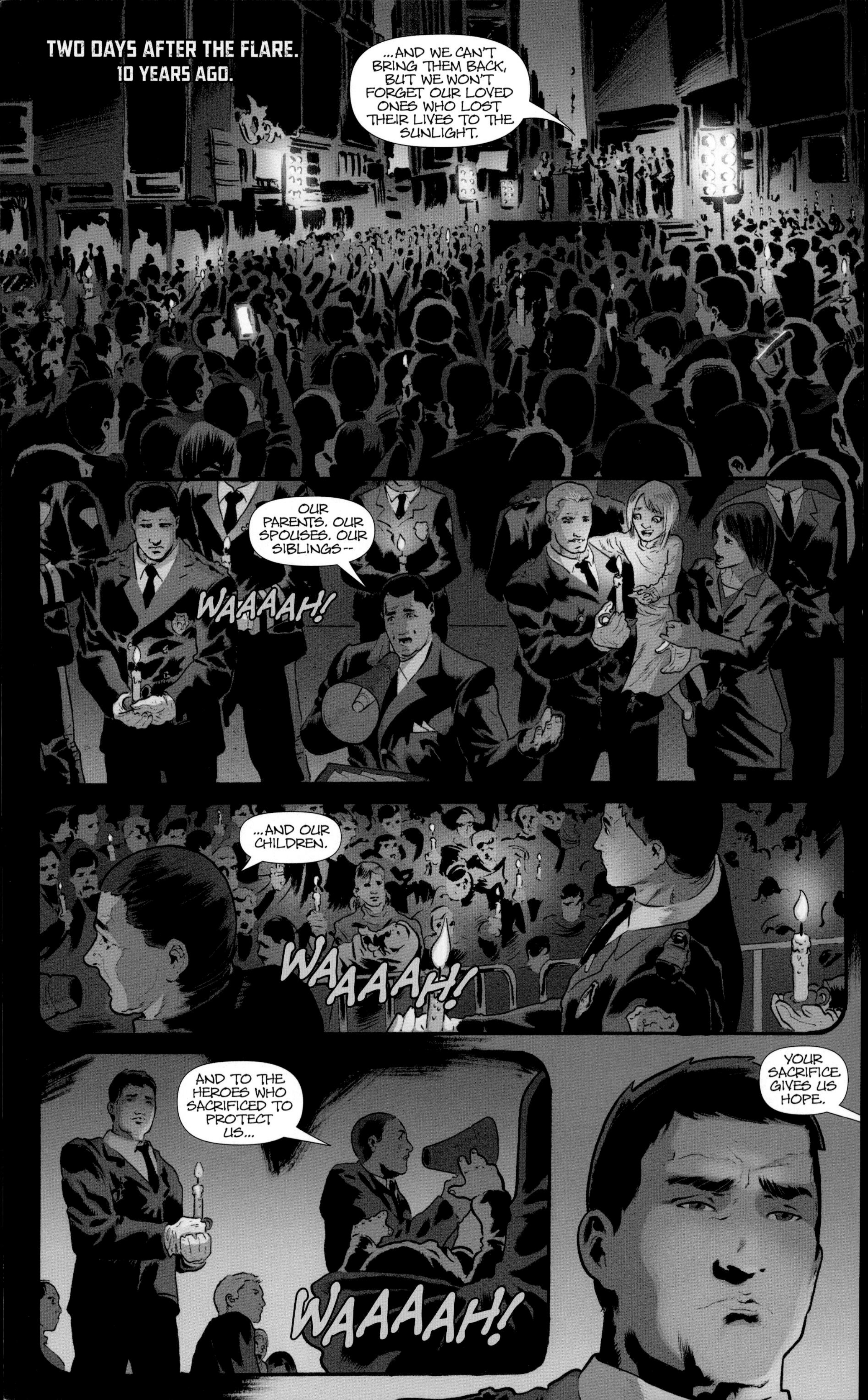
TWO DAYS AFTER THE FLARE. 10 YEARS AGO.
...AND WE CAN'T BRING THEM BACK, BUT WE WON'T FORGET OUR LOVED ONES WHO LOST THEIR LIVES TO THE SUNLIGHT.
OUR PARENTS. OUR SPOUSES. OUR SIBLINGS--
WAAAAH!
...AND OUR CHILDREN.
WAAAAAH!
AND TO THE HEROES WHO SACRIFICED TO PROTECT US...
WAAAAH!
YOUR SACRIFICE GIVES US HOPE.

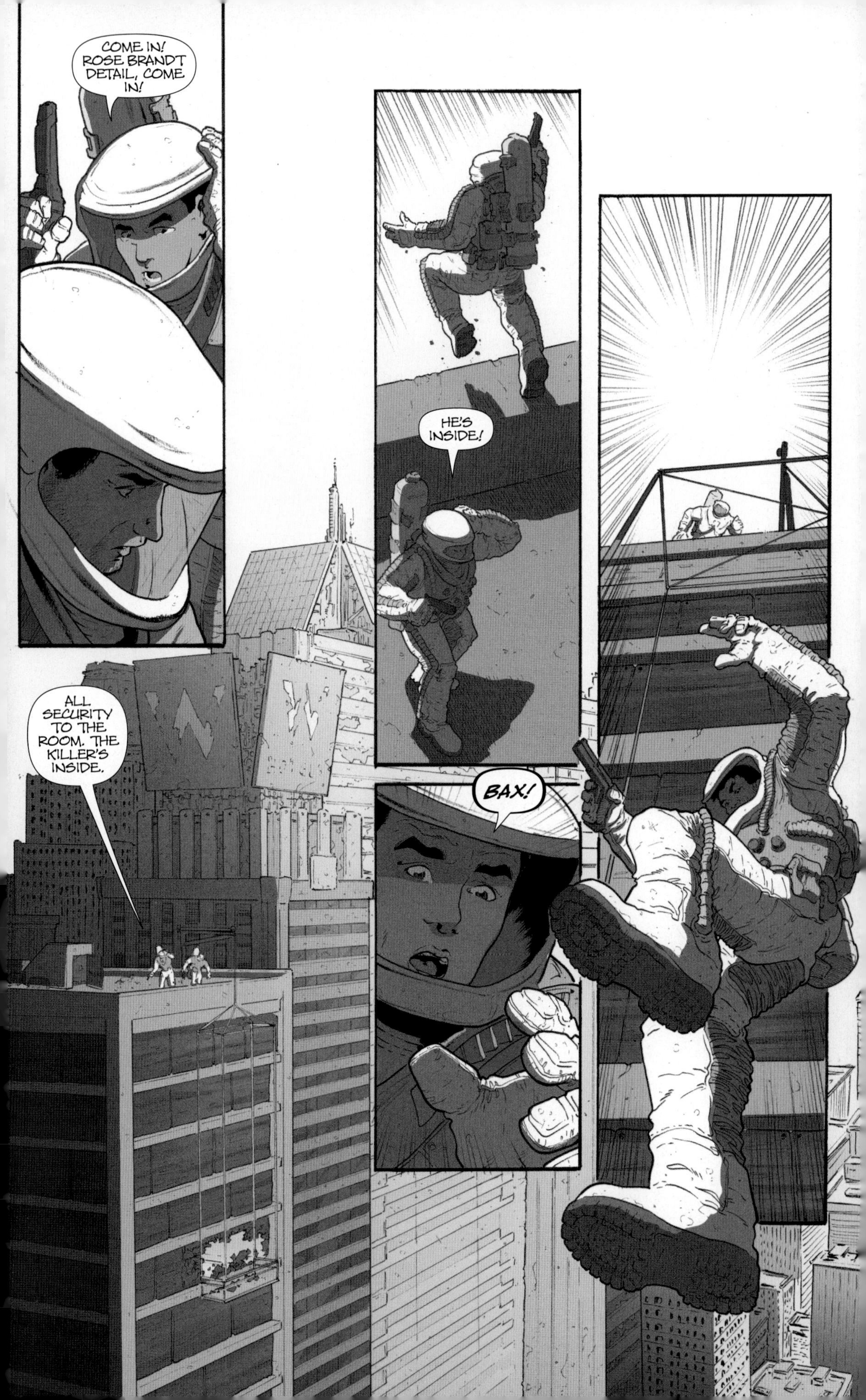
COME IN! ROSE BRANDT DETAIL, COME IN!
HE'S INSIDE!
ALL SECURITY TO THE ROOM. THE KILLER'S INSIDE.
BAX!

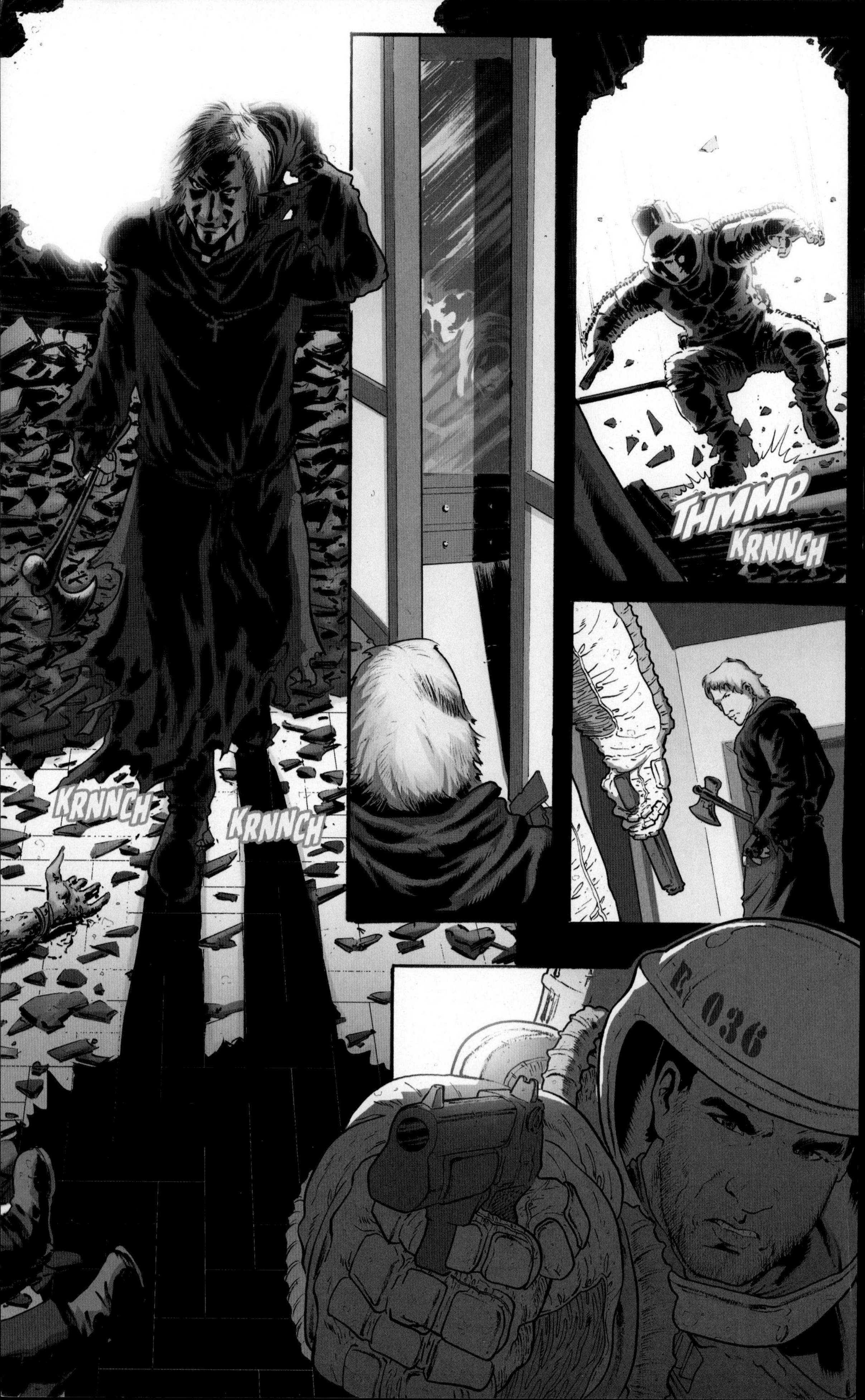
THMMP
KRNNCH
KRNNCH
KRNNCH
E 036

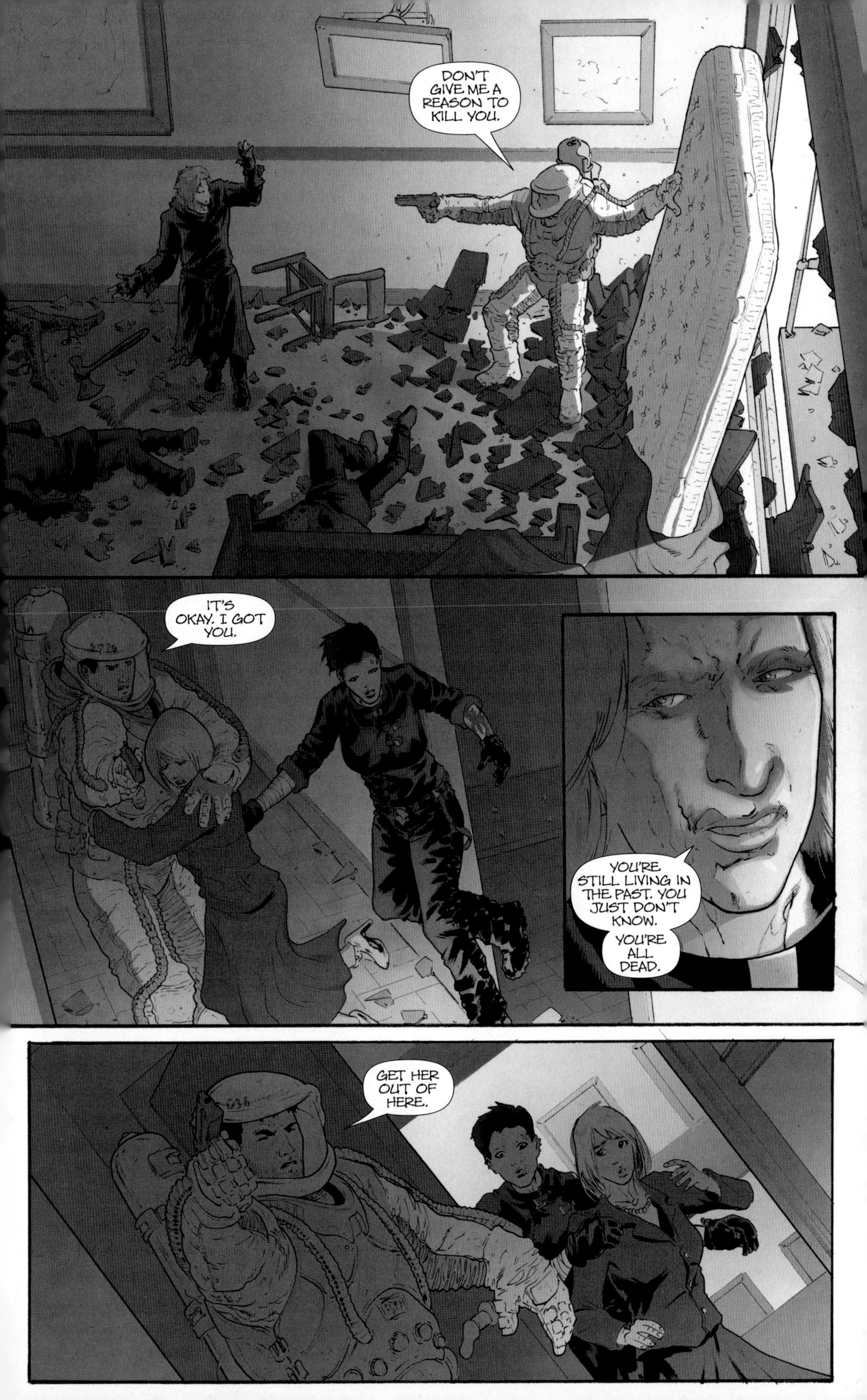
DON'T GIVE ME A REASON TO KILL YOU.
IT'S OKAY. I GOT YOU.
YOU'RE STILL LIVING IN THE PAST. YOU JUST DON'T KNOW.
YOU'RE ALL DEAD.
GET HER OUT OF HERE.

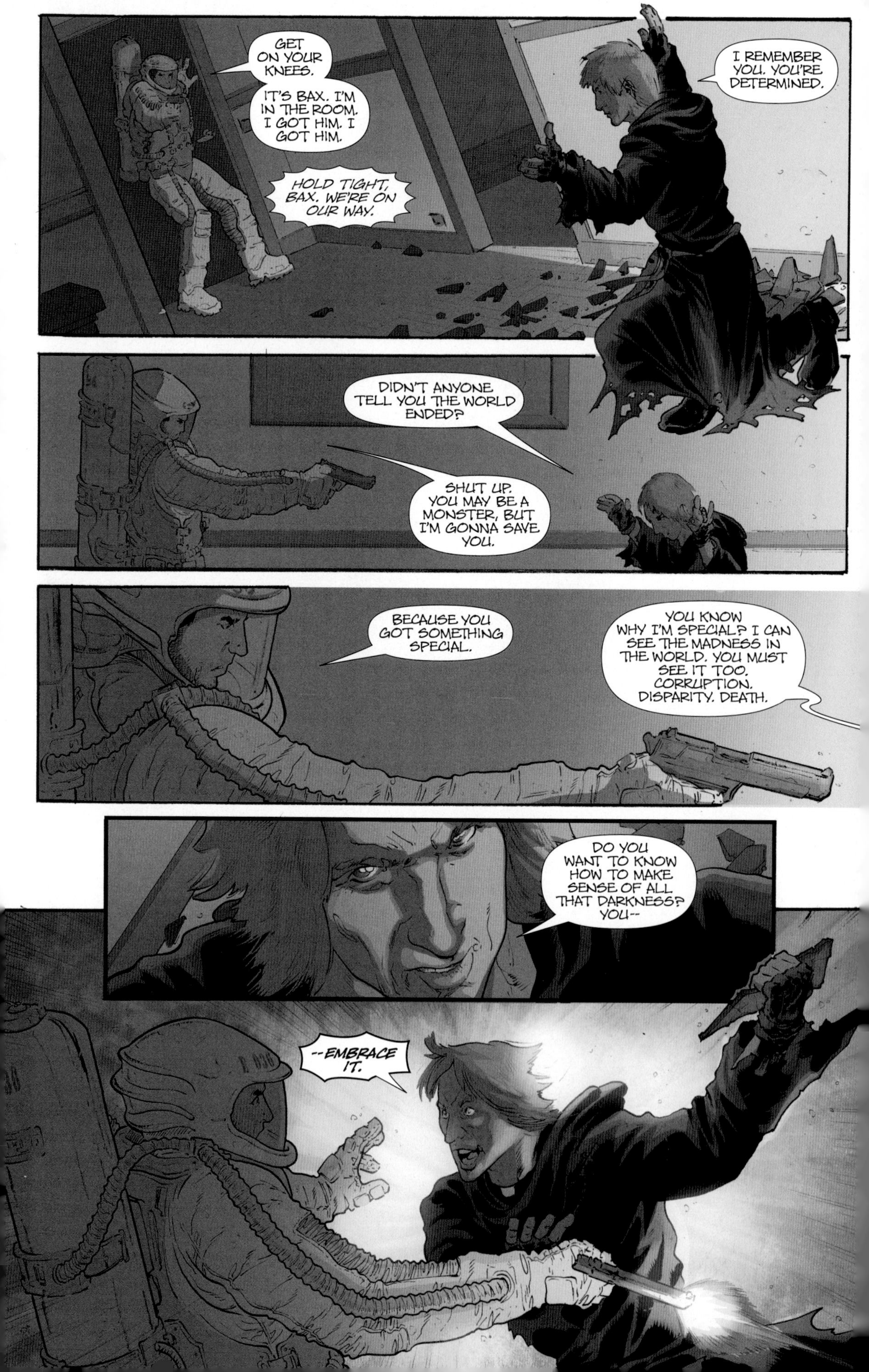
GET ON YOUR KNEES.
IT'S BAX. I'M IN THE ROOM. I GOT HIM. I GOT HIM.
HOLD TIGHT, BAX. WE'RE ON OUR WAY.
I REMEMBER YOU. YOU'RE DETERMINED.
DIDN'T ANYONE TELL YOU THE WORLD ENDED?
SHUT UP. YOU MAY BE A MONSTER, BUT I'M GONNA SAVE YOU.
BECAUSE YOU GOT SOMETHING SPECIAL.
YOU KNOW WHY I'M SPECIAL? I CAN SEE THE MADNESS IN THE WORLD. YOU MUST SEE IT TOO. CORRUPTION. DISPARITY. DEATH.
DO YOU WANT TO KNOW HOW TO MAKE SENSE OF ALL THAT DARKNESS? YOU--
--EMBRACE IT.

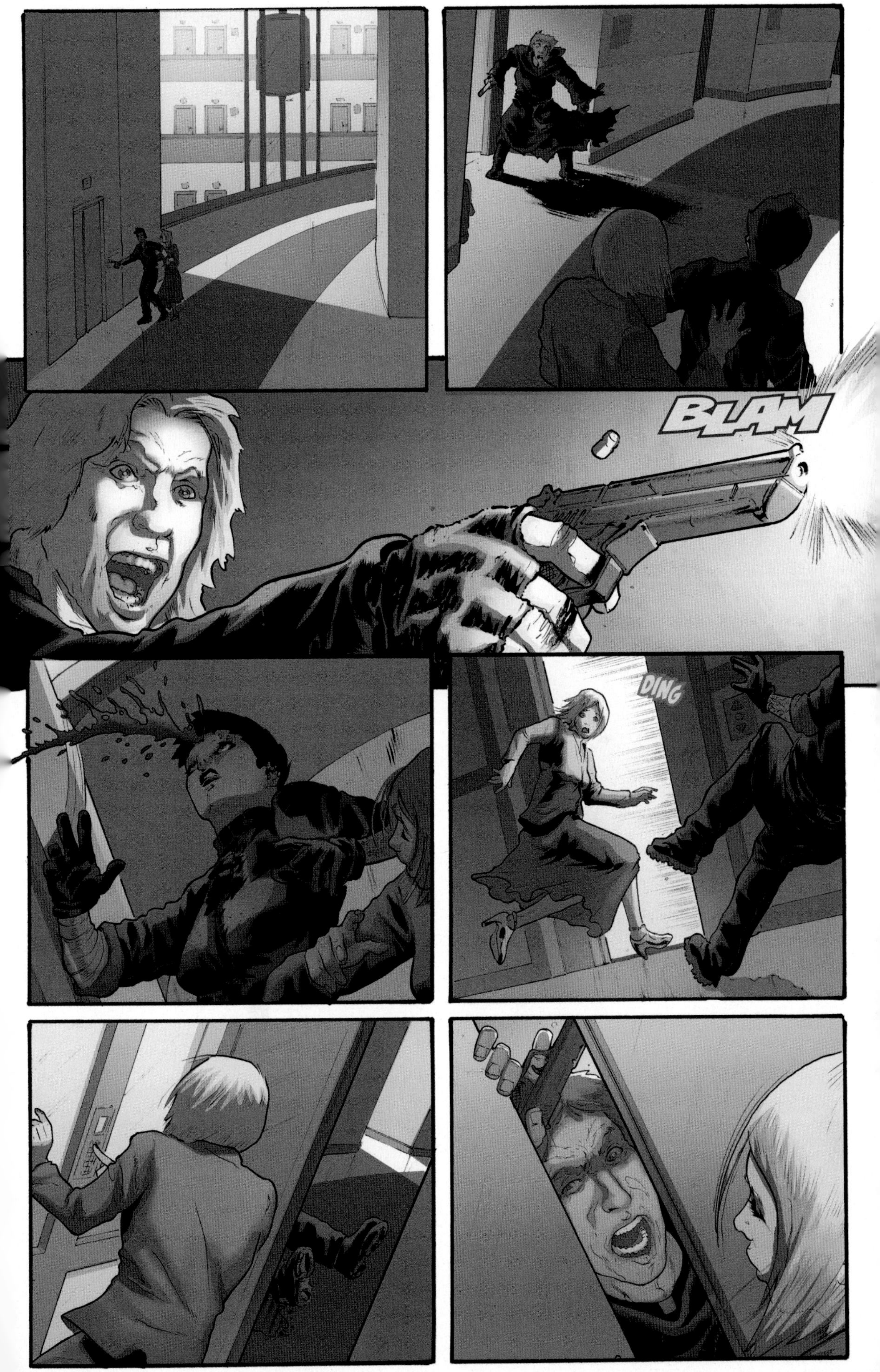
BLAM
DING

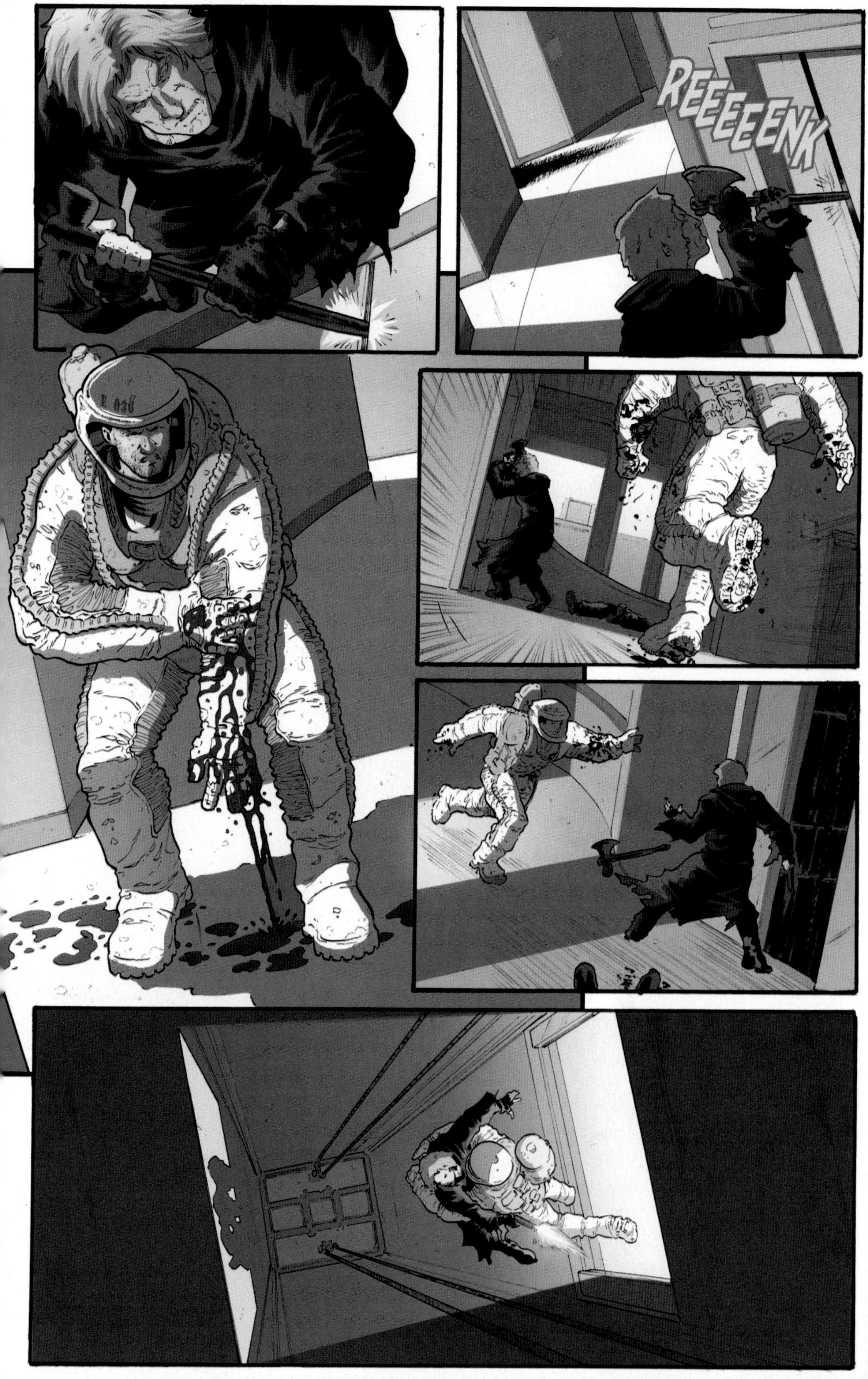
REEEEENK

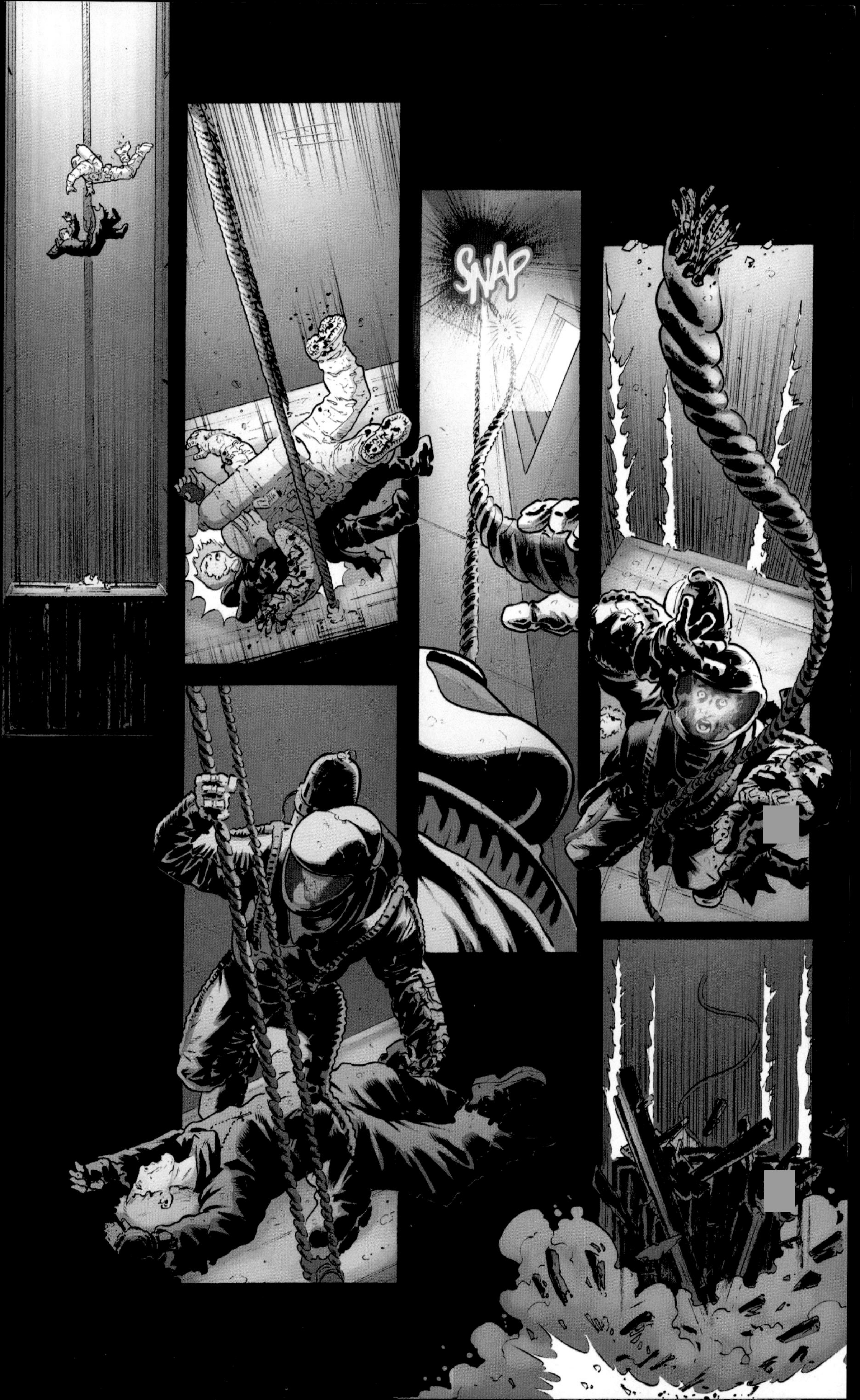
SNAP

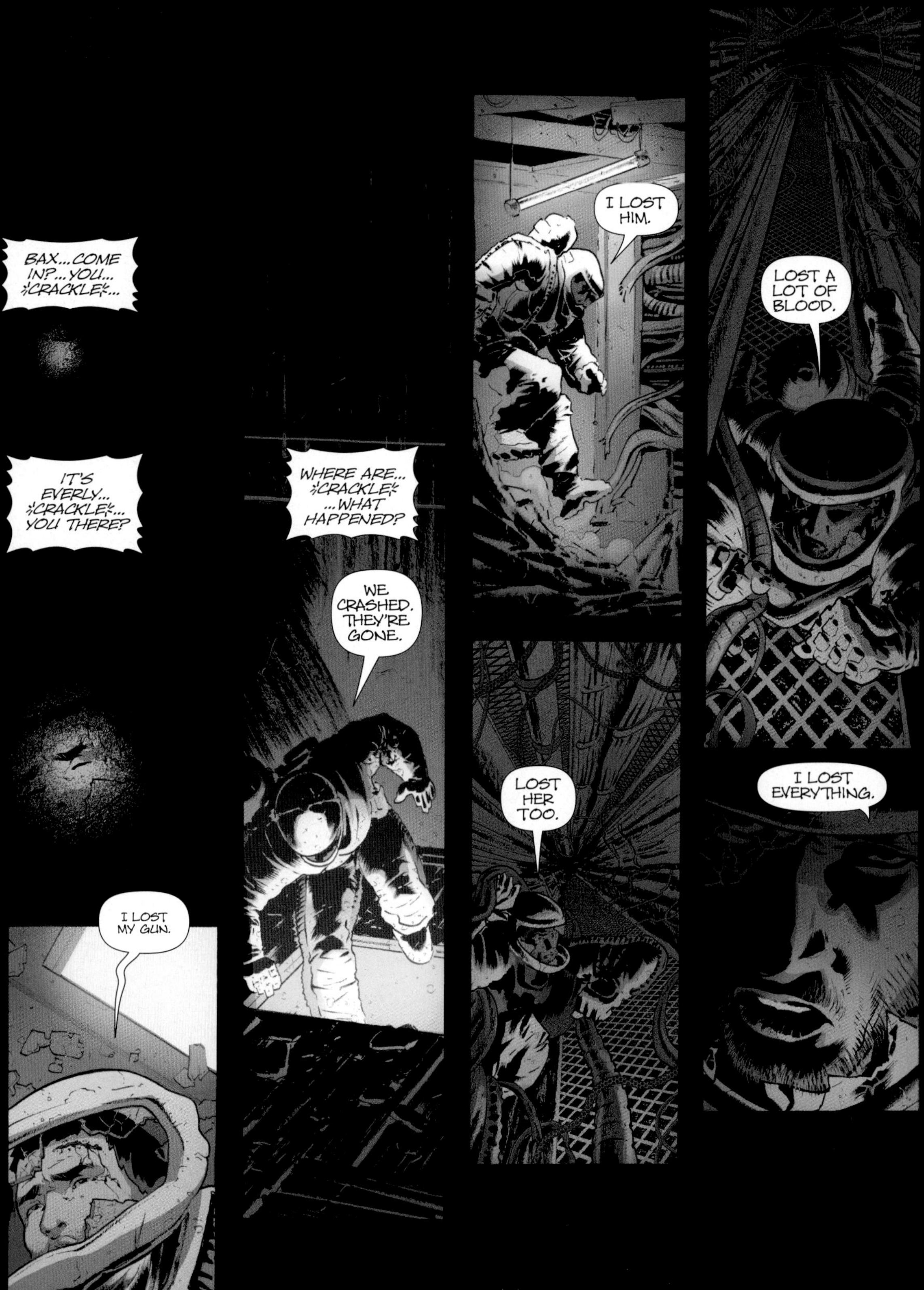
BAX...COME IN?...YOU... *CRACKLE*...
IT'S EVERLY... *CRACKLE*... YOU THERE?
I LOST MY GUN.
WHERE ARE... *CRACKLE* ...WHAT HAPPENED?
WE CRASHED. THEY'RE GONE.
I LOST HIM.
LOST HER TOO.
LOST A LOT OF BLOOD.
I LOST EVERYTHING.

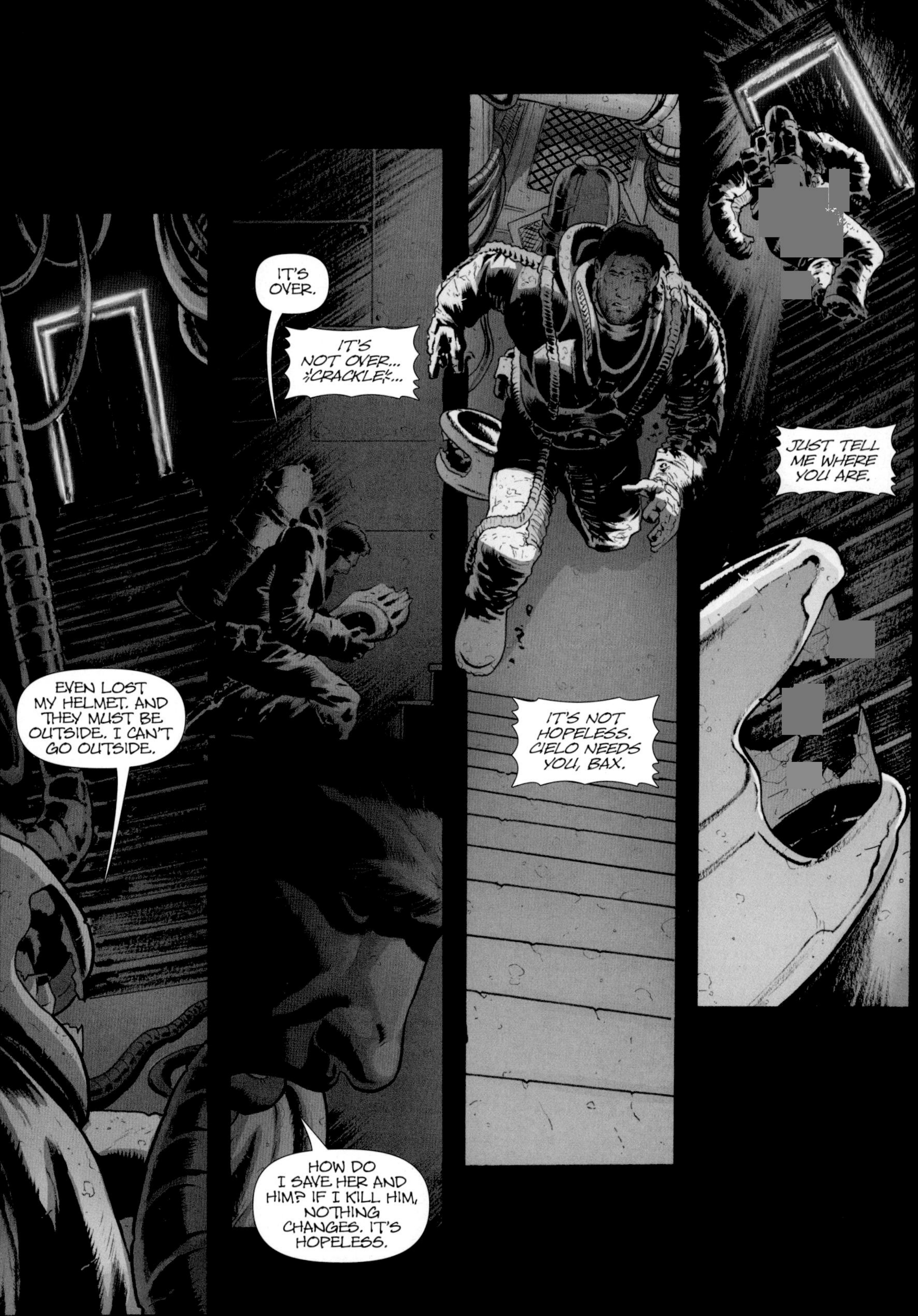
IT'S OVER.
IT'S NOT OVER... *CRACKLE*...
EVEN LOST MY HELMET. AND THEY MUST BE OUTSIDE. I CAN'T GO OUTSIDE.
HOW DO I SAVE HER AND HIM? IF I KILL HIM, NOTHING CHANGES. IT'S HOPELESS.
IT'S NOT HOPELESS. CIELO NEEDS YOU, BAX.
JUST TELL ME WHERE YOU ARE.

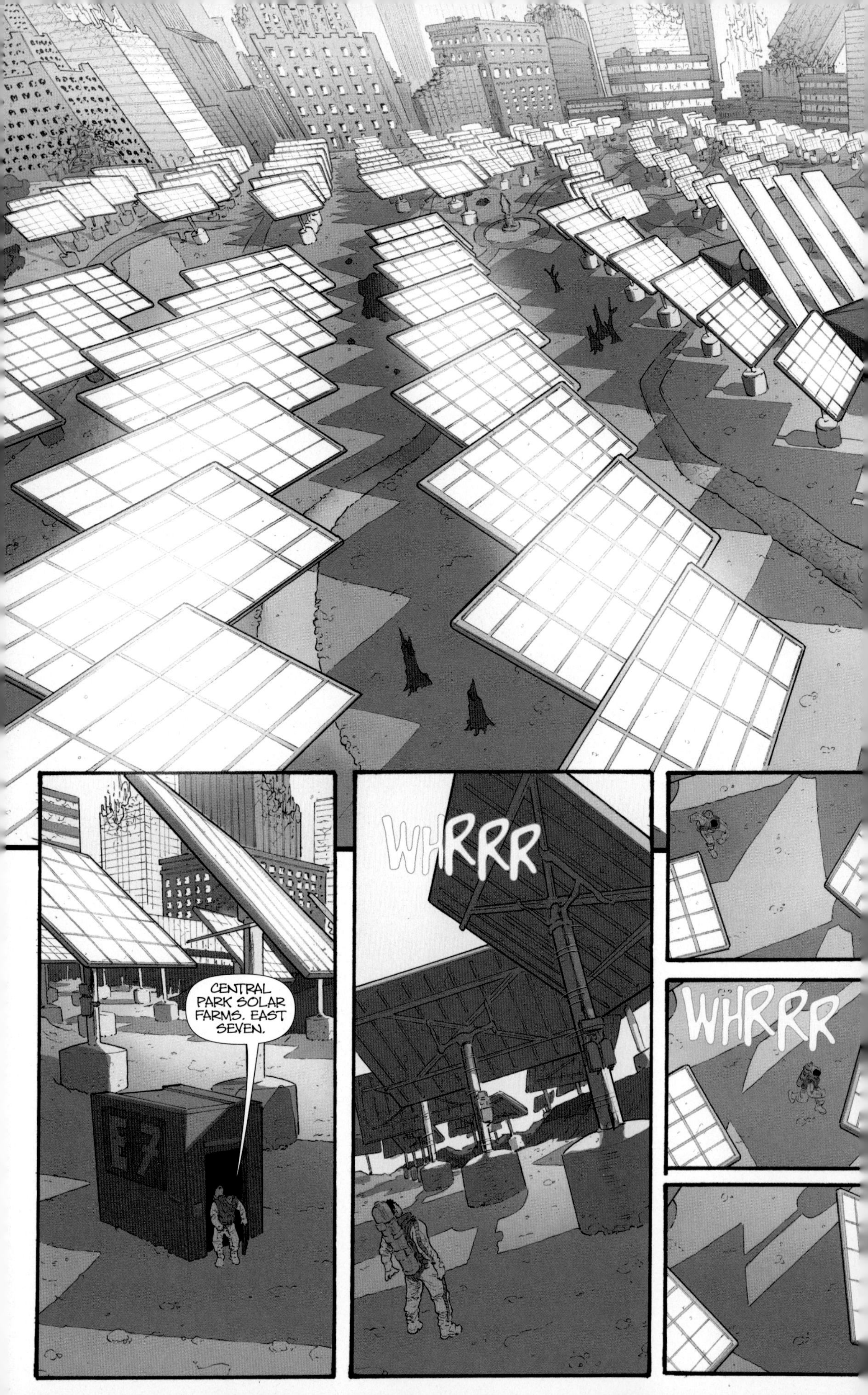
CENTRAL PARK SOLAR FARMS. EAST SEVEN.
E7
WHRRR
WHRRR

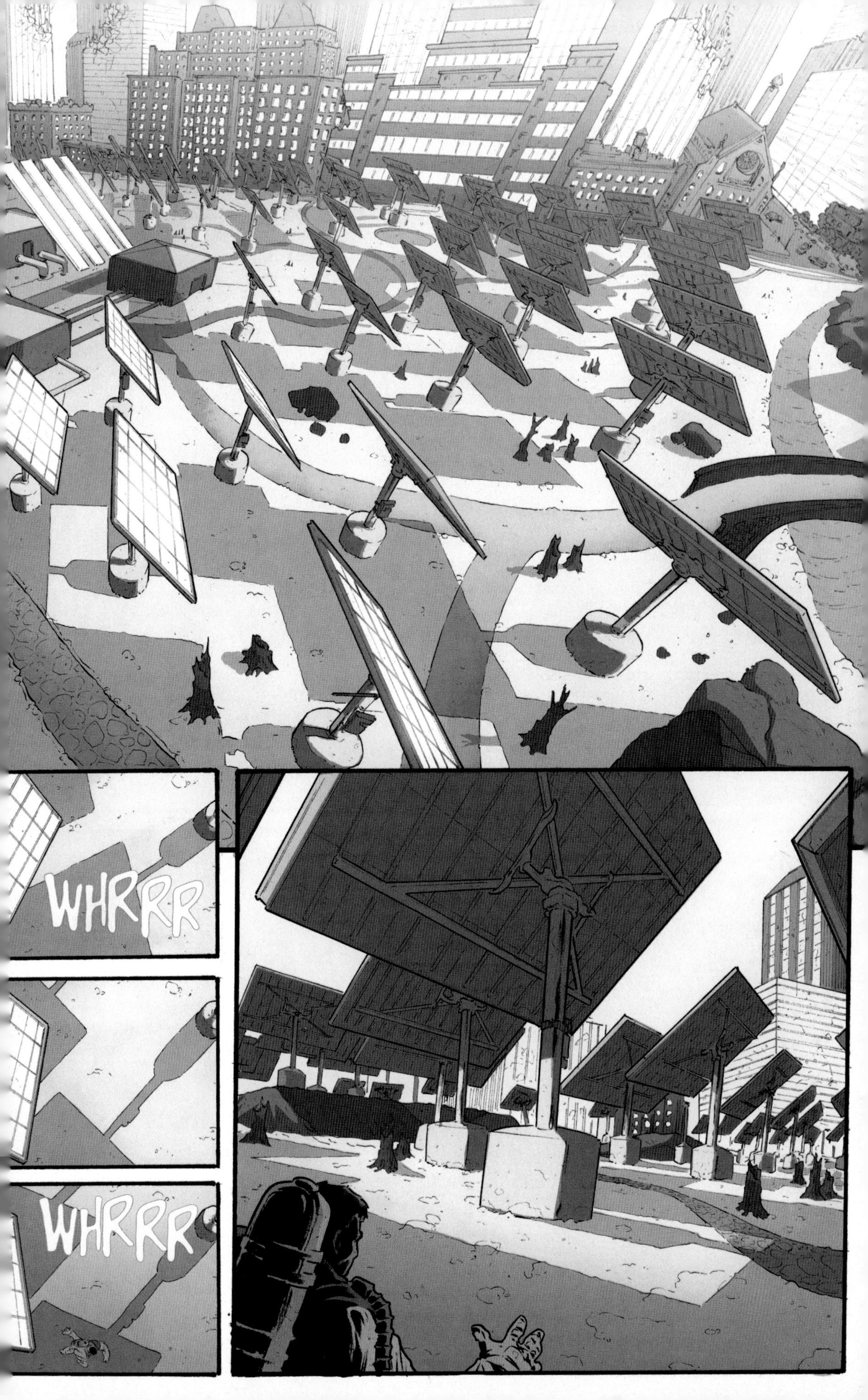
WHRRR
WHRRR

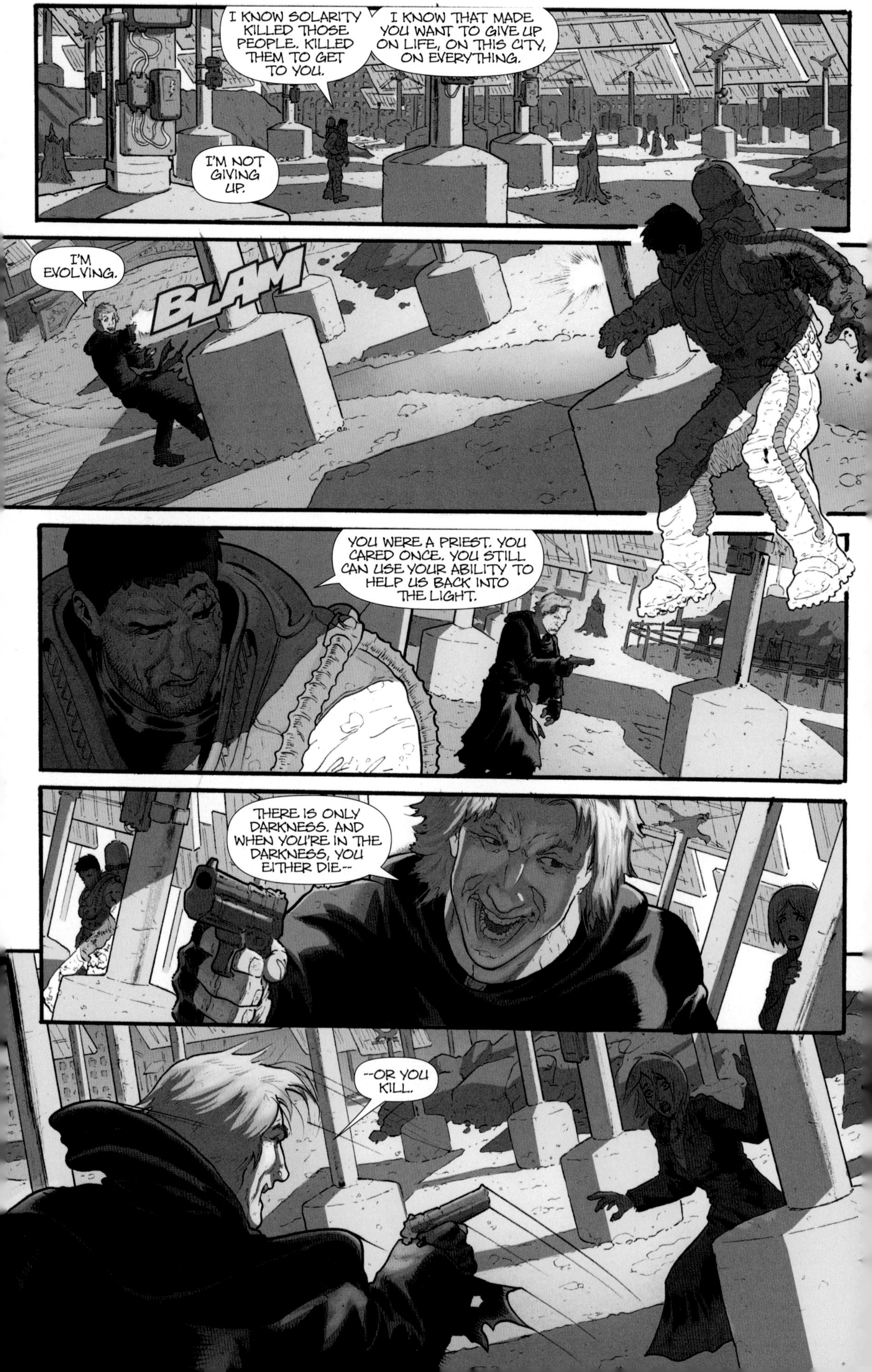
I KNOW SOLARITY KILLED THOSE PEOPLE. KILLED THEM TO GET TO YOU.
I KNOW THAT MADE YOU WANT TO GIVE UP ON LIFE, ON THIS CITY, ON EVERYTHING.
I'M NOT GIVING UP.
I'M EVOLVING.
BLAM
YOU WERE A PRIEST. YOU CARED ONCE. YOU STILL CAN USE YOUR ABILITY TO HELP US BACK INTO THE LIGHT.
THERE IS ONLY DARKNESS. AND WHEN YOU'RE IN THE DARKNESS, YOU EITHER DIE--
--OR YOU KILL.

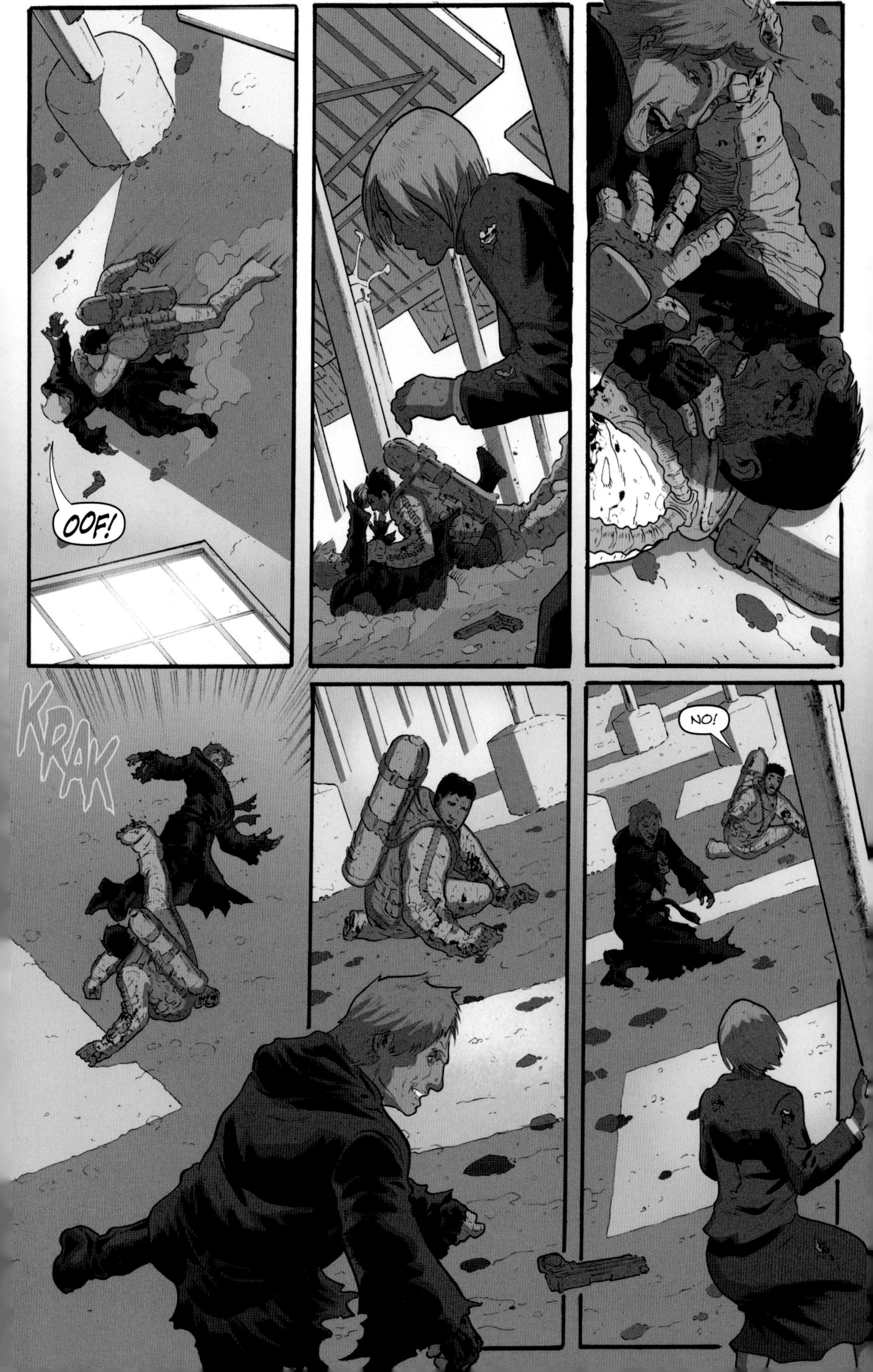

OOF!
KRAK
NO!

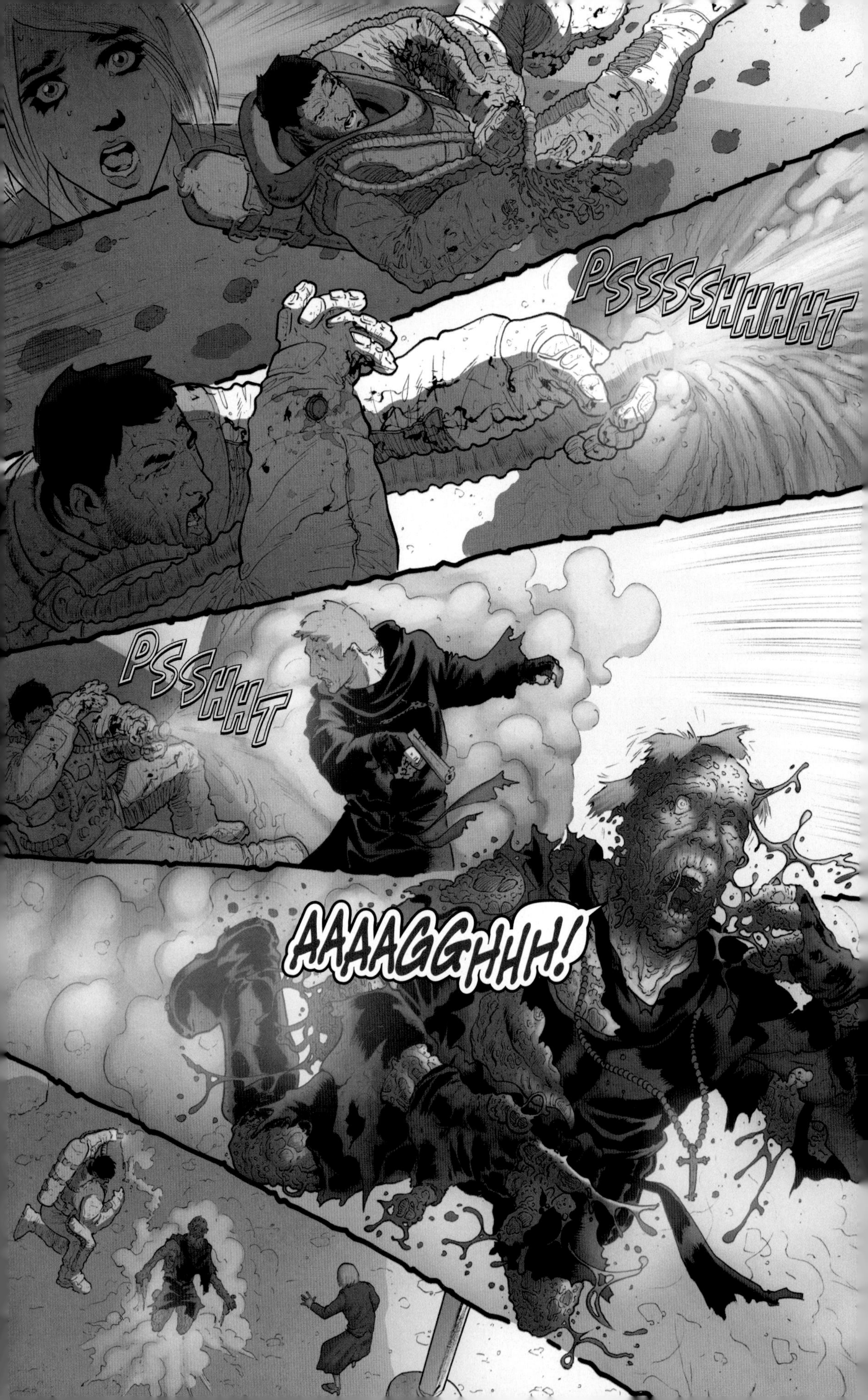
PSSSSSHHHHT
PSSHHT
AAAAGGHHH!

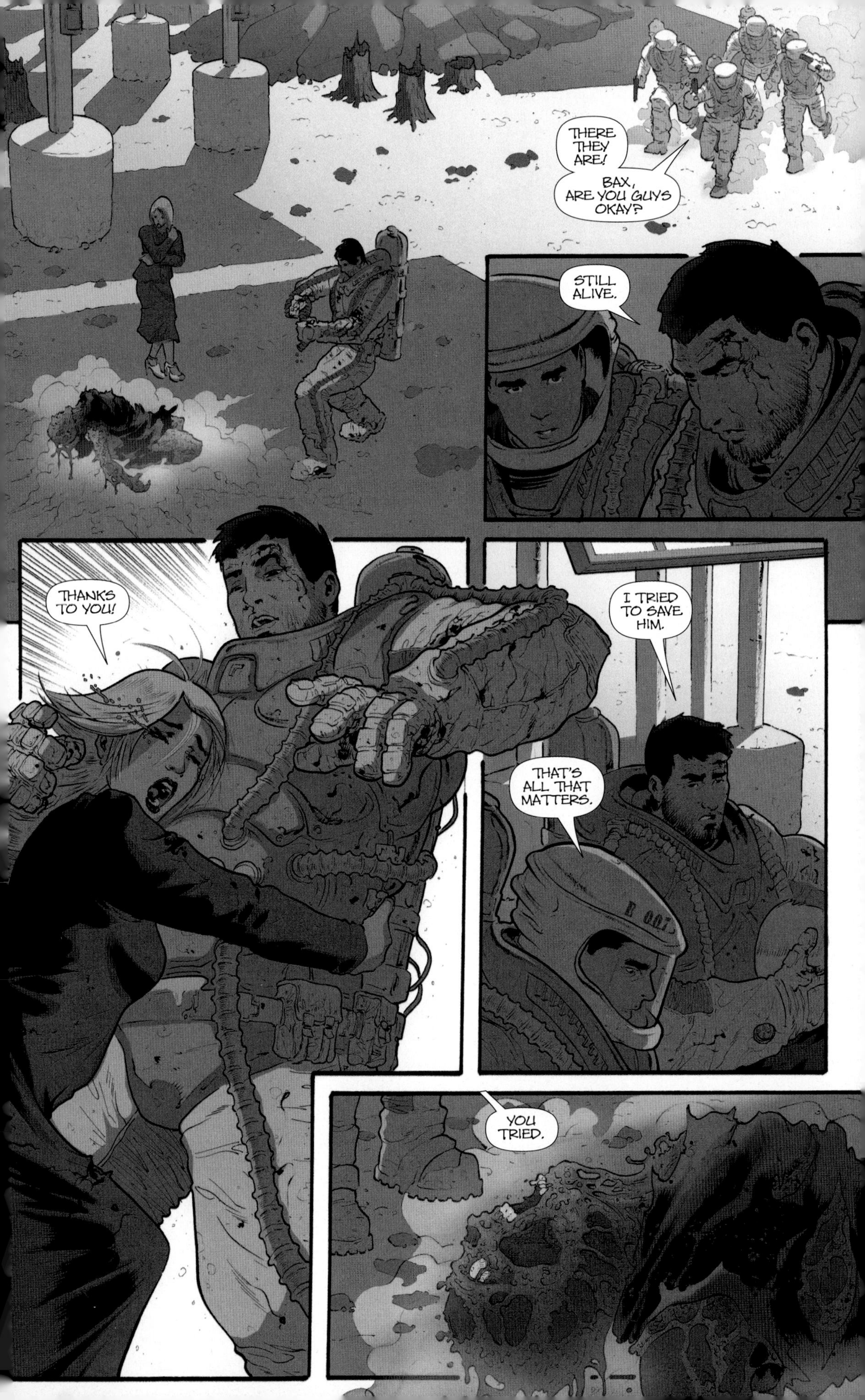
THERE THEY ARE!
BAX, ARE YOU GUYS OKAY?
STILL ALIVE.
THANKS TO YOU!
I TRIED TO SAVE HIM.
THAT'S ALL THAT MATTERS.
YOU TRIED.

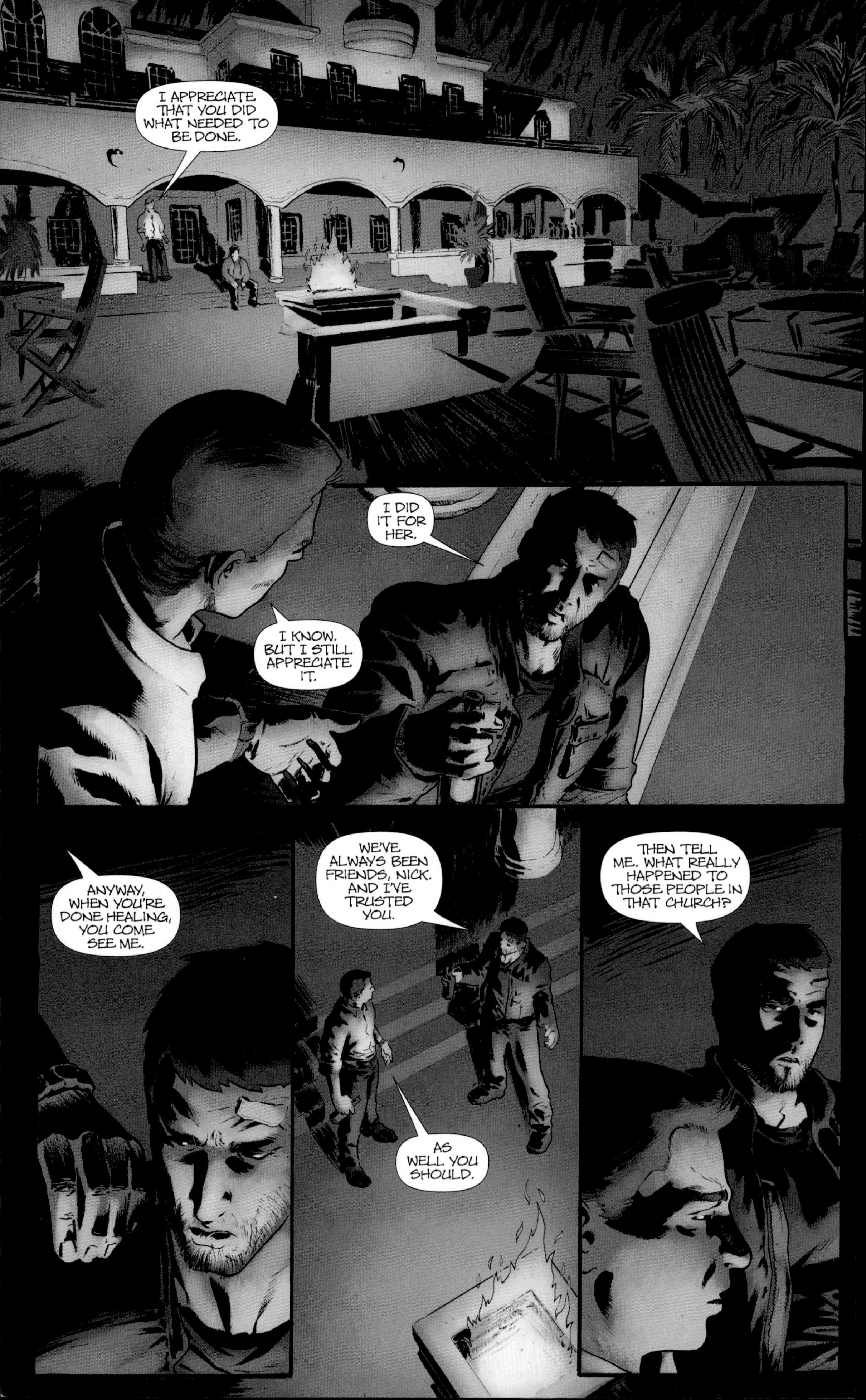
I APPRECIATE THAT YOU DID WHAT NEEDED TO BE DONE.
I DID IT FOR HER.
I KNOW. BUT I STILL APPRECIATE IT.
ANYWAY, WHEN YOU'RE DONE HEALING, YOU COME SEE ME.
WE'VE ALWAYS BEEN FRIENDS, NICK. AND I'VE TRUSTED YOU.
AS WELL YOU SHOULD.
THEN TELL ME. WHAT REALLY HAPPENED TO THOSE PEOPLE IN THAT CHURCH?

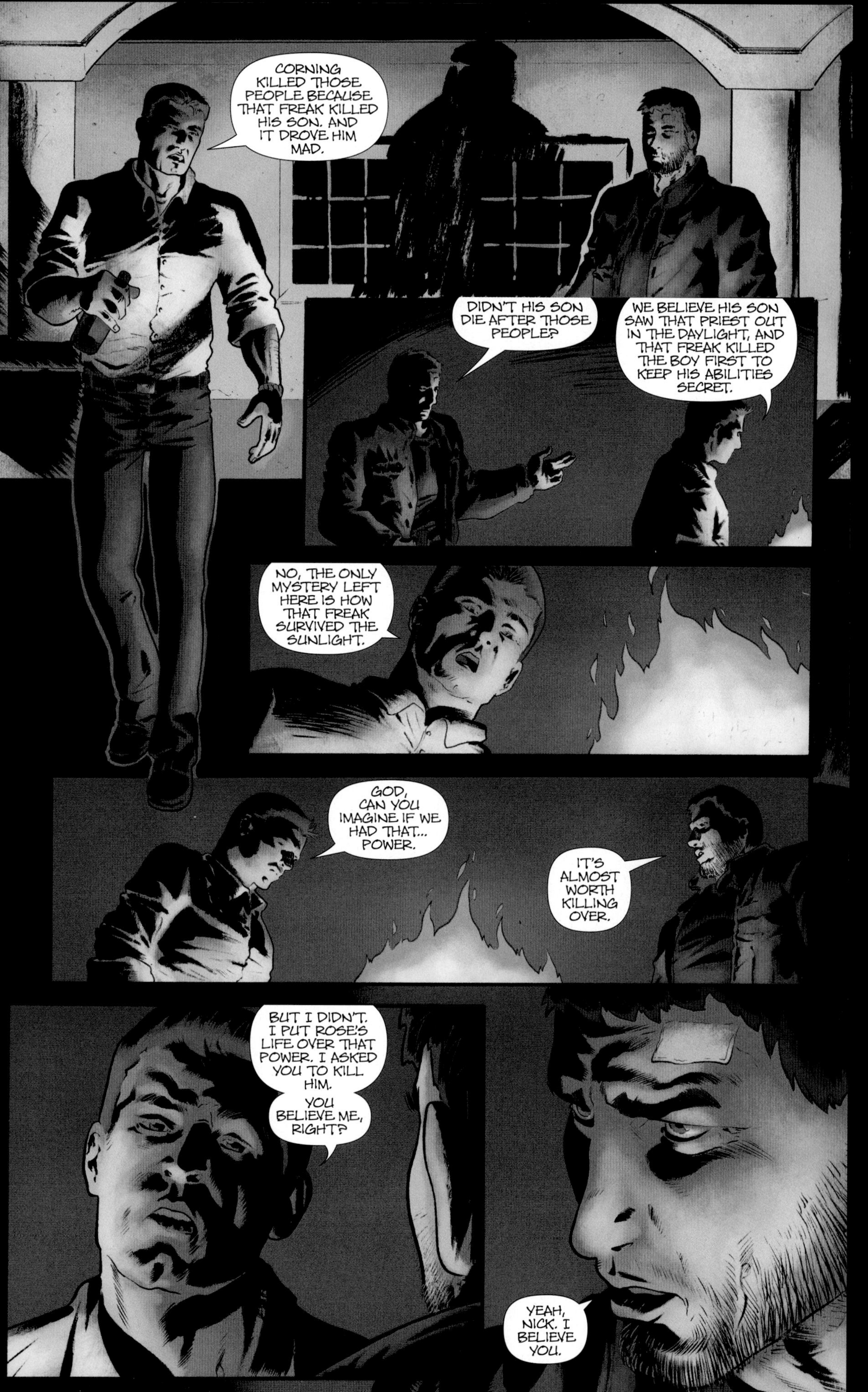
CORNING KILLED THOSE PEOPLE BECAUSE THAT FREAK KILLED HIS SON. AND IT DROVE HIM MAD.
DIDN'T HIS SON DIE AFTER THOSE PEOPLE?
WE BELIEVE HIS SON SAW THAT PRIEST OUT IN THE DAYLIGHT, AND THAT FREAK KILLED THE BOY FIRST TO KEEP HIS ABILITIES SECRET.
NO, THE ONLY MYSTERY LEFT HERE IS HOW THAT FREAK SURVIVED THE SUNLIGHT.
GOD, CAN YOU IMAGINE IF WE HAD THAT... POWER.
IT'S ALMOST WORTH KILLING OVER.
BUT I DIDN'T. I PUT ROSE'S LIFE OVER THAT POWER. I ASKED YOU TO KILL HIM.
YOU BELIEVE ME, RIGHT?
YEAH, NICK. I BELIEVE YOU.

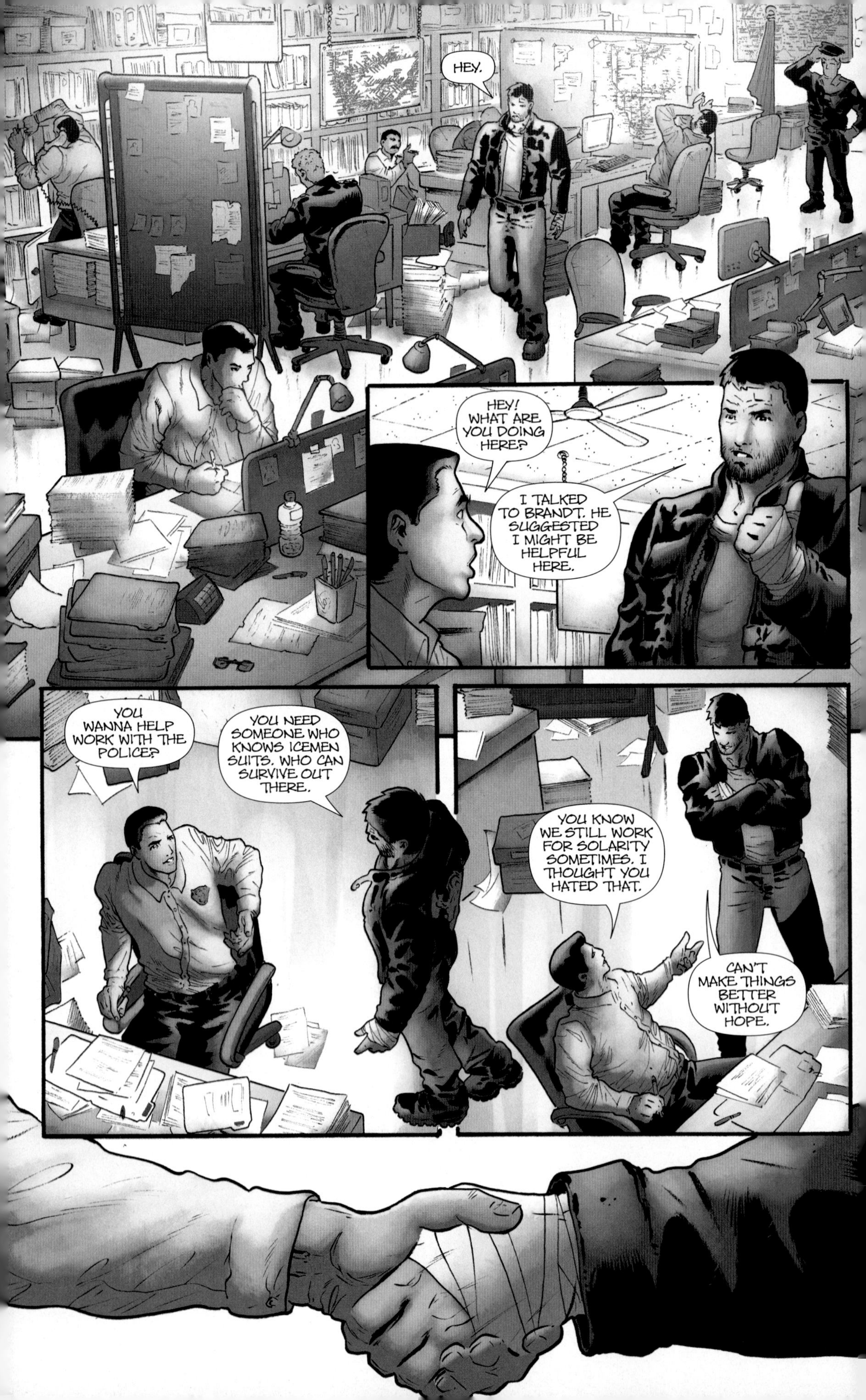
HEY.
HEY! WHAT ARE YOU DOING HERE?
I TALKED TO BRANDT. HE SUGGESTED I MIGHT BE HELPFUL HERE.
YOU WANNA HELP WORK WITH THE POLICE?
YOU NEED SOMEONE WHO KNOWS ICEMEN SUITS. WHO CAN SURVIVE OUT THERE.
YOU KNOW WE STILL WORK FOR SOLARITY SOMETIMES. I THOUGHT YOU HATED THAT.
CAN'T MAKE THINGS BETTER WITHOUT HOPE.

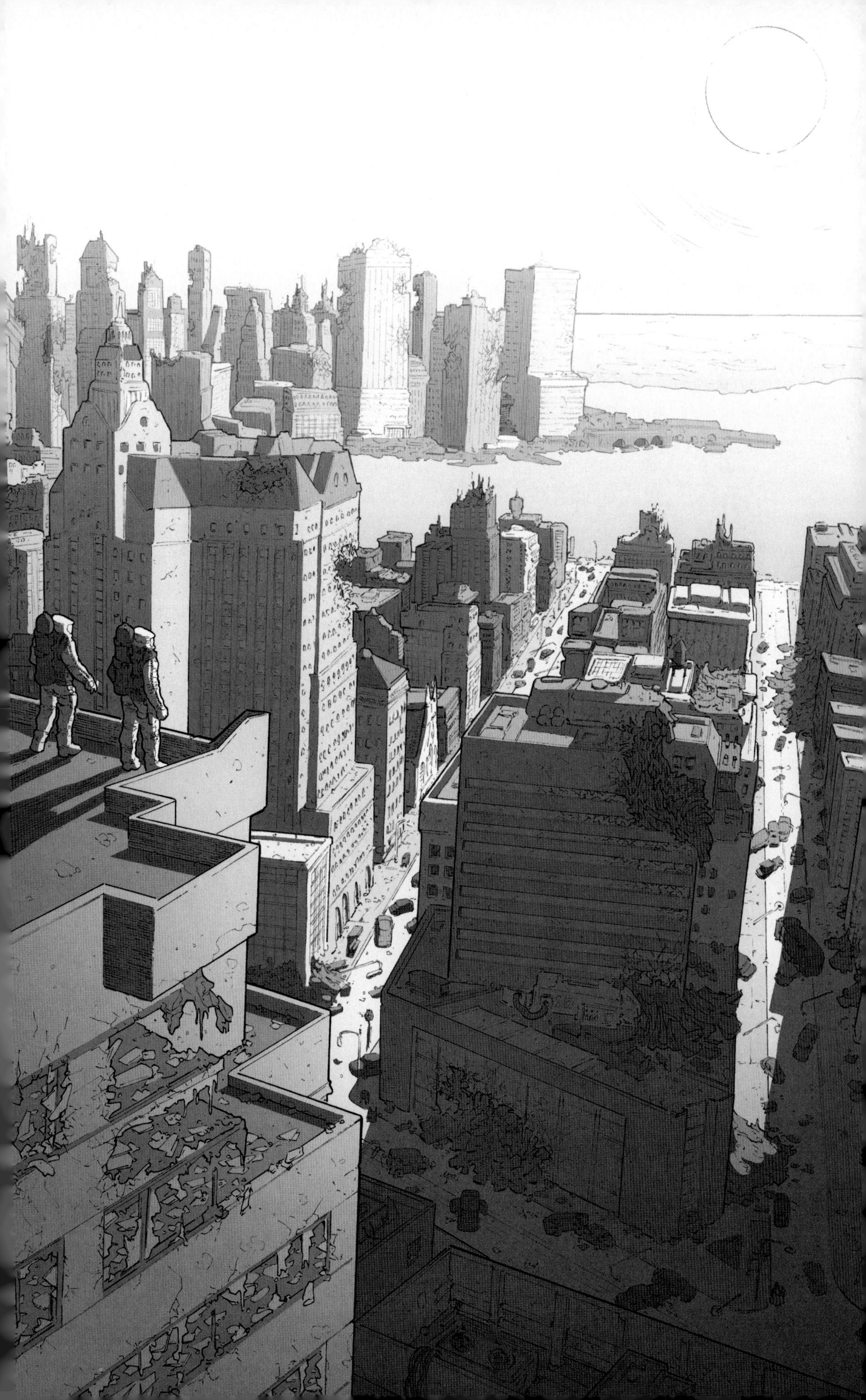

A PEEK BEHIND THE SCENES OF THE CREATIVE PROCESS OF ECLIPSE!

ECLIPSE

Cover Comments:

Zack Kaplan: We spent a lot of time discussing the Issue #1 Cover. It was vital to introduce this new threatening sun, strong and dominating in this empty landscape. We had to capture the post-apocalyptic elements, which come through in the crumbling infrastructure. It was very important to convey the science fiction thriller genre to potential readers. The Iceman suit feels sci-fi, and Gio was the one who pushed, and rightfully so, for the burnt hand in the foreground, to give us that feeling of danger. It required care on Gio's part to draw the burnt hand so as not to confuse it in any way with a zombie or monster. And finally, it was important to meet Bax, and Gio did a great job of giving him a heroic pose.

Giovanni Timpano: This was the tenth concept I sketched for the cover of Issue #1, and now I wonder why I did not think about it at the second or third try. It's so perfect to me because it captures on four levels what you'll find in *Eclipse*: death with the hand in the foreground; our main character with the suit; our city, New York, after the solar event; and our other main character: the sun. All this in the classic frontal "John Cassaday" approach, which I'm a huge fan of.

Giovanni Timpano: I think I took more than a couple of days to do this, but the page deserved it. Zack pointed out how important this page was for the book. There is no sign of full black, just pen lines for the borders of the people/objects. I wanted to show everything I could, at the cost of being blind, without hiding anything under full blacks.

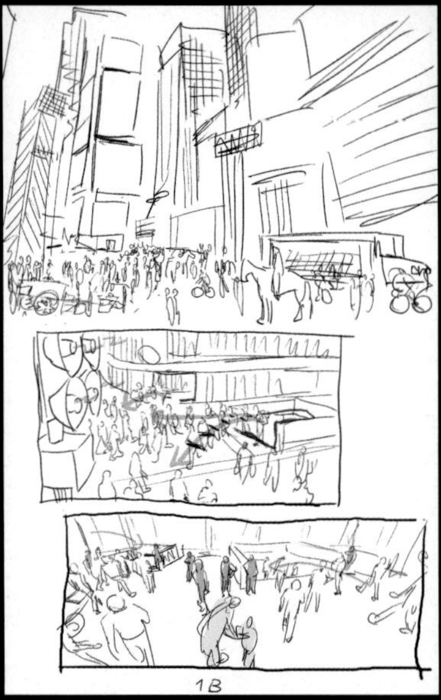
1B

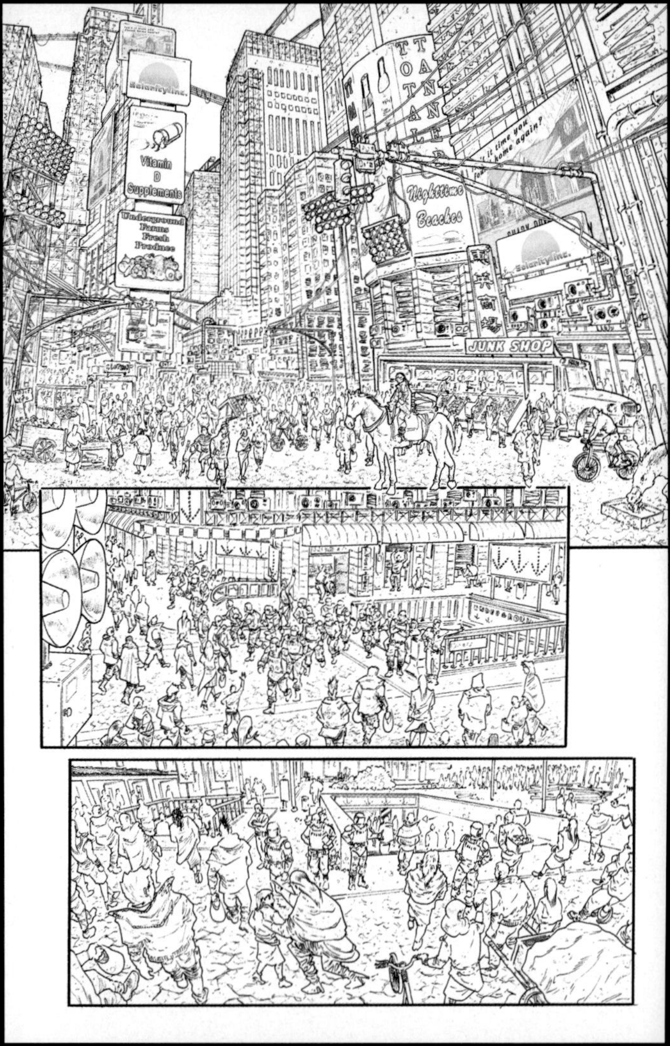
Vitamin
D
Supplements
Underground
Farms
Fresh
Produce
Nighttime
Beaches
JUNK SHOP

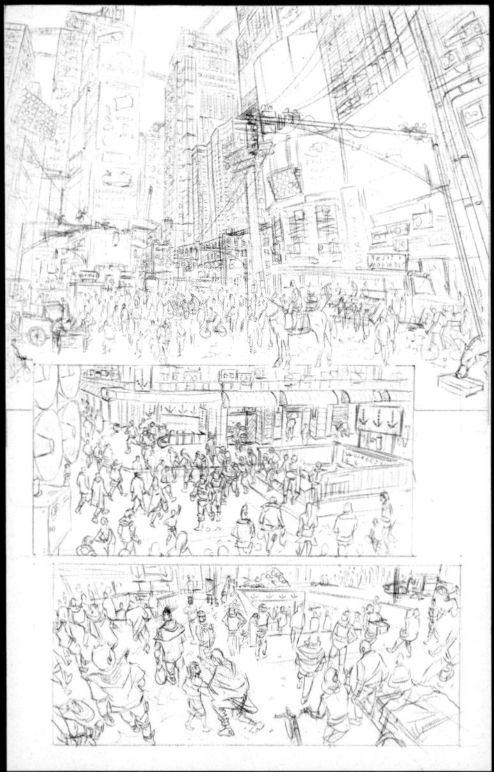

Page 7 Comments:

Zack Kaplan: Even though we've seen Bax in his suit, this is where we first see his face. And it almost feels like Bax is melting under the water. I wanted to open the scene with Bax naked in the shower, as vulnerable as we can see him. He had to be isolated from the rest of these Icemen, who have a sense of brotherhood. And these guys all had to be real macho and the kind of men who do the dirty jobs in society. And that's who Bax is now. The layout is smart because the eye goes from the top left and lands on Bax in the bottom right, where he seems very small and powerless, and he's looking away, capturing his isolation.

Giovanni Timpano: I love to draw these kinds of pages, no action, no big revelations, no fight, no back and forth conversations. It's basically a zoom out from the nose of Bax to the ceiling. But for me it tells more than words can tell.

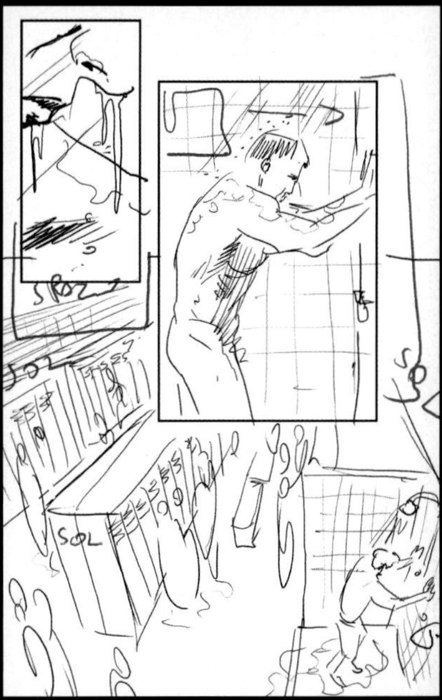
SOL

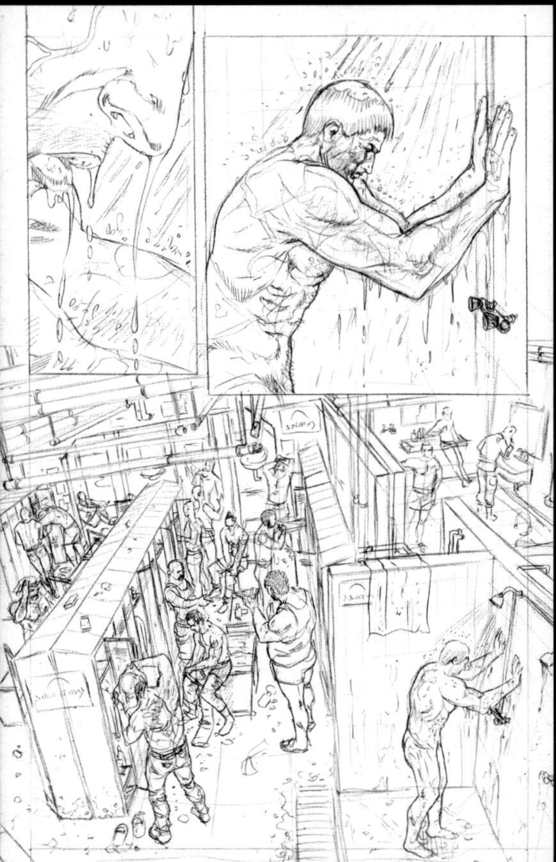

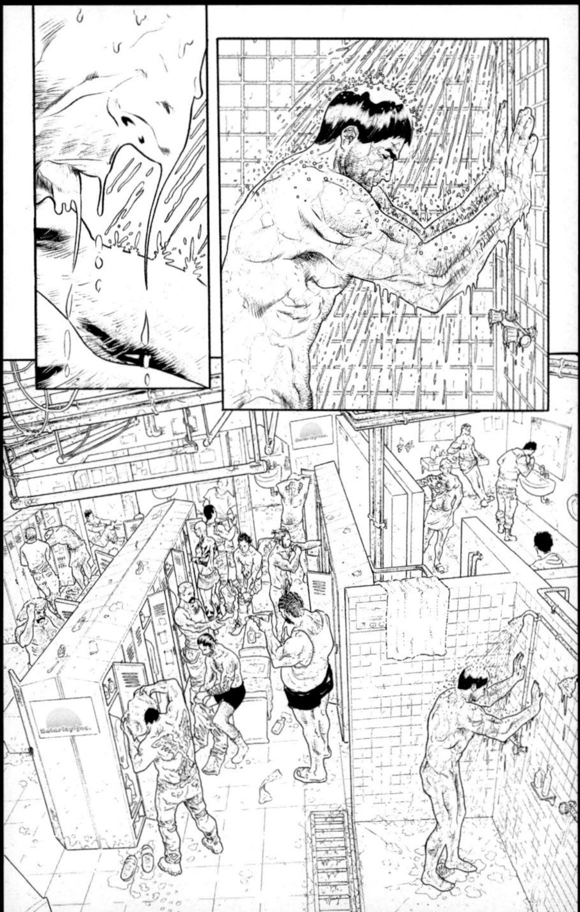

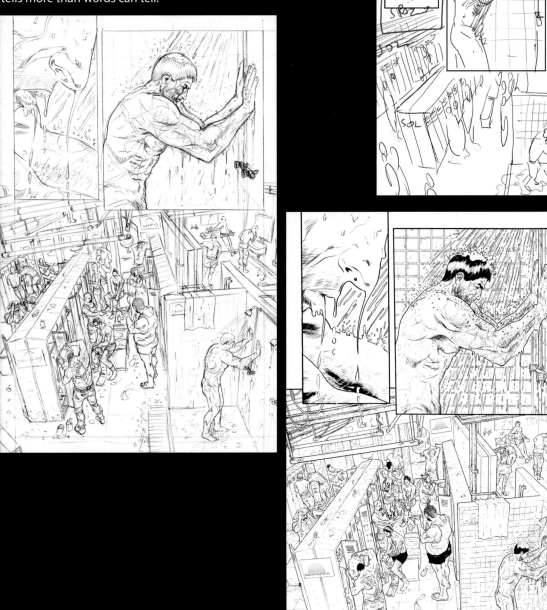

Page 8 Comments:

Zack Kaplan: We open on Bax as just a face in the crowd, because at this point, he wants to be lost. Then we have this big panel where we capture the underground world, which was demanding conceptually and artistically. Gio tells a story with every little section, from the homeless sleeping on the cots to the girls peddling sex. Then Bax walks by a poster for Shady Dome homes, and there's juxtaposition between the comfort of these happy families and Bax's isolation. Then we have two panels that tell the story of Bax turning his back on a mugging, and he's so unwilling to get involved, that his closed door tells us all we need to know.

Giovanni Timpano: This was another page where I spent a lot of time, inspired by the work of the master Moebius, who was my biggest inspiration for *Eclipse*. The large panel does not simply show a crowd of people. Everyone is doing something. They are not put there randomly, and like Bax, everyone is unique and has his or her own story.

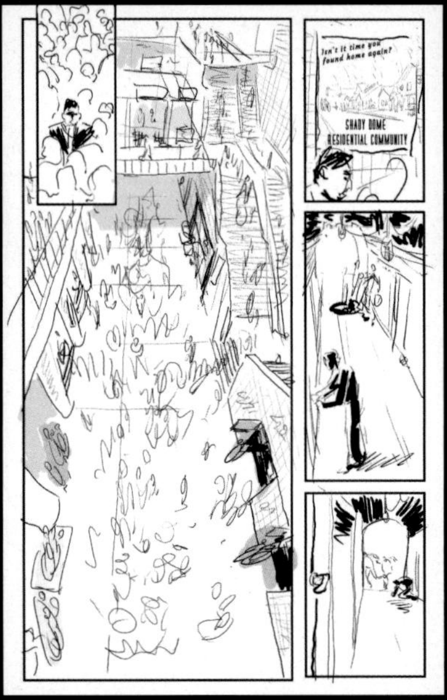
Isn't it time you found home again?
SHADY DOME
RESIDENTIAL COMMUNITY

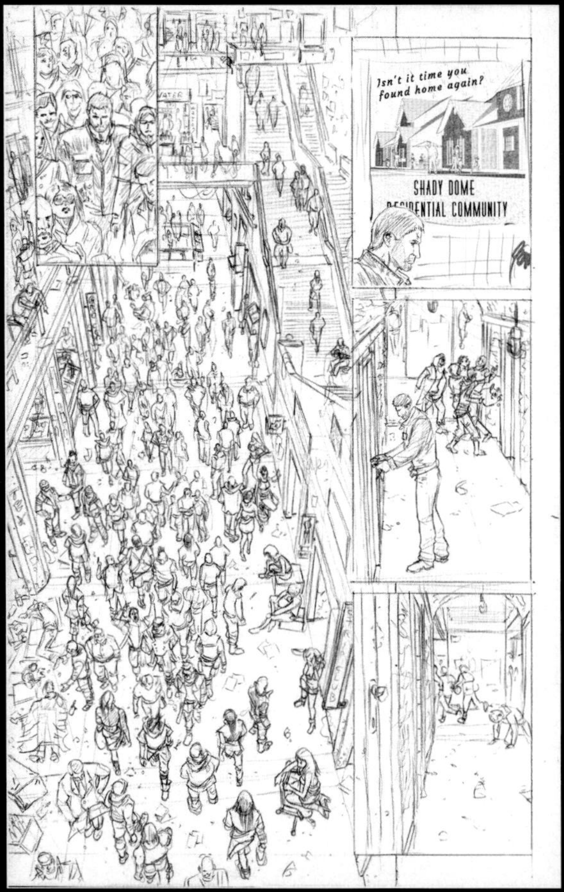
Isn't it time you found home again?
SHADY DOME

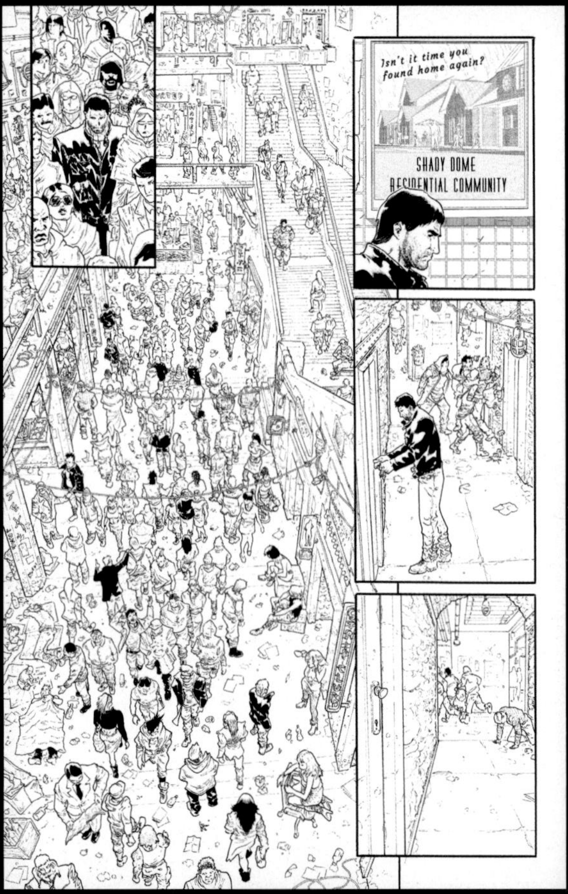
Isn't it time you found home again?
SHADY DOME
RESIDENTIAL COMMUNITY

Page 17 Comments:

Zack Kaplan: I think what is most interesting is that this page is the first time we see sunlight as a weapon. The light had to move. Shadows had to disappear. And then we had to see what happens when sunlight first hits flesh and how these people begin burning. And it was really important to give Bax two panels at the end, because by going from a long shot to a close-up, we are coming into Bax, and we are realizing that this moment is impacting him emotionally. He's making a decision.

Giovanni Timpano: This was a tricky page. To show the sun as a weapon is not an easy thing to do in a page, but we made it, and I think it's great. The page needed various layouts before the final one, and if I'm not wrong, I also added more panels than the number written in the script. The action needed to be clear and readable at the first sight, because it was a sort of "first time" when in a comic book the reader might see a truck carrying mirrors and using them as death beams. As I said, I think at the end, this element works perfectly.

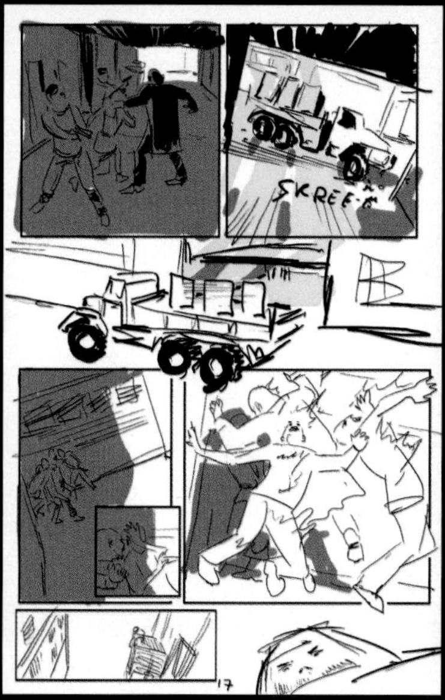
SKREE-E

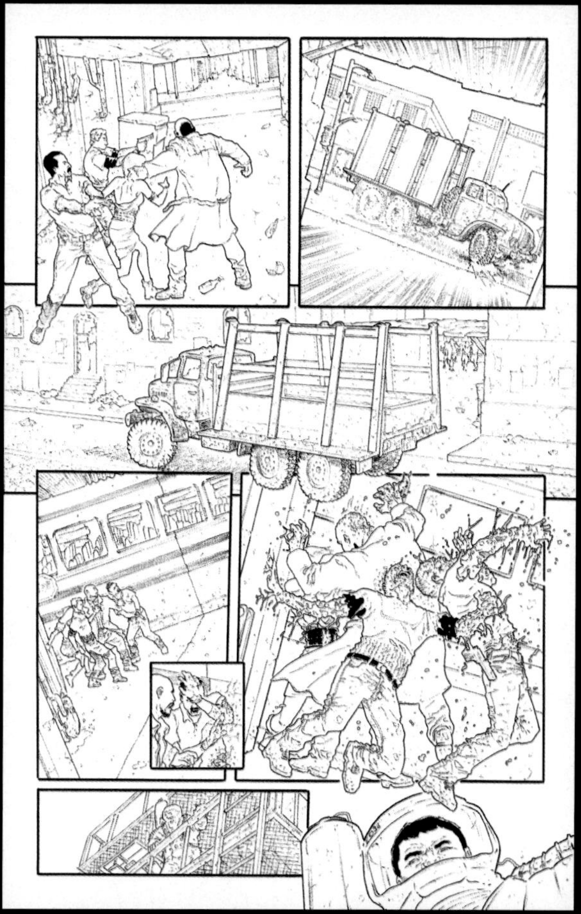

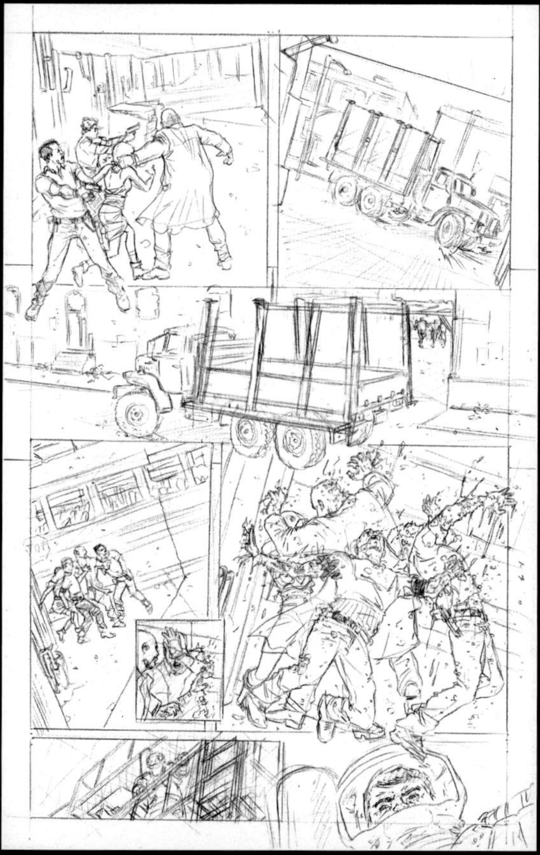

Zack Kaplan: This page was fun. The entire script, Bax has been isolated and avoiding any action. But here, Bax has made his choice to take a heroic step, and so we can leave his story and see his heroism from Cielo's point of view. We actually switch POV as we come in on Cielo's eyes in Panel 2, and then Panel 3 and 4 are her view. And this is the only time in Issue #1 that we switch away from Bax's POV. And then there's this big look at Bax, arm stretched out, saying he's there to help.

Giovanni Timpano: Much like some other pages in this series, I like to oppose the panels where the Icemen suits are drawn with tiny fine pen lines, with panels where they are drawn with big brush strokes, as in the large panel of this page. It helps to create contrasts between the moments and situations, and in this page, it worked very well.

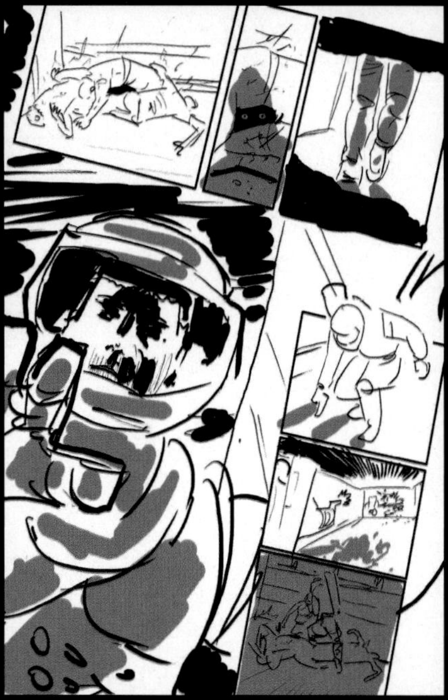

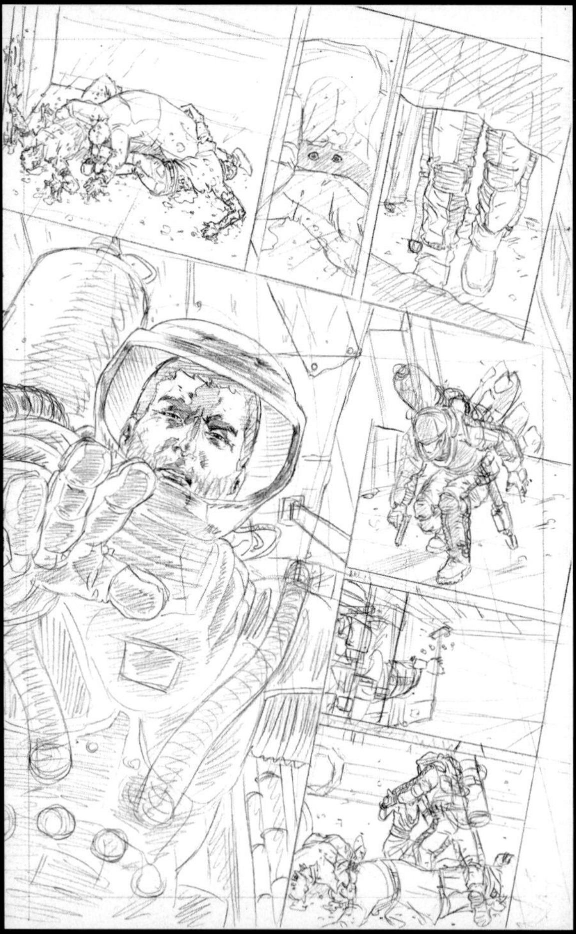

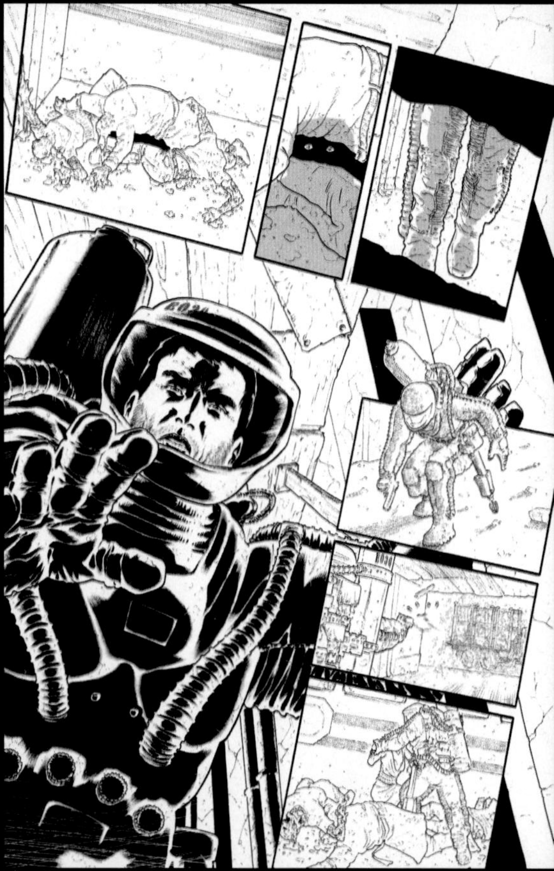

Page 19 Comments:

Zack Kaplan: Gio did something really cool with the last three pages. He gave each character, Bax, Cielo and our killer, a large presence. This page was Cielo's turn. It's our first look at her. I like that we're looking down on her to make her still feel young. She's holding Bax's hand, which is his first contact with another person in the story. And then Gio came up with this cool shot from below the manhole looking up at Bax and Cielo making their escape. And we had to end on Cielo's face, looking shocked because she's seeing what we're going to see on Page 20: this man, our killer, standing in the sun and not burning.

Giovanni Timpano: I'm surprised how much stuff I was able to put in just this page and how detailed it was. I never doubted that Panel 1 needed to have at least half of the page, but the actions inside the others were not simple. That's why it was a challenging page. And yes, the one from inside the manhole was the most fun to draw, even more than the large Cielo panel.

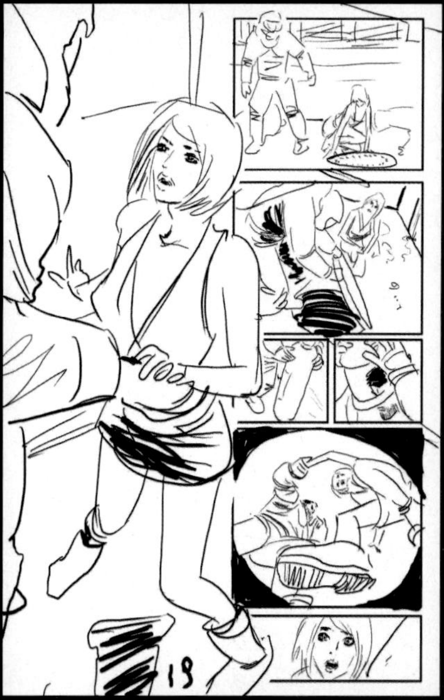
19

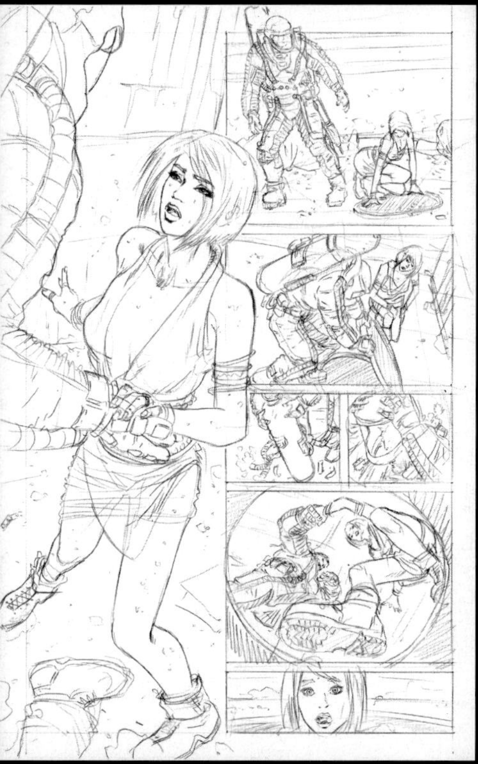

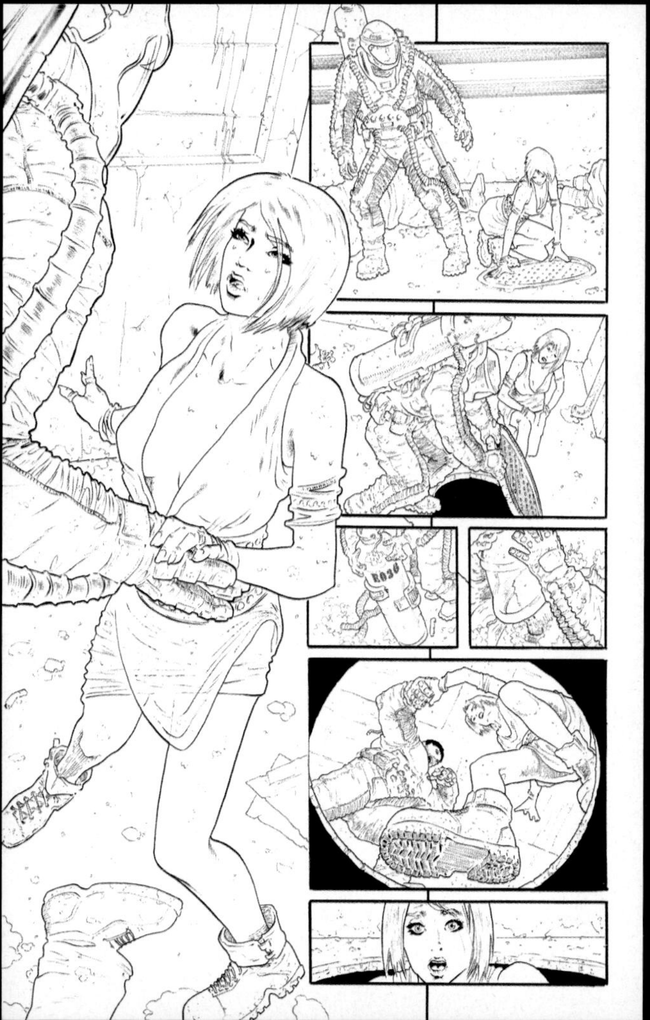

Character Sketches and Development:

DAVID "BAX" BAXTER

Script: This is the rugged face of our hero, DAVID "BAX" BAXTER (30s), our Iceman. Tom Hardy-looking. Brooding.

Giovanni Timpano: While Bax is our hero and deserved our time, it was not a long process to find him. Zack described him to me very well. We got his face from the beginning, and just adjusted his jaw and the length of his face a little, but the rest fell into place. Then, Zack wanted to give Bax a unique clothing piece, and he said that the hero wears a cool jacket, [illegible]mething to that effect. As I thought about it, I was reminded about the movie *Drive* and that hero's jacket. So we worked on various ideas, and after several tries we found this leather jacket with the firefighter symbol on the back, something unique and particular for a hero, but that also captured what Bax is (and was).

BAX 2

Zack Kaplan: Bax comes across in what he doesn't say. He's removed and distant. He's masculine. He had to be a unique blend of depression and courage, indicative of a reluctant hero. It didn't take long for us to get his look. Gio gave hi[illegible]hleticism and broad shoulders because he's been carrying heavy equipment on his back for years. But I knew that he needed a signature element to make him stand out. Gio insisted on a jacket. Did he say I said a jacket? Well, whoever came up with the jacket, Gio was the one who transformed the piece by realizing that it should be his firefighting jacket with Bax's old station house emblem. We even looked at countless firefighting logos to find the right one.

FIRE
DEPT.

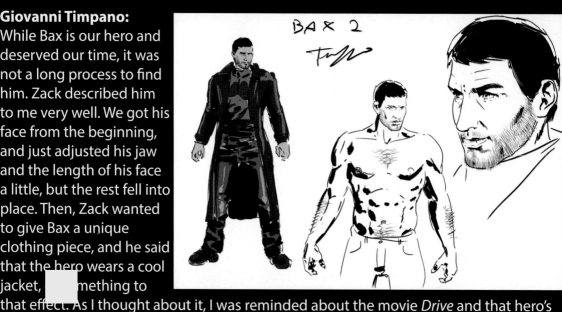

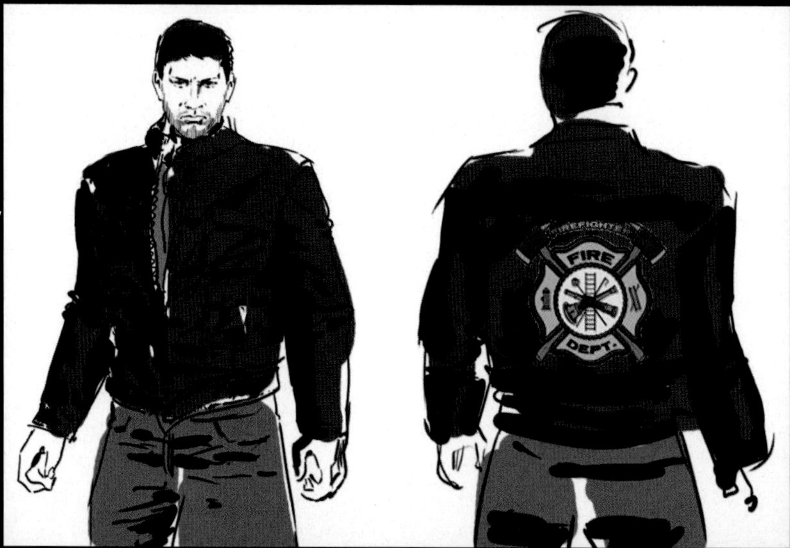

ROSE "CIELO" BRANDT

Script: ROSE "CIELO" BRANDT (16), porcelain skin, risqué club outfit, standing on a block, go-go dancing, her hair whipping about, her face away from camera. Her style is unique, provocative and sexy for her age, a mixture of deep club trends and post-apocalyptic fashion.

CIELO

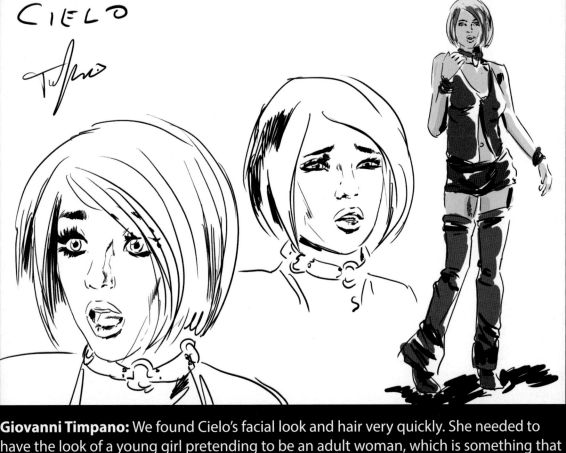

Giovanni Timpano: We found Cielo's facial look and hair very quickly. She needed to have the look of a young girl pretending to be an adult woman, which is something that a lot of girls do at that age. What took a longer time was finding Cielo's clothing. We took a lot of passes at a lot of sketches before finding the right one, because basically Cielo was our window into her generation and their style in *Eclipse*. Zack had a precise series of clothing choices in mind and sent me a folder with a ton of options, like maybe a hundred. In the end, I found something in the folder, but it was worth the time because it was really important for the book.

Zack Kaplan: Cielo was a tricky character because her look had to straddle a fence. On the one hand, she's fun and alive, and lives in the moment, but she's also bitter at her parents and disillusioned by life. She's pretty, sensitive and clever all at once. She's a party girl, rebellious and edgy, but also she's a rich girl raised in the lap of luxury in this world. So her outfits and styles might vary depending on which area in her life she was catering to. I wanted the book to have its own unique feel, and knew that feel required its own fashion style as well. I found a lot of looks I liked by Rick Owens, a fashion designer who's got th[redacted]ban post-apocalyptic thing going. E[redacted] definitely gave Gio a lot to work with, yes, probably a hundred references, everything from high-end looks to office looks to street looks. And we ultimately found a style for Cielo that worked great.

SCRIPT: Solarity's visionary CEO, NICHOLAS BRANDT (30s), well-kept, intellectual, in a crisp suit, all smiles and sugar.

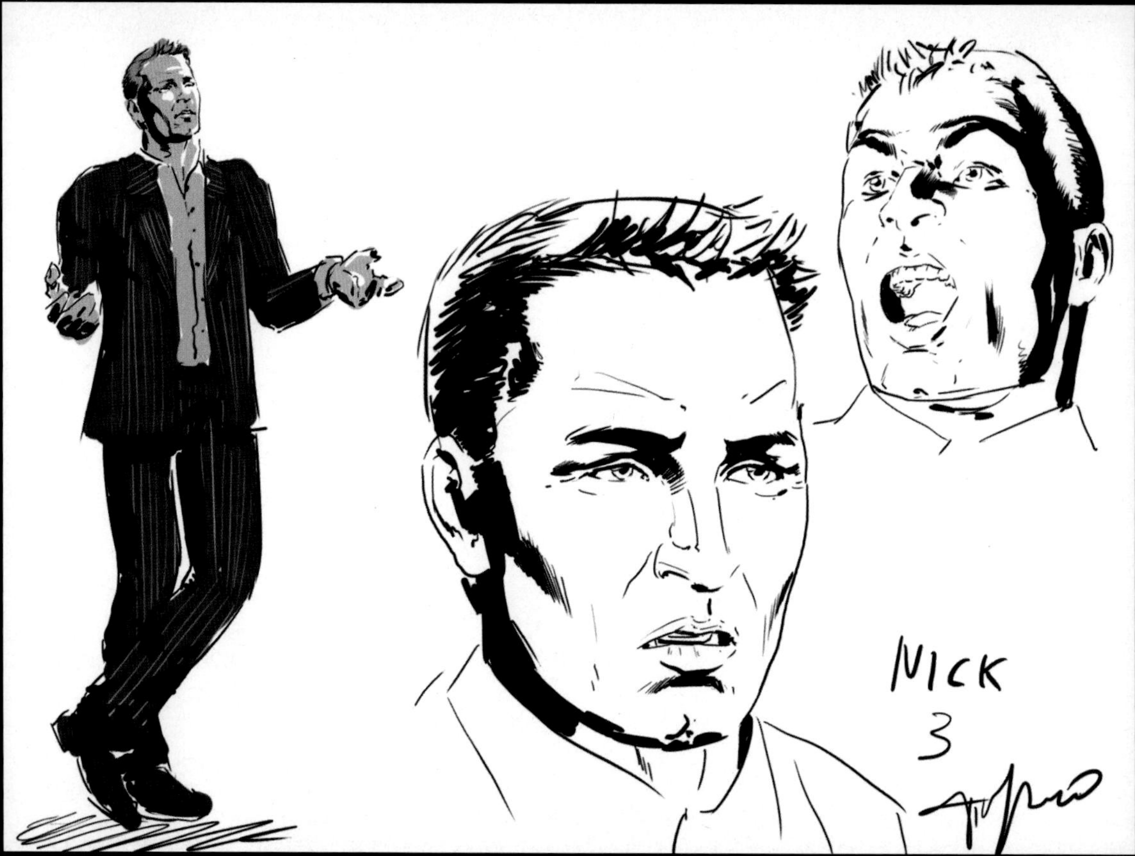
NICK
3

Giovanni Timpano: Nick took a few versions to find the right one, because it's quite tricky for a face to say, "I am a former firefighter, but after a solar flare cataclysm, I fought for and formed a company that basically owns New York City." But Nick's look needed to show all of this, and that's why we worked on a few sketches to get the right one.

Zack Kaplan: I remember several conversations about Nick's overall look, because he had to be a certain type of CEO. He wasn't just exuding power or domination. He was exuding vision. He was a mix between a Silicon Valley tech CEO and a venture capitalist. I remember referencing Elon Musk, but Nick couldn't be quirky or international. Nick had to be the type who used charm and persona to your face, but used cutthroat tactics behind closed doors. And ultimately, he's idealistic, because he's still trying to rebuild this society. We finally found this blond, magnetic version that was perfect.

Script: We see JAMES EVERLY (20s), athletic but thin, a dark streak in a poor kid grown up, drive and ambition in his eyes. He wears plain clothes, a high collar on his coat.

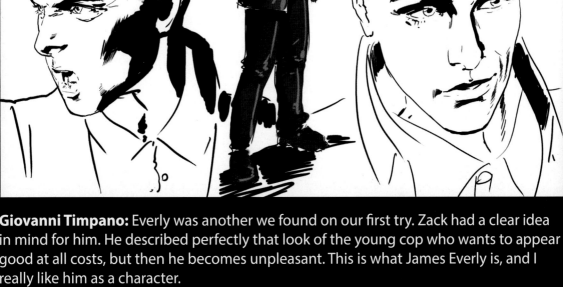

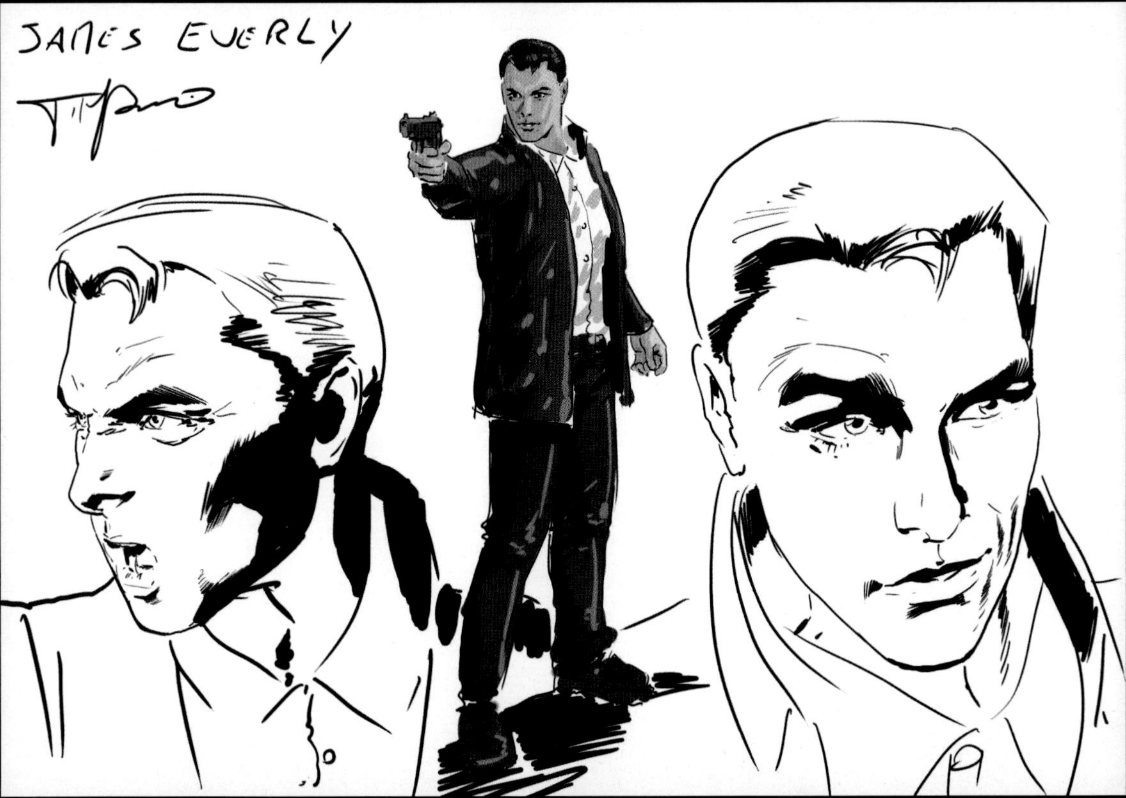
JAMES EVERLY

Giovanni Timpano: Everly was another we found on our first try. Zack had a clear idea in mind for him. He described perfectly that look of the young cop who wants to appear good at all costs, but then he becomes unpleasant. This is what James Everly is, and I really like him as a character.

Zack Kaplan: Everly for me had to be everything Bax was not. He's upbeat and charming. He's youthful and has optimistic naiveté to him. He's ambitious, but void of charisma. He had to be slighter than Bax to create contrast physically. It was okay for Everly to be in classic detective's clothing because that's the role he's playing, and in fact, he desperately wants to be a hero, at all costs.

SCRIPT: Nick's brother, WALLACE BRANDT (late 30s), more grit and shadow.

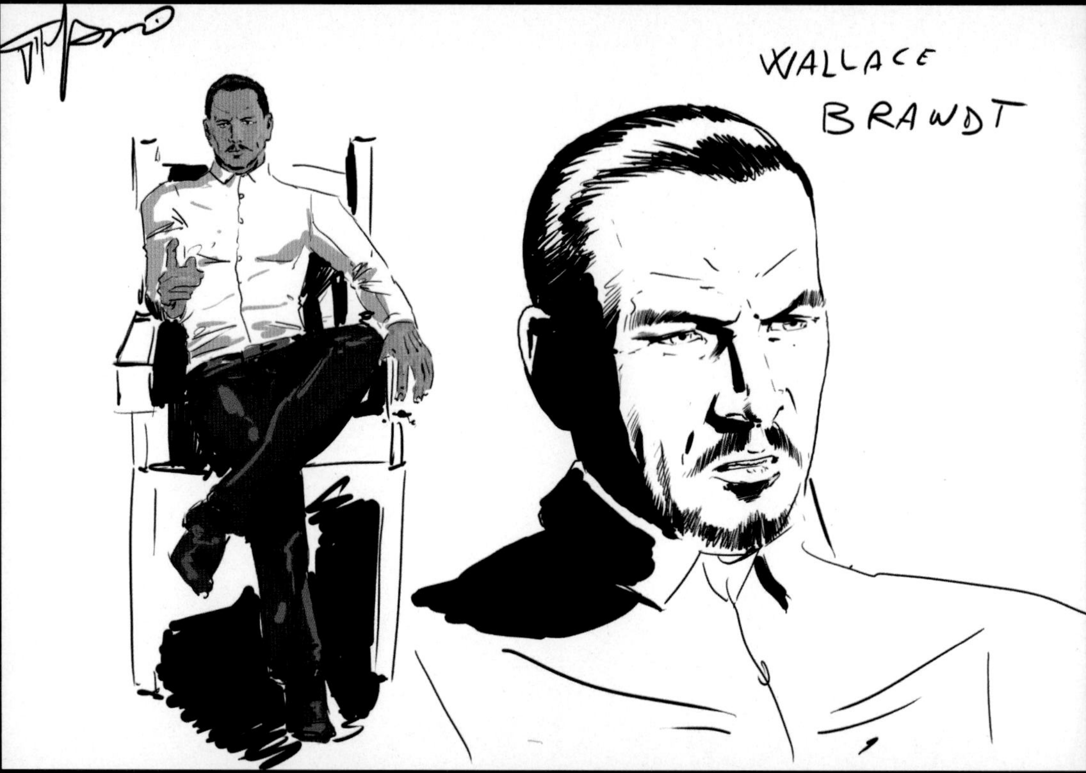
WALLACE
BRANDT

Giovanni Timpano: Wallace is not a nice person, and we needed to show this. That's why I gave to him this devilish look. We just fixed his face a couple times to make him younger, but basically we found him in the first shot.

Zack Kaplan: Wallace Brandt is Nick's brother, and while he has a small role in the beginning of the story, it was important to set up that Nick has someone by his side, in the shadows, who does his dirty work. And giving Wallace that tough look really worked. I described Wallace as having a look that he might stab you in the back at any moment. Nick may fool us, but Wallace reveals that these guys are not just on the straight and narrow.

SCRIPT: Everly stands with two more SECURITY OFFICERS behind him: POOLE (30s), a butch, tattooed chick, hair tight back, angular face, a tough character. MURPHY (50s), a larger guy, perhaps who's let himself go a bit but still has the mass to stop someone, along with clear experience and enough grit to last him a lifetime. These are an odd pairing, but a good security team.

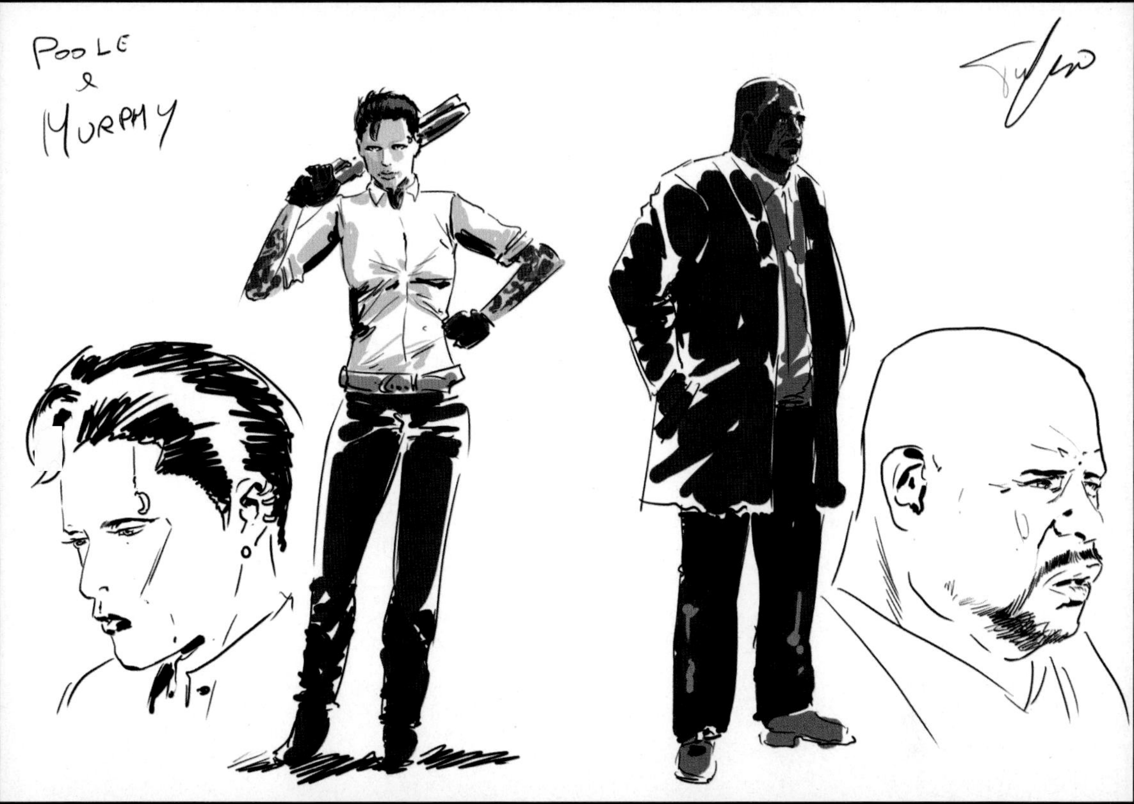
POOLE
&
MURPHY

Giovanni Timpano: I love these two. I mean, Poole wears leather with a white classic shirt under, tattoos on her arms, piercings and earrings (then I had this idea to get rid of her eyebrows) and a shotgun. Murphy is Forest Whitaker for me. So how can I not love them?

Zack Kaplan: I love them too. I actually knew I wanted a woman and a man, separated by age, by physicality, by look. I wanted an odd pair, two bodyguards who are just trying to eke by in this world. Poole had to look like she came from a hard life, so she had to be tight and interesting, while Murphy brought grit and experience, perhaps from a life as a former cop.

SCRIPT: We see VALERIE MCHOME (30s), head-on from the front, mousy quiet scientist in a lab coat, beautiful redhead, her hair pulled back, as she works over some equipment.

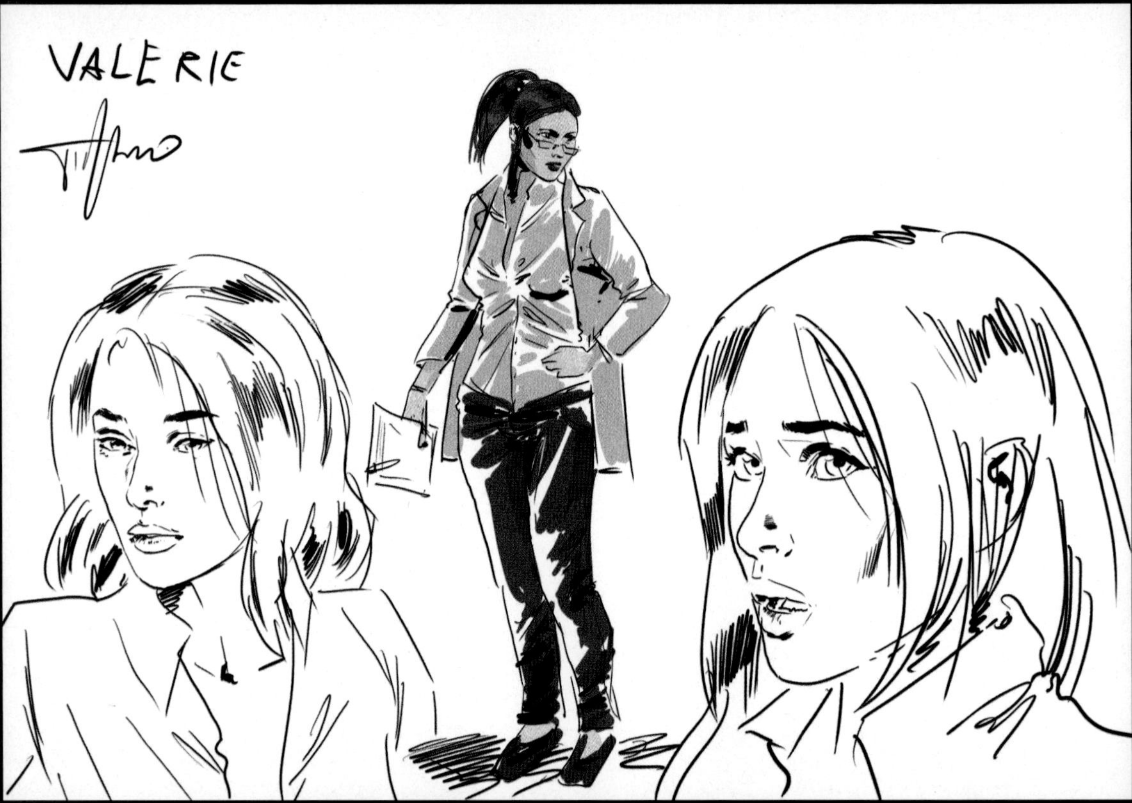
VALERIE

Giovanni Timpano: She's a classic beautiful woman who runs the doctor/technician part on this book. I like how simply beautiful she is.

Zack Kaplan: This is the woman Bax should be with, but isn't. So she had to have a natural beauty and respectable intelligence to her. She had to be soft, and we kind of had to fall in love with her immediately. And she had to let her brain rule her actions, but maybe she's just waiting for true romance in her life. So Gio did a great job of capturing all of that.

PRE-SCRIPT NOTES: The Icemen are the blue-collar workers who go out in the sunlight in protective suits. Their suits might have astronaut components. The helmet is covered in a seemingly opaque tempered visor. There is a hi-tech backpack, maybe more of an NO2 tank or twin tanks with a central box between them. Tubes run from the back and around the suit, pushing super coolant through them. This suit is using coolant to keep the occupant very cool. The Iceman suit should look bulky, hard to move in, but somewhat bad-ass in a grounded sci-fi way, like *Interstellar* meets *Elysium*.

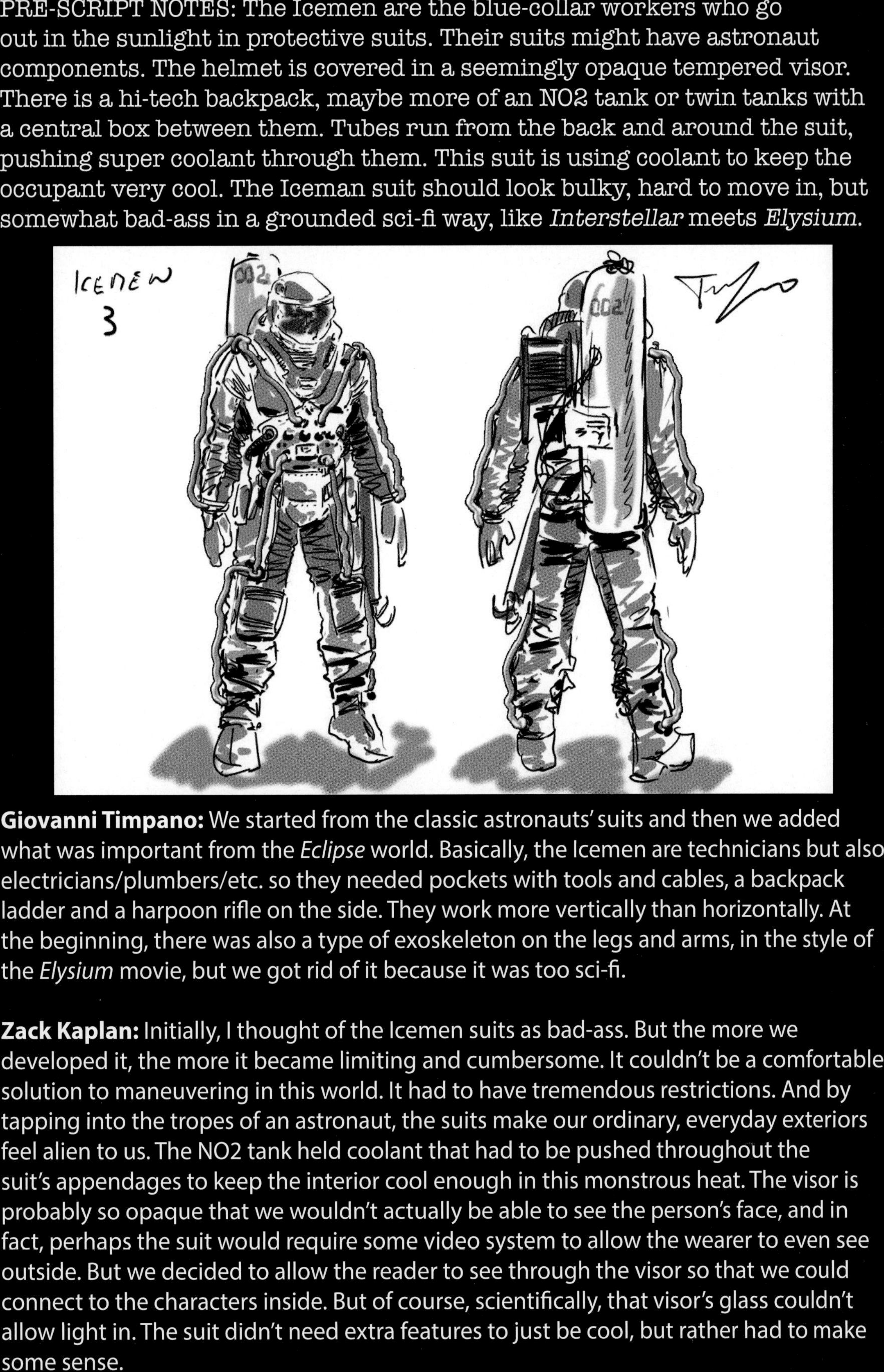
ICEMEN
3
CO2
CO2

Giovanni Timpano: We started from the classic astronauts' suits and then we added what was important from the *Eclipse* world. Basically, the Icemen are technicians but also electricians/plumbers/etc. so they needed pockets with tools and cables, a backpack ladder and a harpoon rifle on the side. They work more vertically than horizontally. At the beginning, there was also a type of exoskeleton on the legs and arms, in the style of the *Elysium* movie, but we got rid of it because it was too sci-fi.

Zack Kaplan: Initially, I thought of the Icemen suits as bad-ass. But the more we developed it, the more it became limiting and cumbersome. It couldn't be a comfortable solution to maneuvering in this world. It had to have tremendous restrictions. And by tapping into the tropes of an astronaut, the suits make our ordinary, everyday exteriors feel alien to us. The NO2 tank held coolant that had to be pushed throughout the suit's appendages to keep the interior cool enough in this monstrous heat. The visor is probably so opaque that we wouldn't actually be able to see the person's face, and in fact, perhaps the suit would require some video system to allow the wearer to even see outside. But we decided to allow the reader to see through the visor so that we could connect to the characters inside. But of course, scientifically, that visor's glass couldn't allow light in. The suit didn't need extra features to just be cool, but rather had to make some sense.

A lot of work and thought goes into a final colored page. When the artwork is finished it is colored, which adds depth and mood. The contrast and color selection draw and guide the reader's eyes across a page and are an important part of the narrative. Below is a look at several pages that artist Giovanni Timpiano and colorist Chris Northrop have picked to share.

Chris Northrop, the colorist of *Eclipse*, gives his thoughts:

PAGE 8 - All of the pages in *Eclipse* are created with a multiply layer being erased or "painted away" over really bright flat colors on a layer below. It's done non-specific at first and then worked away in a more detailed fashion using a brush that is based on dry media (like pastel). A really saturated overlay of highlights is added to create blowout lighting because of the fluorescent lighting. That's what creates the dirty, burned-out look.

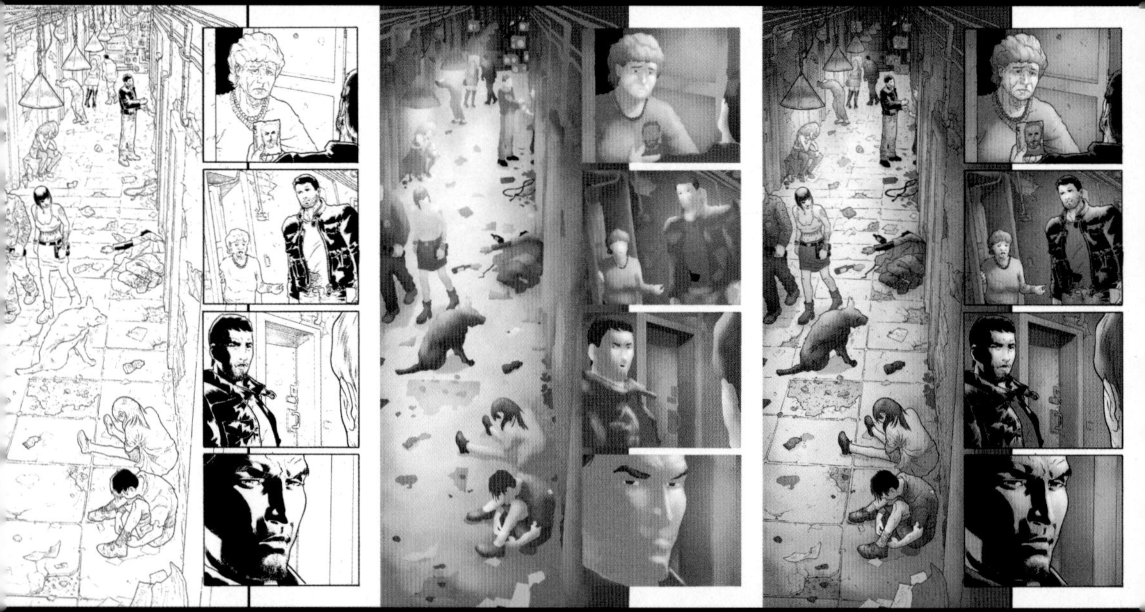

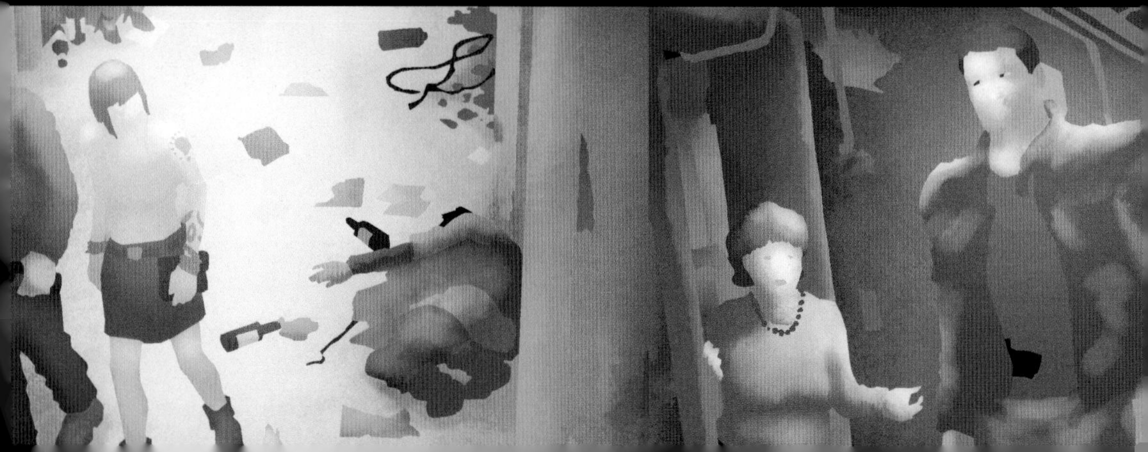

PAGES 11 & 12 - I switched a lot of pages in *Eclipse* to grayscale mode when I was coloring to make sure it looked good in black and white directing the reader's eye. If it looked like a *Twilight Zone* episode in black and white and the tones read well, I was happy. These were probably the most important pages that I looked at when checking contrast because there are so many earth tones in the background and the characters in the foreground are lit by the greenish blue lights from the truck's bar.

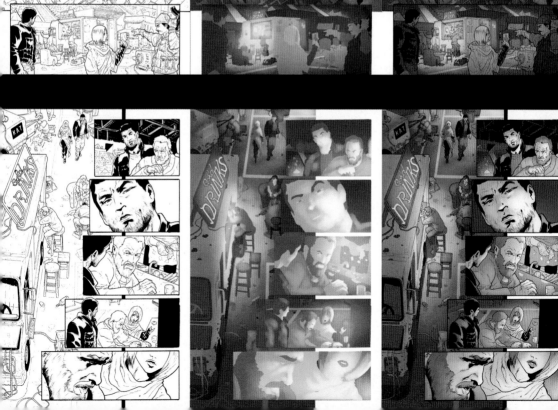

PAGE 16 - Crowds are actually very easy to color, even though this may look like a lot of work. There are so many people in the top panel here.

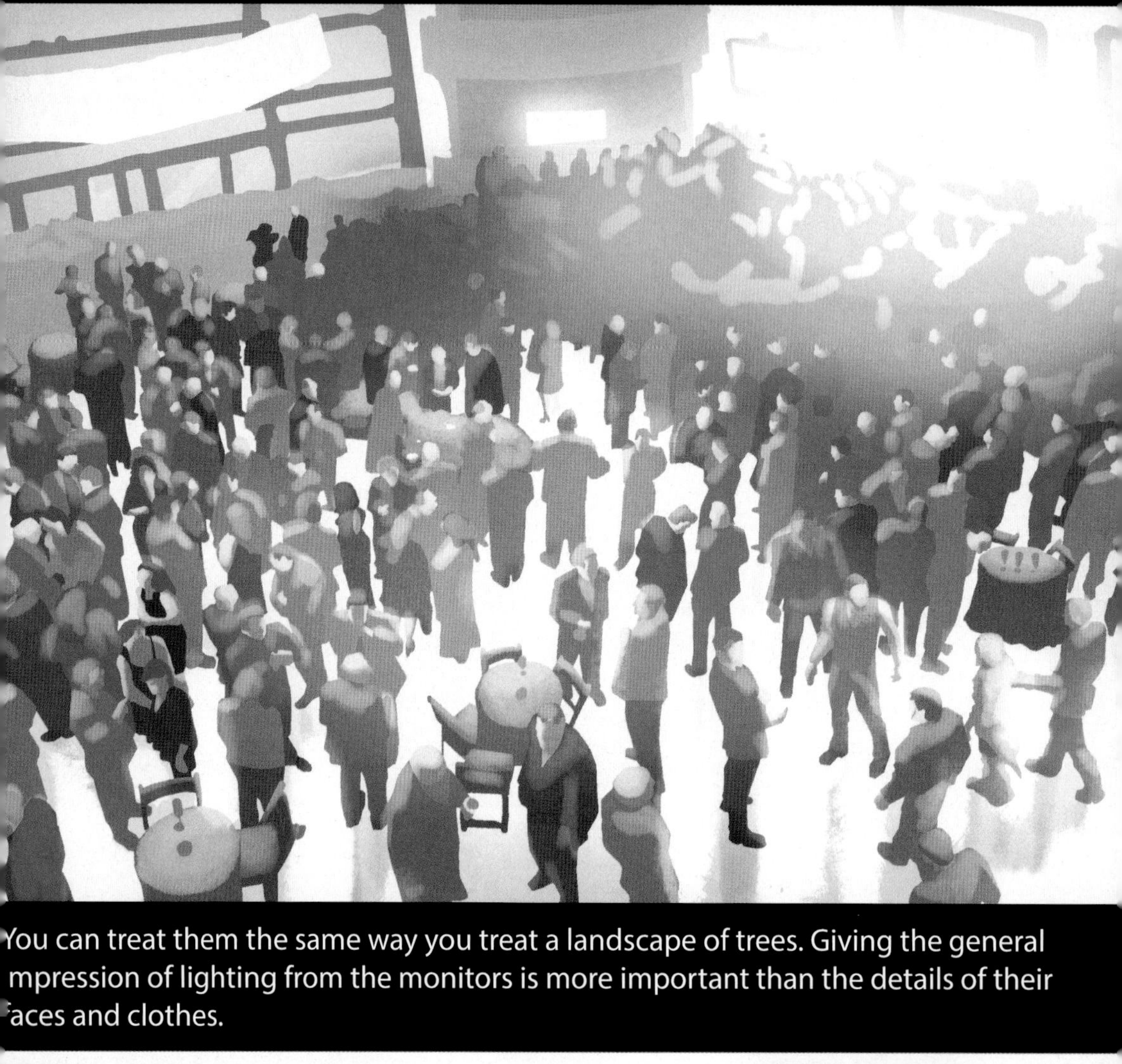

You can treat them the same way you treat a landscape of trees. Giving the general impression of lighting from the monitors is more important than the details of their faces and clothes.

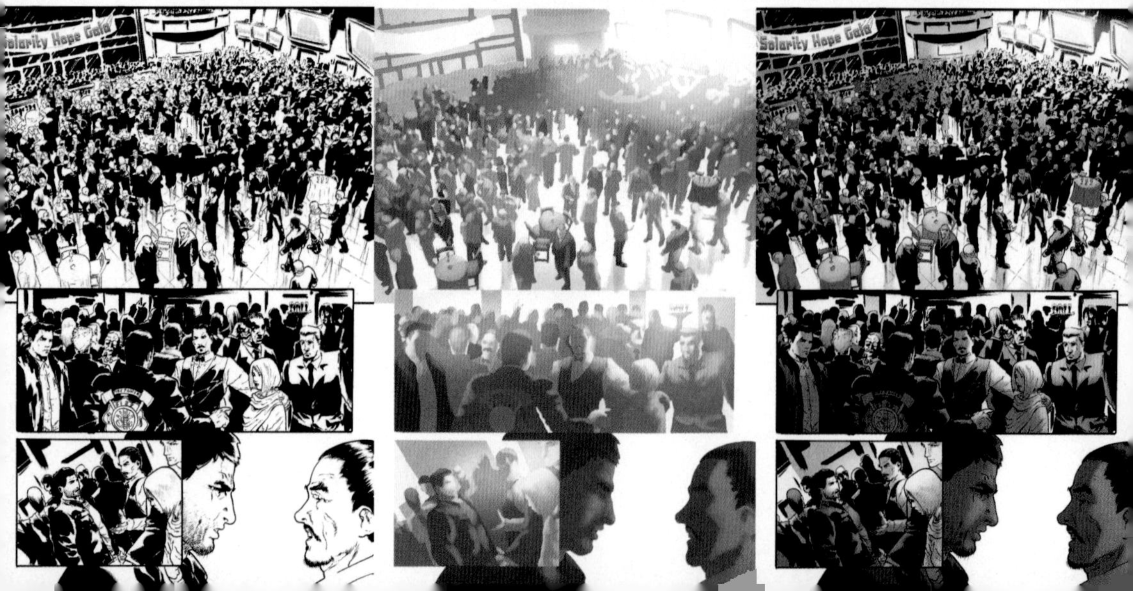

Solarity Hope Gala

AGES 18 & 19 - Sun kills are my favorite thing to color in *Eclipse*. BIG blasts of light. Going from a small crack of light that starts to let the heat in, to a panel that's enveloped in heat.

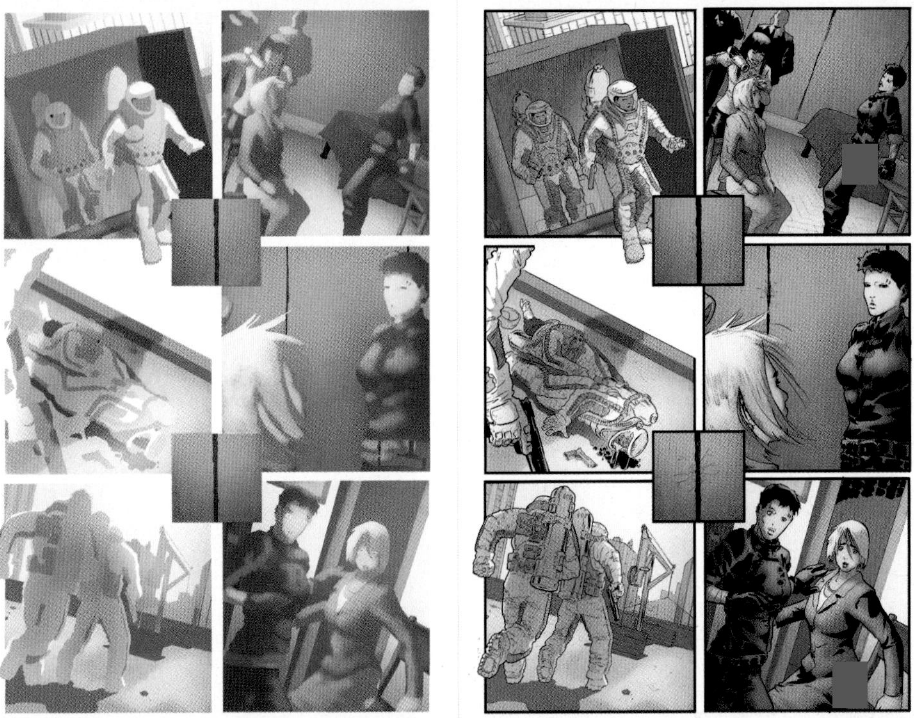

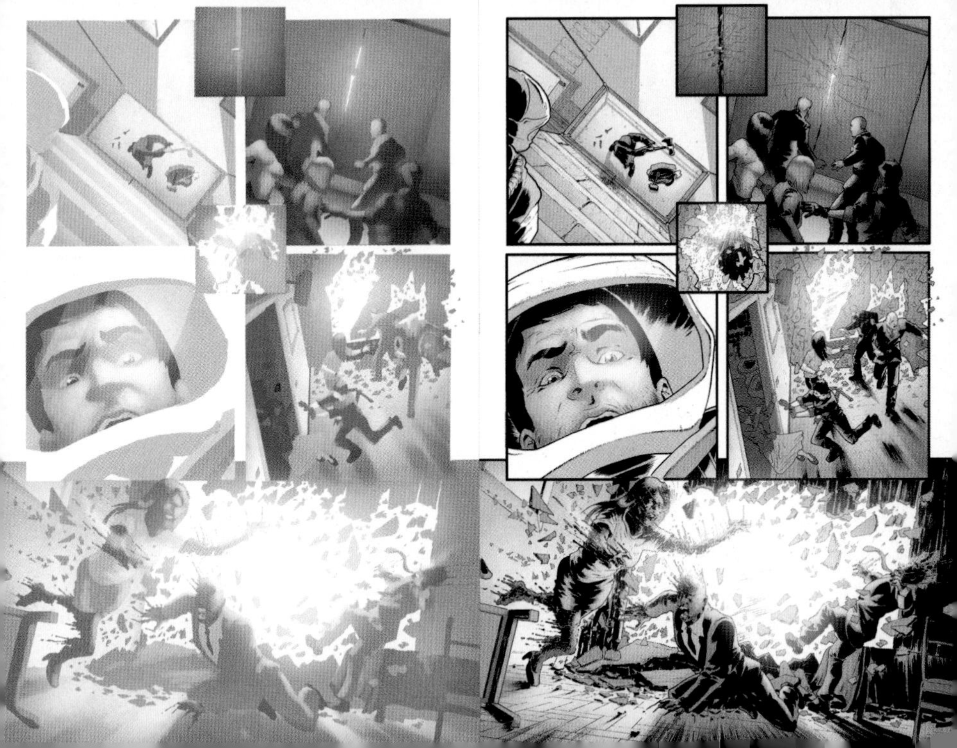

Lettering:

A lot of work and thought goes into lettering each and every comic book page. From the font selected to represent the dialogue, to the words bolded or italicized for emphasis, to the placement of word balloons from panel to panel so as not to obscure Giovanni Timpano's outstanding art.

Troy Peteri, the letterer of *Eclipse*, gives his thoughts:

As the letterer on the majority of Top Cow's titles for the last decade or so (Ouch, that time went quickly!), I don't often have the opportunity to talk about what it is that I do, because I'm too busy doing it. But here goes, there's a method to (most of) my madness.

Any time I start lettering a new series, I decide which fonts and styles will be used based on two things: art style and genre. Knowing that this was a futuristic series with sci-fi overtones, I chose the main fonts and styles because they reminded me of the ones a reader would see in the oversized European sci-fi hardcovers.

Since the title takes place in a kind of postapocalyptic society, all of the establishing captions should look weathered and dilapidated.

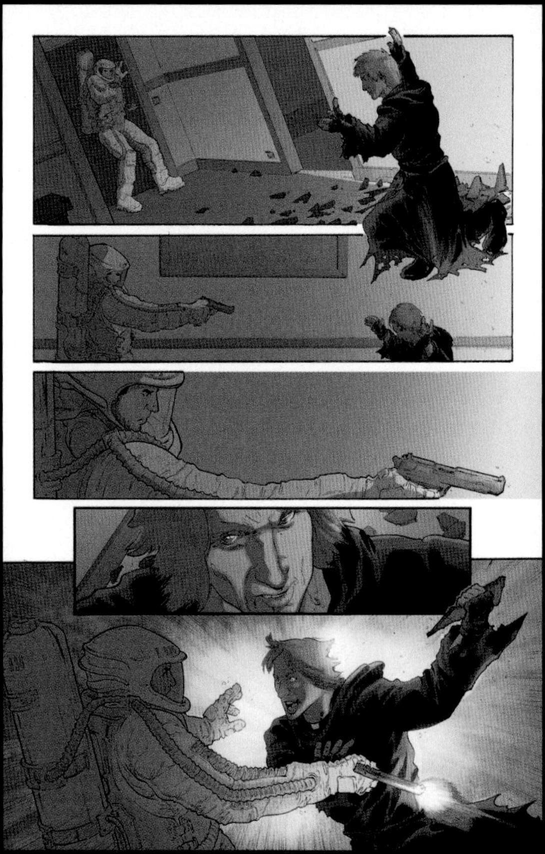

As for the main dialogue font throughout, I chose it with the same logic in mind. It should look organic and relatively "hand-drawn," like many European comics, rather than similar to what's seen in SO many typical monthly comics.

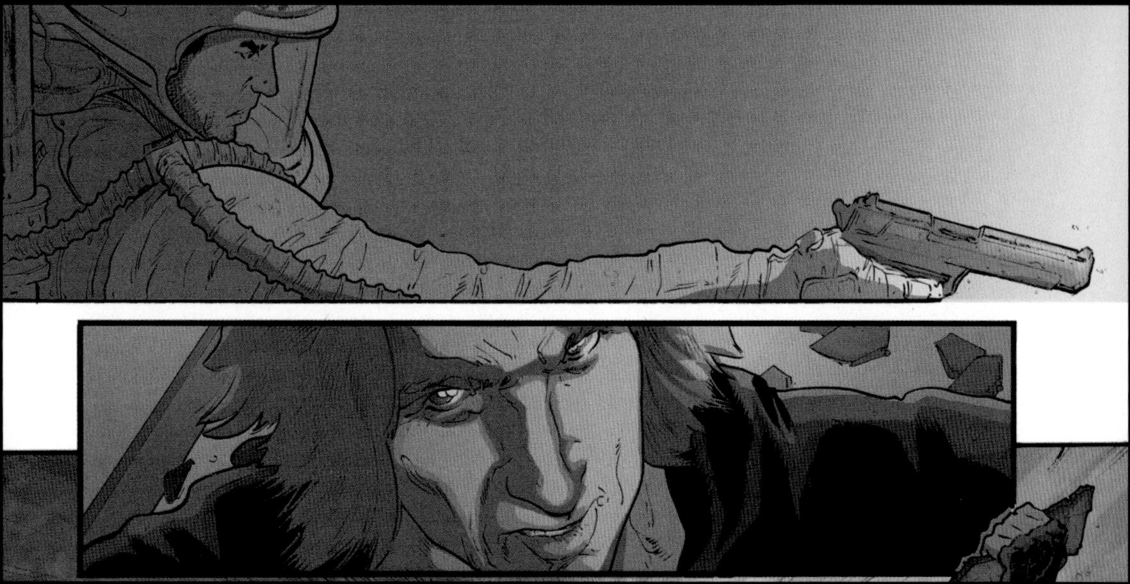

One of my favorite elements of Giovanni's artwork is that it reminds me of classic illustration and has a very cinematic feel, and I didn't want the lettering to be "loud" or overpowering. I'd worked on another book with his artwork recently, where I chose to letter everything with more esoteric word balloons and balloon tails due to the genre of the comic, and I didn't want to copy myself on this book.

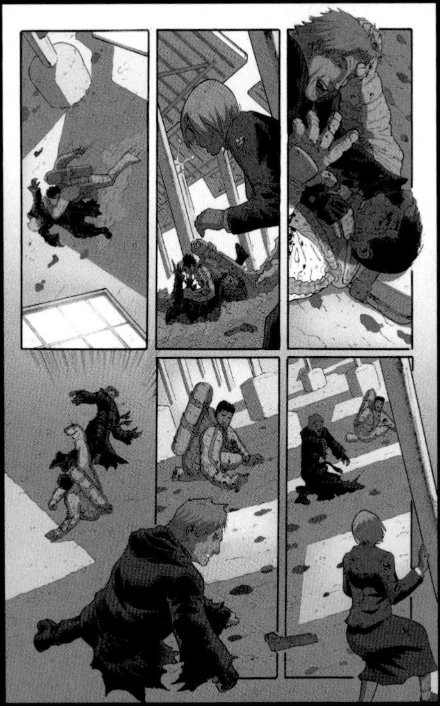

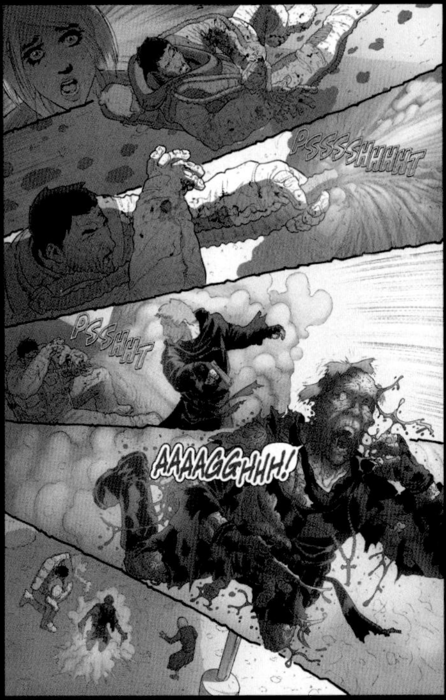
PSSSSHHHHT
PSSHHT
AAAAGGHHH!

So all of the dialogue, electronic balloons, etc. are very basic and staccato, because the vibe of the book itself (to me, humbly) is closer to that of *Alien* or a John Carpenter film rather than a loud *Independence Day*-like sci-fi movie. So, even the loud balloons aren't that loud, and the sound FX are as subtle as I can keep them.

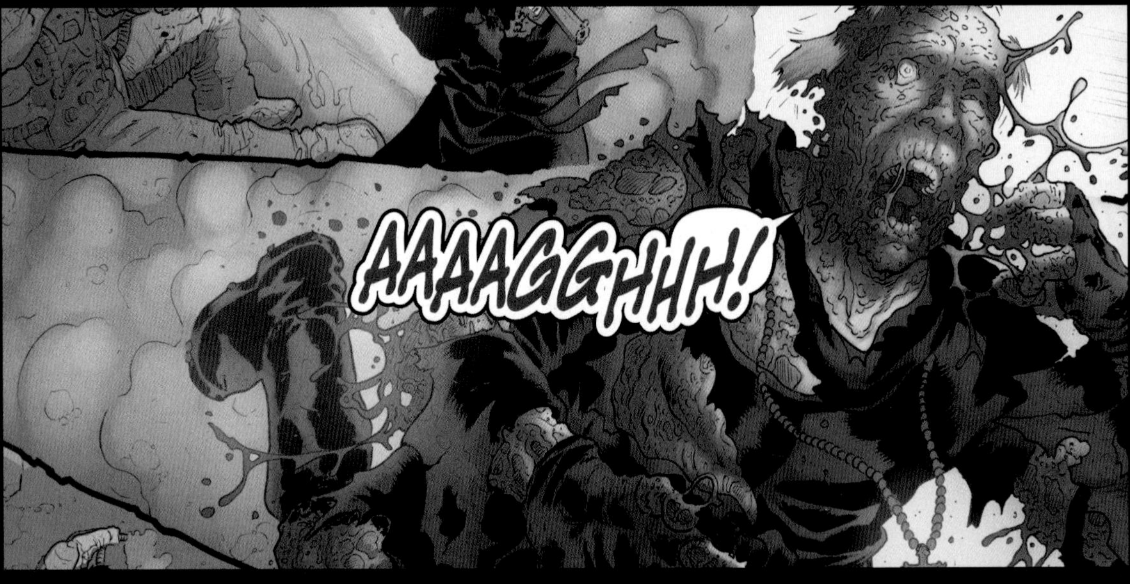
AAAAGGHHH!

My main job as a letterer is to guide the reader's eye through the artwork in the proper order so the readability is clear, and my second most important job is making sure important artwork isn't covered.

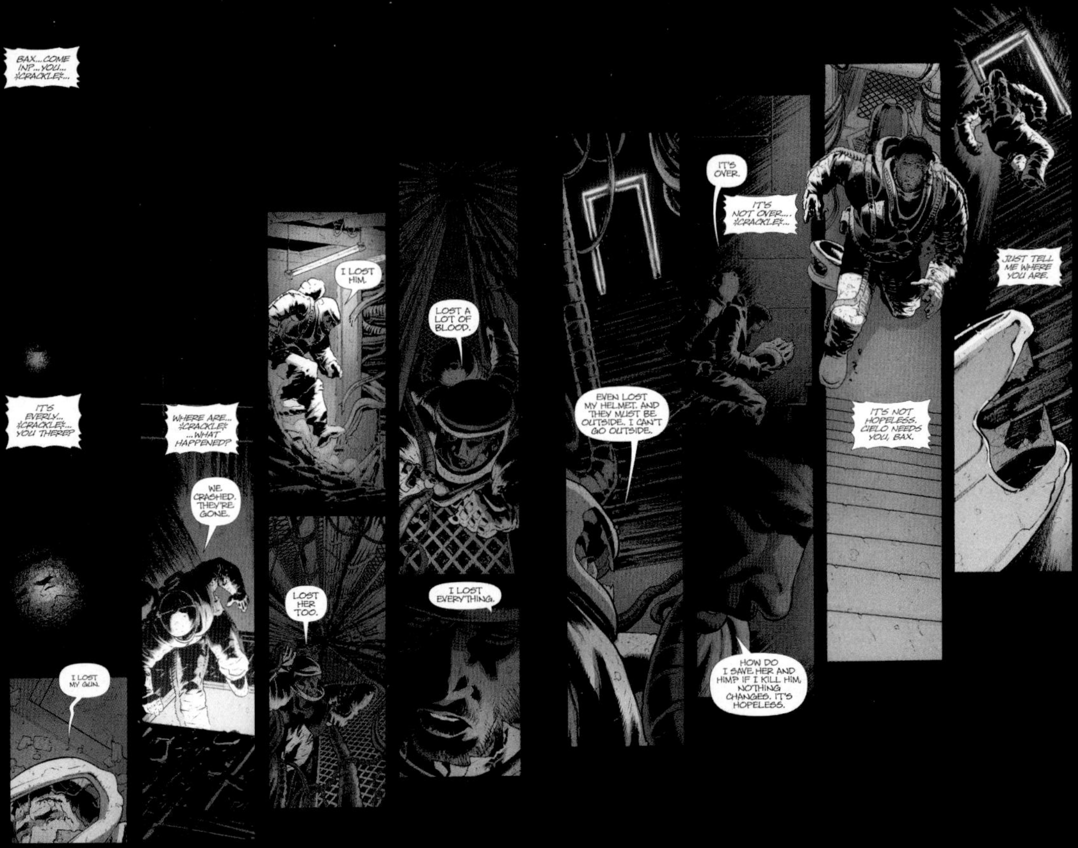
BAX...COME IN?...YOU... *CRACKLE*...
IT'S EVERLY... *CRACKLE*... YOU THERE?
I LOST MY GUN.
WHERE ARE... *CRACKLE* ...WHAT HAPPENED?
WE CRASHED. THEY'RE GONE.
I LOST HIM.
LOST HER TOO.
LOST A LOT OF BLOOD.
I LOST EVERYTHING.
EVEN LOST MY HELMET. AND THEY MUST BE OUTSIDE. I CAN'T GO OUTSIDE.
IT'S OVER.
IT'S NOT OVER.... *CRACKLE*...
HOW DO I SAVE HER AND HIM? IF I KILL HIM, NOTHING CHANGES. IT'S HOPELESS.
IT'S NOT HOPELESS. CIELO NEEDS YOU, BAX.
JUST TELL ME WHERE YOU ARE.

This spread is a good example of me trying to force the reader's eye in one direction, because the artwork is cinematic enough that it really doesn't NEED any dialogue to tell the story, so I wanted to make sure the reader sees everything in the proper order.

We hope that this look inside the lettering process on *Eclipse* (and all other comic books), has been informative and eye-opening!

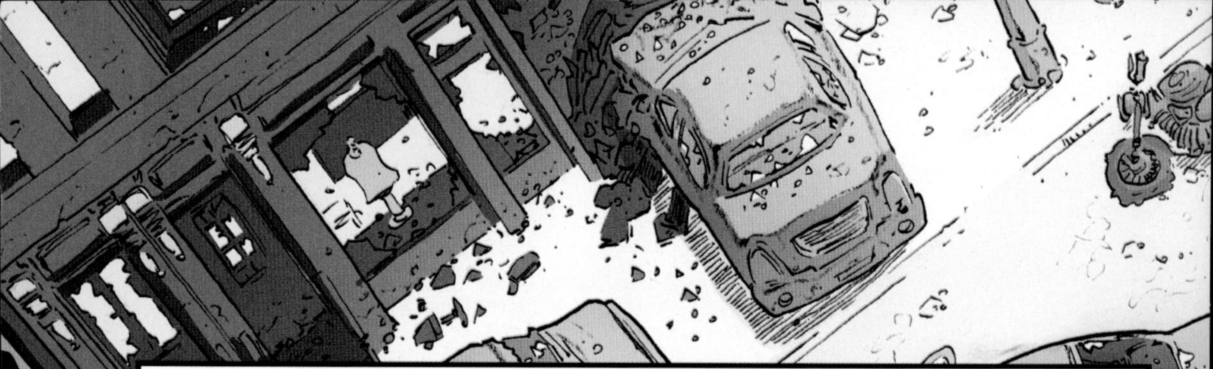

NOTICE TO VACATE

Dear Residents,

In order to continue providing emergency services, such as food and water delivery, shelter and medical attention, the Federal Emergency Management Agency will be focusing our efforts in select cities with the proper underground infrastructure for safety from the sunlight.

You are located in:

WASHINGTON, DC, NATIONAL EMERGENCY ZONE 3

You should IMMEDIATELY RELOCATE to your designated ***Zone 3 Safe Emergency City*** of:

PHILADELPHIA

If this designated Safe Emergency City is not available, seek out one of the appropriate Zone cities.
Zone 1: BOSTON Zone 2: NEW YORK CITY Zone 3: PHILADELPHIA
Zone 4: ATLANTA Zone 5: DETROIT Zone 6: DALLAS Zone 7: CHICAGO
Zone 8: SALT LAKE CITY Zone 9: LOS ANGELES Zone 10: PORTLAND

INSTRUCTIONS FOR TRAVEL

The National Guard will be conducting limited neighborhood sweeps and can pick up and provide any individuals safe transportation to shelter in a designated Safe Emergency City. The National Guard will also conduct stops every 24 hours at local police stations. If you cannot wait for the National Guard in your home or current location safely, please seek out a police station.

If you must travel without the National Guard, AVOID traveling during the hours of 5am – 9pm, as any exposure to SUNLIGHT remains fatal. Do not seek shelter in any vehicles or structures with windows, as even indirect sunlight can cause death.

Be aware that travel at night without the National Guard may be dangerous. Local and state police departments can no longer gaurantee your safety. 911 emergency phone services remain down.

Do not accept assistance from any police or military organizations unless they are authorized by FEMA and the National Guard. There have been reports of individuals abusing abandoned police and military credentials and vehicles.

If you elect to remain in the city of Washington, DC, FEMA will not be able to provide emergency services to you or maintain your safety.

Sincerely,

Thomas Demartin
Deputy Director of FEMA

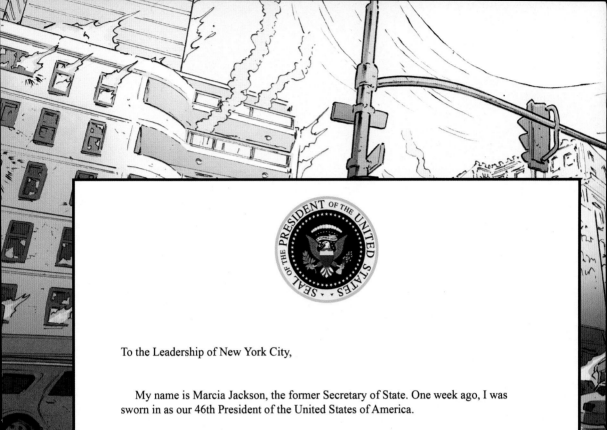

To the Leadership of New York City,

My name is Marcia Jackson, the former Secretary of State. One week ago, I was sworn in as our 46th President of the United States of America.

These are hard times. I don't begin to comprehend the nature or severity of the problems you face. We have heard of tens of thousands of refugees flooding your area. I can only assume that you are doing everything in your power to maintain order and protect those within your city.

However, the national government remains intact. Many emergency zone cities are surviving, along with townships across the countryside. People remain hidden during the day from this strange phenomenon with the sunlight, but we are by no means beaten. We continue to work together to recover from this disaster and rebuild our great nation.

We need your help. We are aware that you have achieved what seems to be the impossible for so many cities. You have restored a solar power supply for your city. Our engineers are ready to learn about whatever techniques you used, and hopefully, bring power to the rest of the country.

We are also aware that you have closed off your borders. You've barricaded the bridges and tunnels, cutting off New York City. We've attempted to send envoys and soldiers, and they have all been fired upon or sent away.

I am writing to appeal to your humanity and ask that you assist us. If you continue to ignore our pleas and remain isolated from the nation, then understand that we will send in our military forces to recover control of New York City.

We will only survive this together if we put the needs of the entire nation before our own. We can only have hope if we are ready to make sacrifices.

Very sincerely yours,

Marcia Jackson
President of the United States

COVER GALLERY
ALL COVERS BY GIOVANNI TIMPANO

SERIES PROMO IMAGE

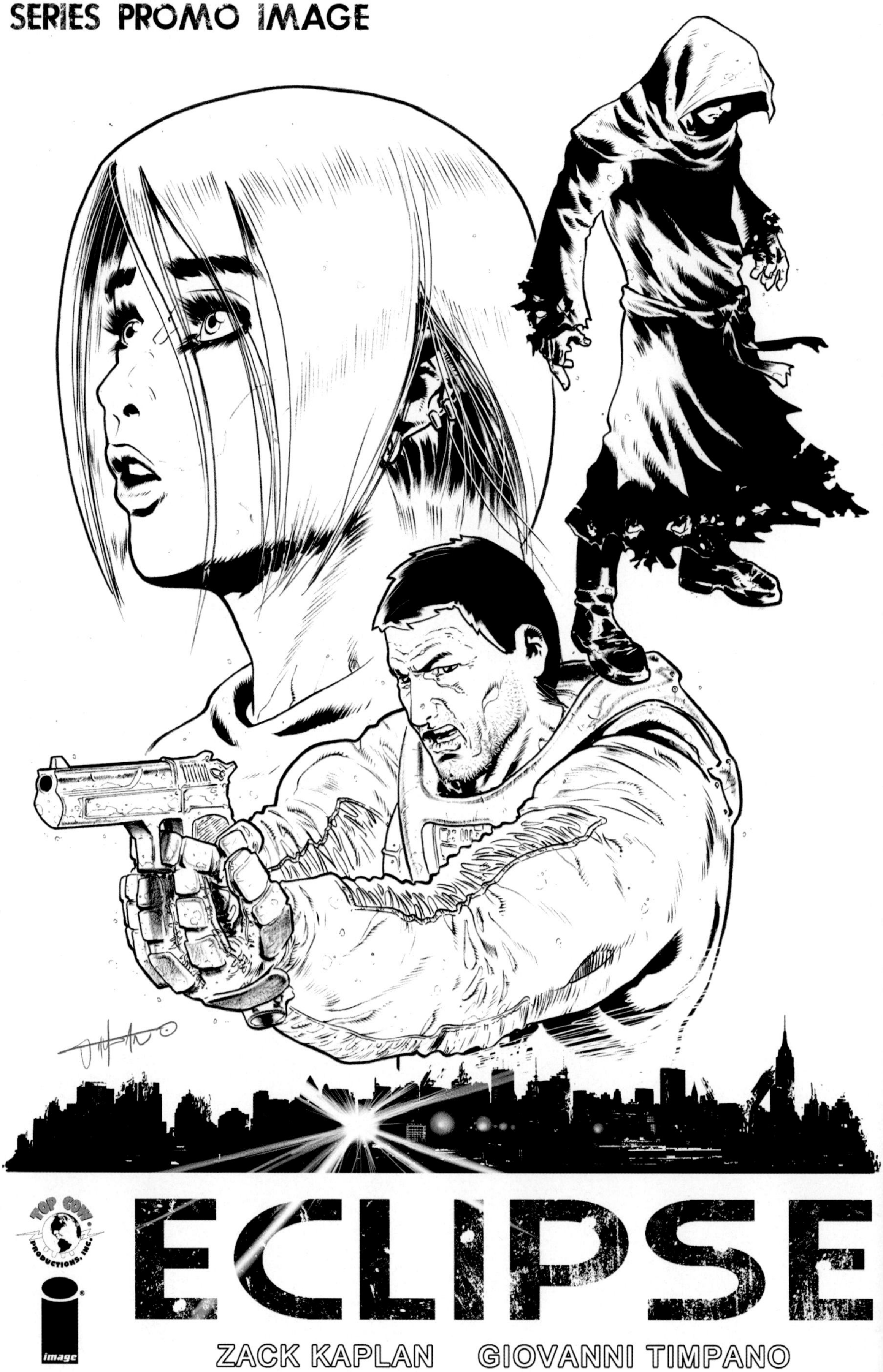
ECLIPSE
ZACK KAPLAN GIOVANNI TIMPANO

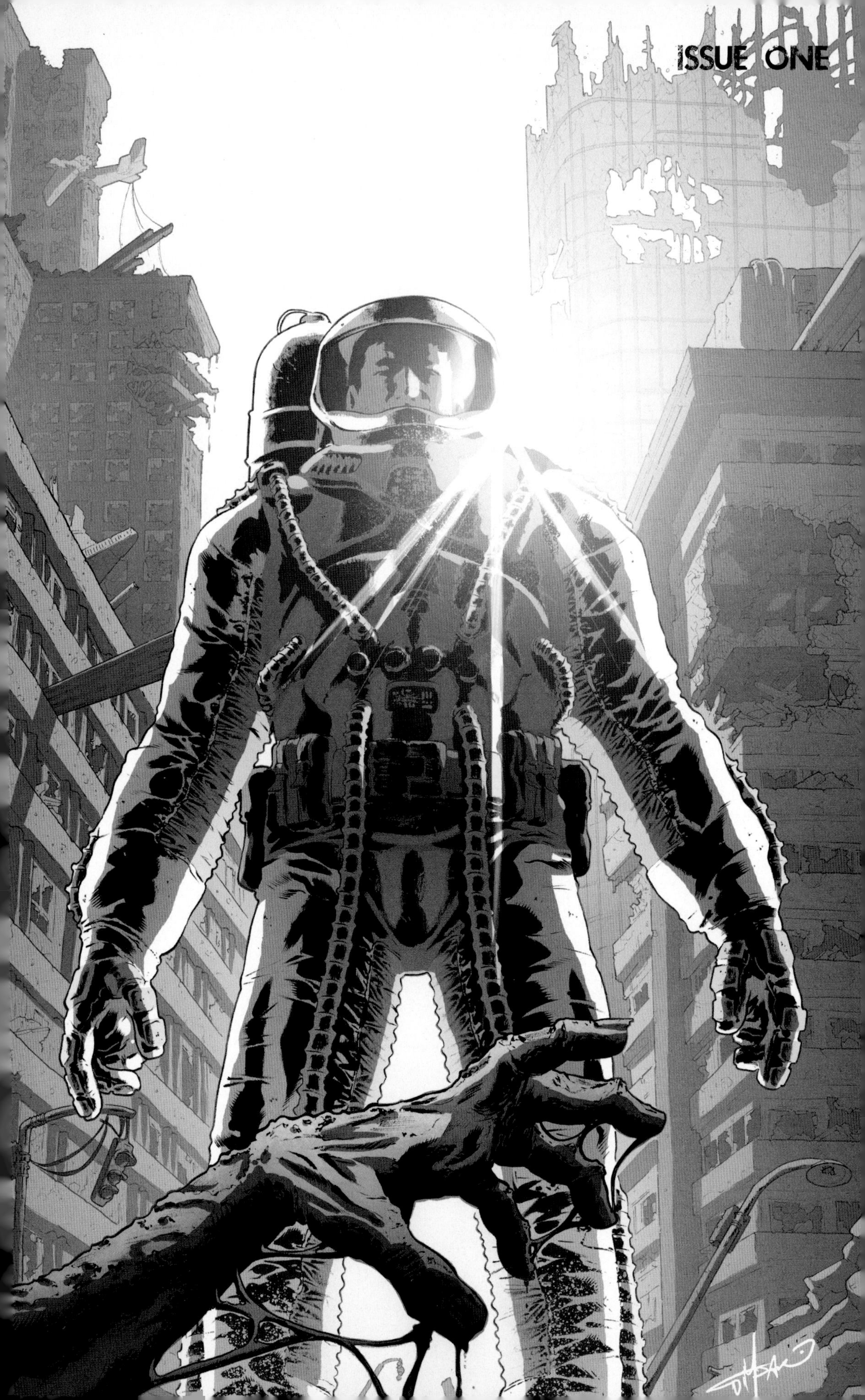
ISSUE ONE

ISSUE ONE SECOND PRINTING

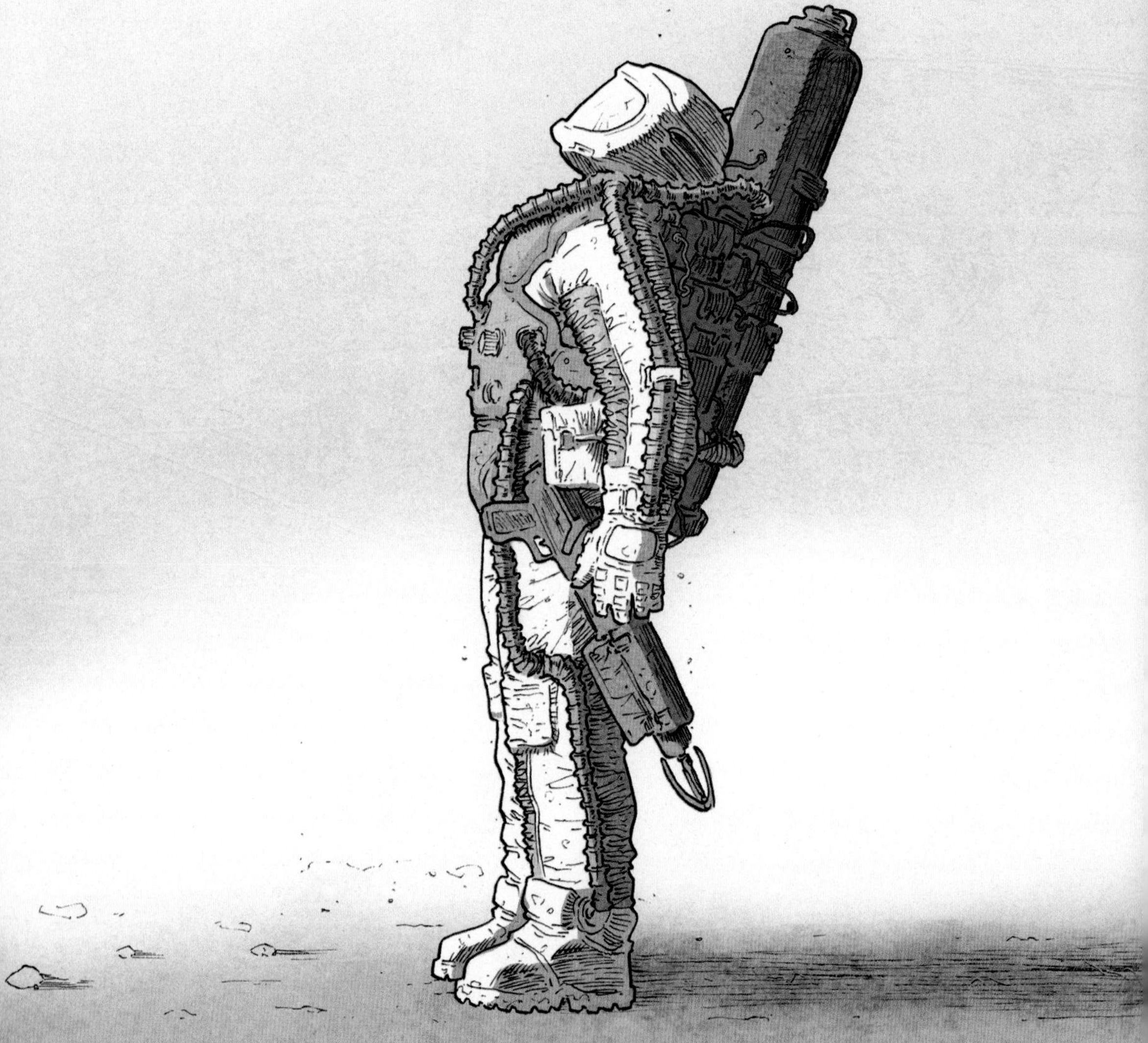

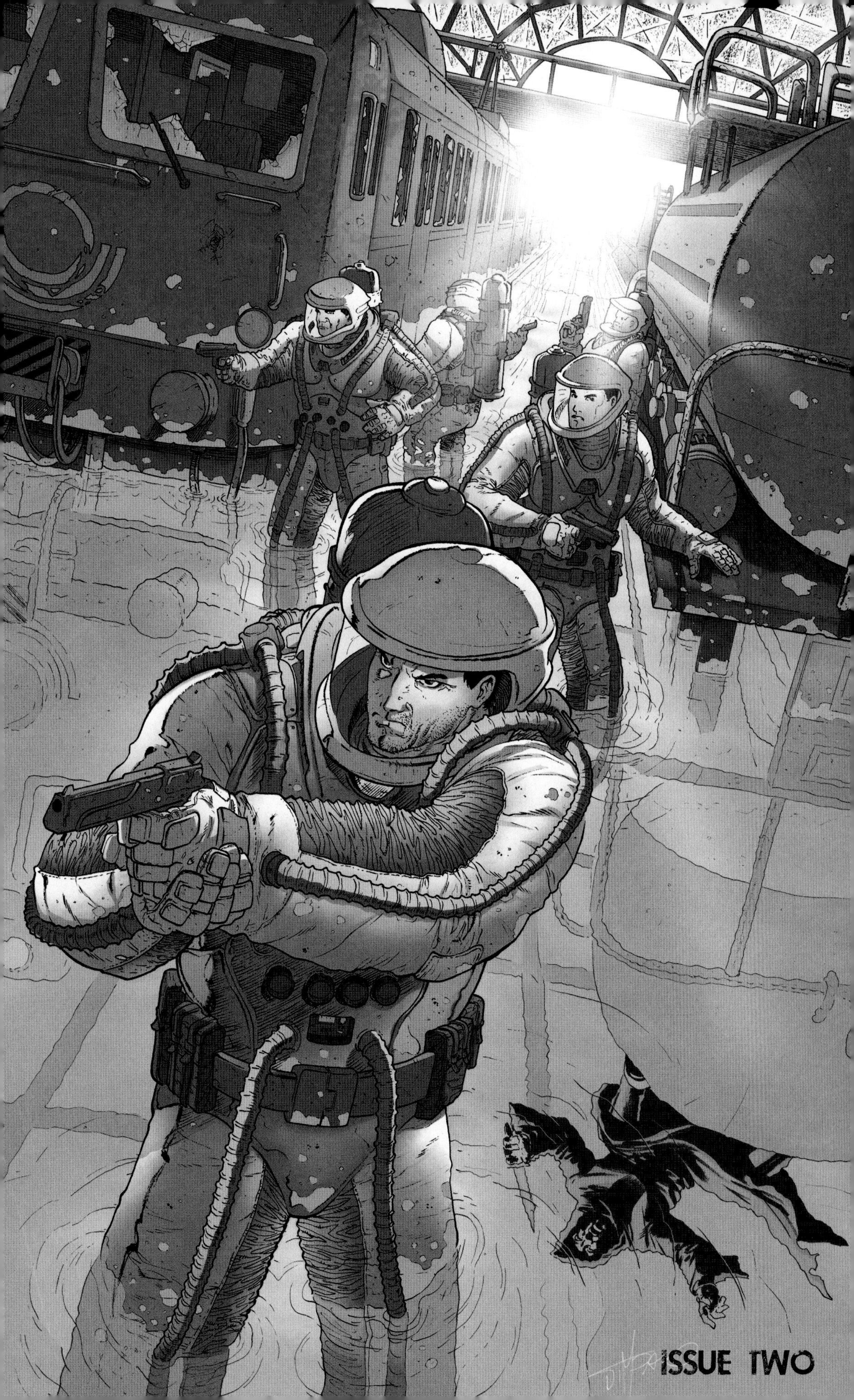
ISSUE TWO

ISSUE TWO UNUSED COVER B

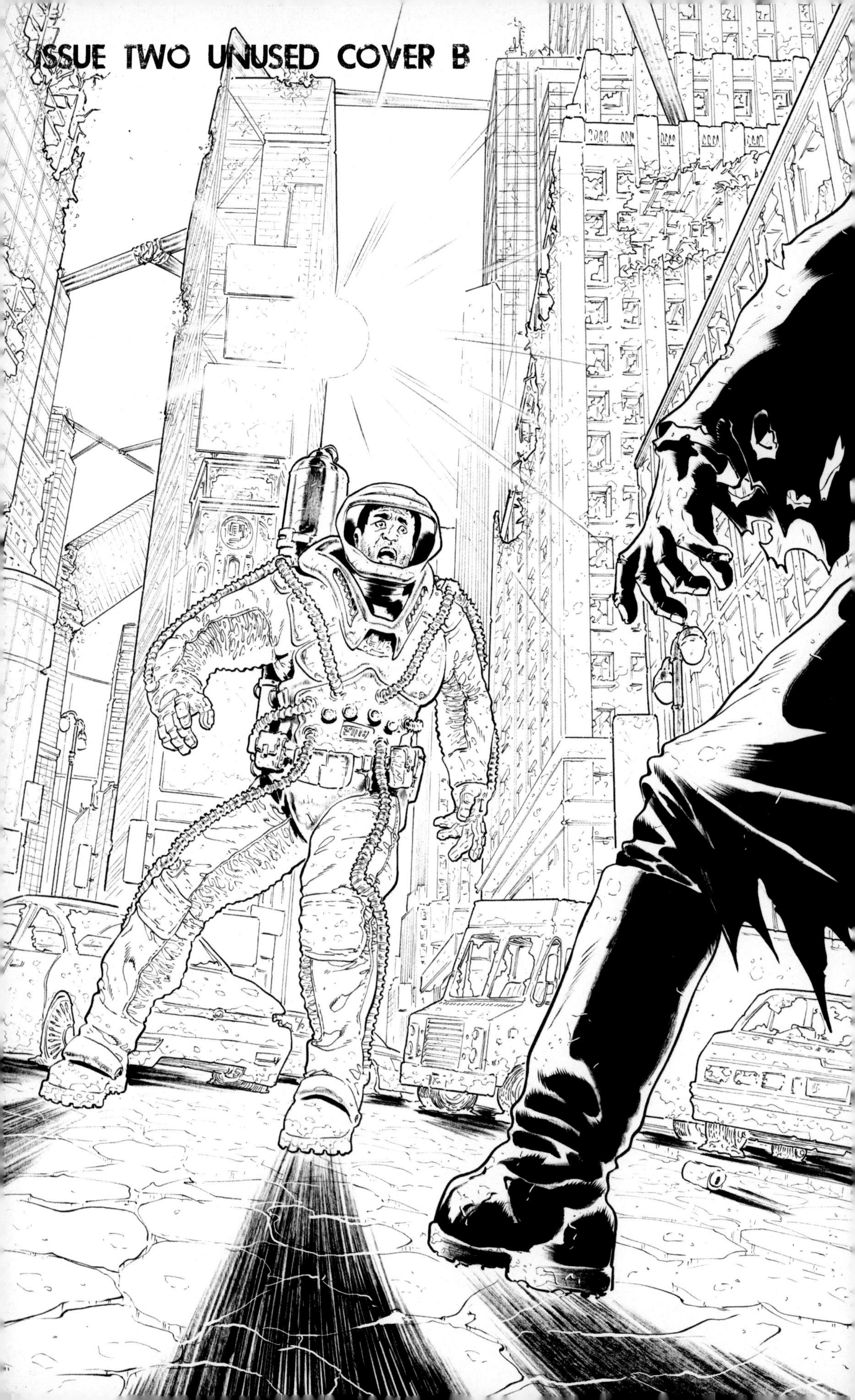

ISSUE THREE

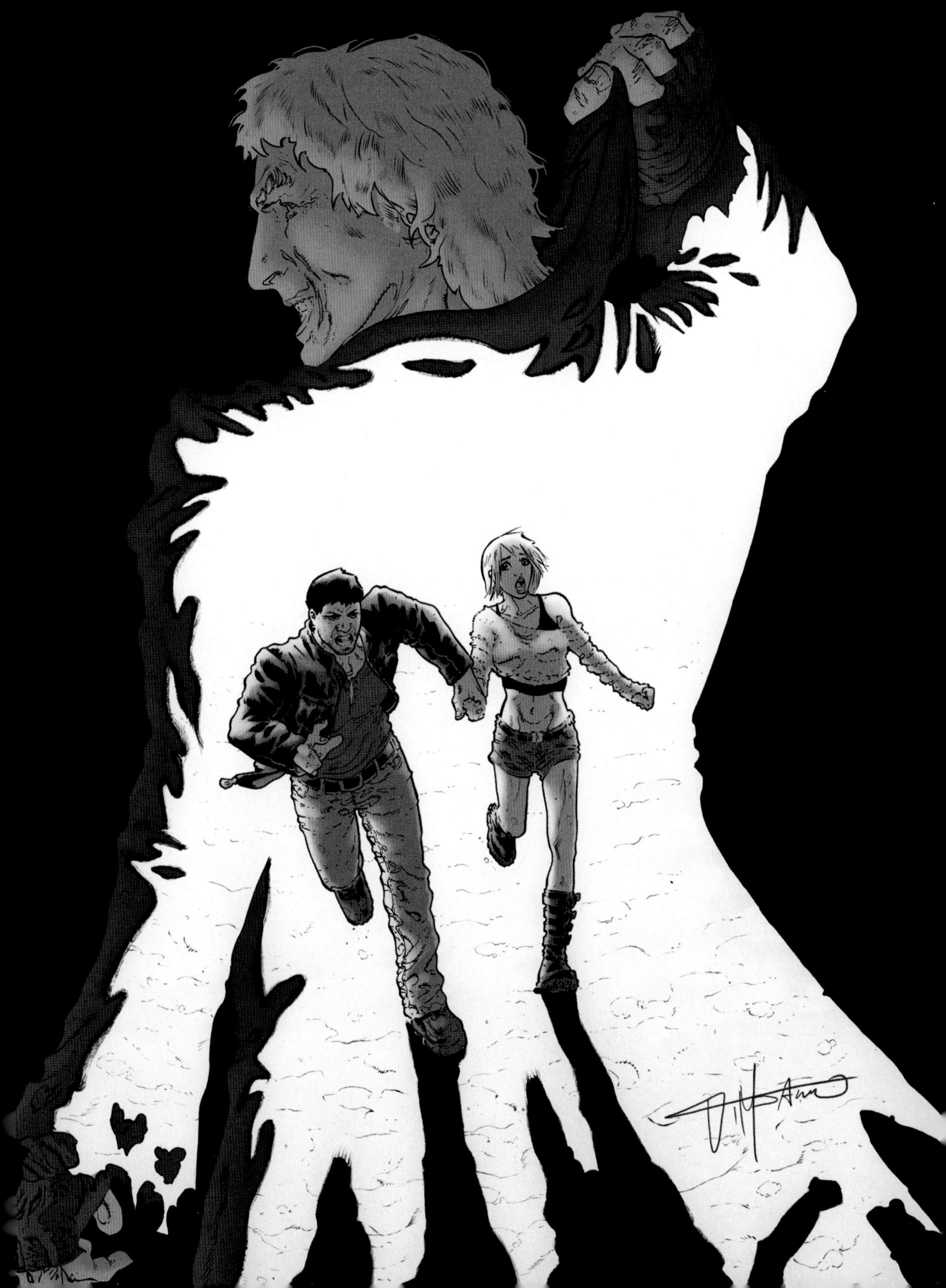

ISSUE FOUR

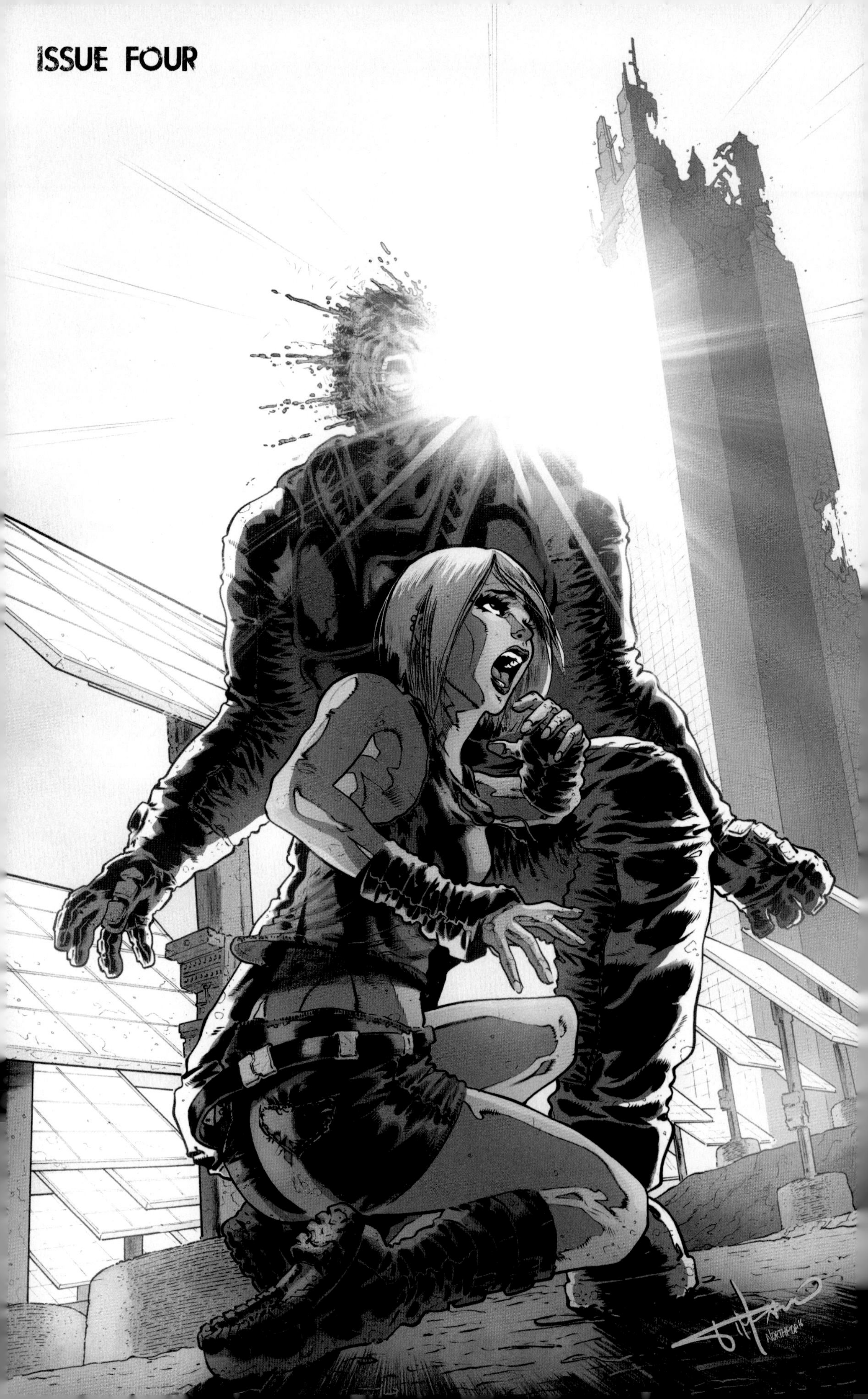

The Top Cow essentials checklist:

IXth Generation, Volume 1
(ISBN: 978-1-63215-323-4)

Aphrodite IX: Complete Series
(ISBN: 978-1-63215-368-5)

Artifacts Origins: First Born
(ISBN: 978-1-60706-506-7)

Broken Trinity, Volume 1
(ISBN: 978-1-60706-051-2)

Cyber Force: Rebirth, Volume 1
(ISBN: 978-1-60706-671-2)

The Darkness: Accursed, Volume 1
(ISBN: 978-1-58240-958-0)

The Darkness: Rebirth, Volume 1
(ISBN: 978-1-60706-585-2)

Death Vigil, Volume 1
(ISBN: 978-1-63215-278-7)

Eclipse, Volume 1
(ISBN: 978-1-5343-0038-5)

Eden's Fall
(ISBN: 978-1-5343-0065-1)

Impaler, Volume 1
(ISBN: 978-1-58240-757-9)

Mechanism, Volume 1
(ISBN: 978-1-5343-0032-3)

Postal, Volume 1
(ISBN: 978-1-63215-342-5)

Rising Stars Compendium
(ISBN: 978-1-63215-246-6)

Sunstone, Volume 1
(ISBN: 978-1-63215-212-1)

Symmetry, Volume 1
(ISBN: 978-1-63215-699-0)

The Tithe, Volume 1
(ISBN: 978-1-63215-324-1)

Think Tank, Volume 1
(ISBN: 978-1-60706-660-6)

Wanted
(ISBN: 978-1-58240-497-4)

Wildfire, Volume 1
(ISBN: 978-1-63215-024-0)

Witchblade: Redemption, Volume 1
(ISBN: 978-1-60706-193-9)

Witchblade: Rebirth, Volume 1
(ISBN: 978-1-60706-532-6)

Witchblade: Borne Again, Volume 1
(ISBN: 978-1-63215-025-7)

For more ISBN and ordering information on our latest collections go to:
www.topcow.com
Ask your retailer about our catalogue of collected editions, digests, and hard covers or check the listings at:
Barnes and Noble, Amazon.com, and other fine retailers.

To find your nearest comic shop go to:
www.comicshoplocator.com